W9-BOO-978

BULLS BEFORE BREAKFAST

MAP OF PAMPLONA AND ENCIERRO COURSE

RÍO ARGA

Calle Santo Domingo
(300 yards)

Ayuntamiento
(40 yards)

Calle Mercaderes
(75 yards)

Calle Estafeta
(320 yards)

la Telefónica
(100 yards)

el Callejón

BULLS BEFORE BREAKFAST

Running with the Bulls and Celebrating Fiesta de
San Fermín in Pamplona, Spain

Peter N. Milligan

Foreword by John Hemingway

St. Martin's Press ☒ New York

To my father, William T. Milligan Jr.,
who most certainly disagreed with John Steinbeck

. . . the dreamers of the day are dangerous men,
for they may act their dreams with open eyes,
and make it possible.

T. E. LAWRENCE,

SEVEN PILLARS OF WISDOM: A TRIUMPH

BULLS BEFORE BREAKFAST. Copyright © 2015 by Peter N. Milligan. Foreword copyright © 2015 by John Hemingway. All rights reserved. Printed in the United States of America. For information, address St. Martin's Press, 175 Fifth Avenue, New York, N.Y. 10010.

www.stmartins.com

Library of Congress Cataloging-in-Publication Data

Milligan, Peter N.
    Bulls before breakfast : running with the bulls and celebrating fiesta de San Fermín in Pamplona, Spain / Peter N. Milligan ; foreword by John Hemingway.
        p. cm.
    ISBN 978-1-250-06573-5 (hardcover)
    ISBN 978-1-4668-7273-8 (e-book)
    1. Running the bulls—Spain—Pamplona.   2. Fiesta de San Fermín.
I. Title.
    GV1108.4.M55 2015
    394.26946'52—dc23   2015013649

Designed by Omar Chapa

Map by Emily Langmade

St. Martin's Press books may be purchased for educational, business, or promotional use. For information on bulk purchases, please contact the Macmillan Corporate and Premium Sales Department at 1-800-221-7945, extension 5442, or write to specialmarkets@macmillan.com.

First Edition: June 2015

10   9   8   7   6   5   4   3   2   1

CONTENTS

FOREWORD

Bulls Before Breakfast is a great book. It's funny, colorful, and chock-full of the kind of insider knowledge that anyone who wants to run with the *toros bravos* (and live to tell the tale) needs to remember. The author, Peter Milligan, is a lawyer from Philadelphia whom I met, fittingly enough, after an *encierro* a few years back. He was standing outside Bar Txoko in Plaza del Castillo with a chocolate Kaiku batido in his hand, and while I knew then that he was a runner and an American, I had no idea until reading this book that he had been coming to the fiesta de San Fermín for over a decade. He and his brother, Ari, are in fact what I would call hard-core runners. They run for the sheer joy of it, for the adrenaline, for the fear, and for the way that it makes them feel when they are close to these wild, almost mystical animals. They also run because it is a part of the fiesta to run, and they love everything about the fiesta de San Fermín. They love the camaraderie, the people you meet, the bullfights, the friends you make, the food, the traditions, the partying, the fireworks, the whole shebang. Finally, they understand that they'll never be able to convey to a newcomer what the fiesta is really like. That is a gift you can only experience and receive firsthand.

I confess that I am not quite as passionate about the *encierros* as Peter and his brother are. I've only run about fifteen times, whereas Peter has over seventy *encierros* to his credit. In this sense I am closer to my grandfather's average (Ernest never ran) than I am to Peter's. Still, with my limited experience, I was pleased to see Peter point out in his book that if you do this long enough you will get hurt, and that there is no safe place on the course. Sometimes, such as the day his brother was gored, you have bulls that get separated from the herd early on and then decide that they're going to attack and try to kill anything and everything that gets in their way. Plowing into a crowd of runners lined up against a wall, they toss grown men into the air the way you might a piece of paper or a plastic fork. They are incredibly strong and agile, and if you are seriously unlucky, a bull might, for reasons known only to him, decide that you, in particular, need to die, and he will hunt you down.

Of course, in the late afternoon all the bulls that run in the *encierro* will fight and die in the bullring. It is, after all, what they were bred and raised for. While Peter doesn't expect everyone to agree with this tradition or understand his *afición*, his passion, for corrida, he does ask his readers to show the proper respect for what many Spaniards consider an art form. Pamplona and all that it offers, he says, is something that can change your life and your way of looking at the world if you give it a chance. It is, as Peter points out, a city that takes tolerance and acceptance of diversity and differences of opinion to new heights. An attitude that perhaps a politically and culturally polarized America could learn something from.

Indeed, the fiesta is a place of contradictions. It is a religious festival; San Fermín was a Christian martyr. At the same time, it is a kind of pagan bacchanal where just about anything goes. It is a celebration of life and of death, of violence during the *encierros* and the afternoon corridas, and yet of amazingly peaceful relations among the more than one million people who come to Pamplona every year. In fact, in the six years that I've been running with the bulls, I don't think I've ever really seen two people beat each other up. If you're feeling that ornery and nasty, all you have to do is find a spot on the 900-meter run, wait for that second rocket to go off, and then start counting. The bulls will find you.

—John Hemingway

INTRODUCTION

Brazos en Jarra (our Pamplona family)

"The hoost . . . set his hond in kenebowe."
—TALE OF BERYN, C. 1400

*Every July, I love to stand in the cobblestoned streets of Pamplona
with arms akimbo, and with my adoptive brother, Ari. It just takes
a minute, and the fiesta finds us. We saddle it, adjust the stirrups,
coax over the bridle, and ride her nonstop 'til sunup on the fifteenth.*

This is the story of our fiesta.

We will hardly sleep. We will talk and laugh ourselves hoarse.
We will eat too much, and permanently damage the muscles used
to smile. We will get sick. We will get injured. We will get lost. We
will damage a rental car. Somewhere, we will stain a carpet.
We will eat too much ham. I will throw up, and Ari will exaggerate
how hard it is to swallow his pills. We will lose money and probably our parking garage ticket, too. We will destroy a shirt, and a
pair of pants or two, or more. I know Ari will go anywhere, do
anything. He will never be the voice of reason. He will never suggest reserve.

Until the end, it will seem he never needs to find a seat, cool down, take it easy, get a jacket, take a nap, rest just a bit, sleep, find a bathroom, adjust his shoes, take an aspirin, get a soda, or suffer any foibles of a rational man.

If the fiesta was a contest of stamina, Ari would win annually. He is the machine. He walks just as fast in the last minutes of the fiesta as the first. It's a badge of honor if you can just keep pace.

We go to Pamplona with plans. I make them; Ari enforces them. He makes sure I do not beg off amidst fiesta. Many people aimlessly meander through fiesta, which is perfectly fine. They waste time and miss the details. They would not recognize our experience. Equally, we have friends in Pamplona with experience and knowledge that grossly outpace ours. They love and protect the fiesta, and have for decades. They look out for us and have helped us enjoy our time in Pamplona more than we deserve. We look to them for advice and guidance, and hope to carry on traditions they've created for decades to come.

When you run with the bulls in Pamplona, you are running with bona fide Spanish fighting bulls—*los toros bravos*—that are, at least in a literary, romantic sense, if not actually, brothers. They are not animals but beasts. They foam at the mouth, snort, and dig at the sand with their cloven hooves. When they leave their paddock, the herd bursts out into the morning sun, running together for the last time. Most likely, they will all die in the bullring late in the afternoon. By running with the bulls, you are joining the herd for at least a metaphysical moment, and this idea cannot be over-sentimentalized. I am not a joiner—I don't sit on committees or go to meetings. I don't sign up for things. I am fiercely independent. Yet I happily join in this group and run with these bull brothers, and our bull-running brothers, and my actual but adoptive brother, and it is like drinking from the Pierian Spring. We all run together, and I find this stirring. Joyously, we together put our lives on the line with bulls whose lives will imminently end. It is a true honor.

Don't kid yourself—they are killers. They will chase you down for sport and in anger, with malice aforethought. Spanish *toros bravos* are among the most dangerous animals on the planet. They are killer whales on cobblestones. Most do not comprehend the capacity of a *toro bravo* to kill a man—sometimes by mistake but often on purpose. These are not rodeo bulls that will simply toss your unconscious body in the air and walk away. *El toro bravo* will come back and finish the job.

After the morning run, the bulls are penned together underneath the aging bullring, and then they mill about in a small enclosure with their comforting steers and some of the cowboys from their ranch watching from the catwalks above. Some stand in the sun, while others loll in the shade of the tree that blocks my view a little more every year. Seriously, can they trim that tree back for me?

At noon, the cowboys use a system of pulleys and levers and the steers to separate the bulls from each other into smaller stalls under the ring. This should be the first time these bulls have been apart since near birth, and during this sorting (the *sorteo*), you can see the anger and concern in their eyes.

Barring something extraordinary, under the late sun of the afternoon, each of them will be killed in the ring by a famous matador, or maybe just a new young buck in his first feria. It is bloody and barbaric and exhilarating and pluperfect. Sometimes a bull will show such extraordinary bravery that he will be afforded recognition as great as, or greater than, the matador. A precious few will be pardoned. We pray for the same every morning.

In Pamplona, from our 5:00 a.m. alarm until we collapse in bed at 2:00 a.m., the twenty-one-hour day of the fiesta de San Fermín is without flaw. It is a diamond we will forever view through a golden haze.

Even Ernest Hemingway found it difficult to describe a fiesta day. Usually, he made a run at it from the periphery, such as in *The Sun Also Rises*, which is not about the fiesta, and only uses graphic descriptions of the running and the feria as a backdrop. In 1924,

Hemingway witnessed the death of bull runner Esteban Domeño. In 2009, we had a similar experience, witnessing the death of Daniel Jimeno Romero; however, we were running in the street. Hemingway was not, and never did. Ari was inches away from the fatal goring in 2009. *Inches.* It is not unusual for us to wake up in the middle of the night thinking about Daniel. He was a Pamplona friend, and he is missed on Pamplona mornings.

No one (including Hemingway) has yet written a comprehensive account of the rocket that starts the morning bulls running, or the taste of aluminum at the back of your throat for hours afterward. An accurate depiction of the camaraderie among runners is even more elusive. Unlike Hemingway, I know what happens in the San Fermín running of the bulls, or *encierro*. It is more complex than most assume, and it changes a person. I am not an adrenaline junky. It is not about adrenaline, but everyone asks if it is. It is not about machismo, either, but it helps if you bring a little bit. The running of the bulls, and the entire Pamplona fiesta, has become an embodiment of my brotherhood with Ari, and an outlet and extension of our friendship. All of the bull runners, and I mean those that return every year they can (and not the onetime sightseer), feel the same way about one another.

But, to truly understand it, you must get down into the streets of Pamplona. Grand philosophical discussions transpire on this subject during the fiesta. A few summers ago a friend stopped me in the street and said, "The three basic ingredients of the festivities are the joy and good humor; the noise and the noise; and the open nature of the fiesta." Add the bulls, and he was close.

For me, the strong underlying and authentic leitmotif of the fiesta of San Fermín is fellowship and family. I cannot get over the idea of joining the herd of brothers with my brother, and our new brothers, whom we gain daily. Notwithstanding the snippets shown on ESPN, or the debauchery portrayed in British newspapers, it is a family fiesta. It is all about the family experience.

Ari and I do not look alike nearly at all. In fact, we get more than a few *Mutt and Jeff* comments on the differences. Yet, after spending just a little time with us, no one retains any doubts that Ari is my brother. It's clear in the way I mercilessly taunt and torment him, as is my legal obligation as the older and larger, stronger, and more strapping sibling. And taller. I am the taller brother. This will be obvious to you.

And, every time we run in Pamplona, our family gets a little bigger. Before Game 6 of the 1974 Stanley Cup finals, Philadelphia Flyers legendary head coach Fred Shero wrote on the locker-room chalkboard, *"Win together today and we walk together forever."*

In Pamplona, we join the herd, and all run together forever. Eight times every July.

We look forward to welcoming you to the family in the streets of Pamplona someday.

BULLS BEFORE BREAKFAST

1

Breakfast After Bulls
(a perfect day)

"When you wake up in the morning, Pooh," said Piglet at last,
    "what's the first thing you say to yourself?"
"What's for breakfast?" said Pooh.
"What do you say, Piglet?"
"I say, I wonder what's going to happen exciting today?" said
    Piglet.
Pooh nodded thoughtfully.
"It's the same thing," he said.

— A. A. MILNE, *WINNIE-THE-POOH*

*In 1988, then fourteen-year-old Aryeh Leib Deutsch (whom every-
one calls "Ari"; it rhymes with "Atari" and not "Larry") put in a job
application at our family store in the Echelon Mall in Voorhees, New
Jersey. Then, he came to live with us. It's a long story. We moved
my desk out of the bedroom and down to the basement to make room
for another bed, and kept our clothes in boxes under the box springs.
We worked together all day, and at night watched* Letterman *on a
black-and-white television with old vacuum cleaner parts we used
to jury-rig an antenna. We've been inseparable ever since. He is my
little brother. I know Ari better than anyone in the universe. This*

makes him nervous, and he asked that in writing this book, I keep information "not relevant" to our travels to myself. For instance, he would rather I not tell you he can throw a perfect spiral with a Nerf football, but cannot catch anything thrown in his direction. He does not want anyone to know that he broke his glasses laughing at Urkel on Family Matters *in 1992. Or that his catchphrase is "put a visor on it," which makes no sense no matter how many times he explains it. He can pump gas better than anyone I know. He can also walk very fast. But he thinks a foul ball with two strikes "should be" a strikeout. He thinks Roger Moore was the best James Bond. Obviously, there will be a debate as to what is "relevant."*

On July 14, 2011, Ari and I slept later than any other day that fiesta. We had reached that transient state of exhaustion one finds only during the Pamplona fiesta. In nine days we had less than thirty-six hours of sleep. It was the last day of the famed Navarran festival, and then everything would come to an end at midnight. Tossing aside our lassitude, we stepped out onto the cobblestones in high spirits wearing crisp, brand-new, perfectly ironed white linen pants. This would be our fiftieth run with the bulls together in the streets of Pamplona. We made our way to the town hall, and there was already a human traffic jam waiting to enter the course at the entrance we usually use. But we caught the eye of a member of the Policía Foral who had gotten to know us from our morning frolics during prior years. He waved us over to the side and held everyone back to let us climb under the barrier. We shook hands with him and pantomimed a discussion, and thanked him, and we told him we would see him next year. *"Próximo año, mi hermano!"* We would say this over and over during the day to our huge Pamplona family, before the day ended with burnt fingers and firework ashes raining down into our tear-filled eyes.

Together Ari and I had set this artificial fifty-run goal sometime during our third fiesta, but privately. It is bad form to brag about how many times you've run, and what really matters to those who run annually is having one perfect run in a lifetime. An artist does not brag about the quantity of his art but the quality. My children have (and probably yours will or have) brought home hundreds of "artistic" creations, but this does not make them artists. Pablo Picasso only needed *Guernica* to be considered great. To wit, there are ballet lessons, and then there's Baryshnikov.

In our forty-nine runs up until that date, we'd come close to what could be considered a perfect run (to us), and we had also just horrifically missed but always longed for better. At the very least, a good run requires one to get close to the bulls, to place one's body and soul in front of the herd and the horns, and to run a good distance in front of these marvelous killers. A perfect run? Well, I have no idea what that will be as I still rally my old bones from a couple hours of sleep and roll into the streets to find out.

That morning, Ari and I briskly walk down calle Estafeta, decorated festively with all its bunting and flags, and with the hordes of locals and visitors who have come to watch and (unsafely) hang from balconies the entire stretch of the street. There are thousands and thousands of onlookers. For some that morning, merely coming *to see and not run* is a lifetime dream come true. We run. We look for friends above and wave to them, and find friends in the street and hug them and quietly wish them *suerte* as we continue down the cobblestones. We make our way down to the end of calle Estafeta to where the road gets wider on the right-hand side. This is where we have agreed to wait. All around us runners are elasticizing their legs and jumping high into the air and checking their watches. They are stretching their necks and arms and taking small practice dashes down the middle of the street. As 8:00 a.m. approaches, activities stop; there is less and less talking, and even less eye contact among the brothers who have gathered this morning to face this charge together. Ari and I clear the street where we are standing for the moment of the last few pieces of debris. He wanders over to the left side of the street and I stay on the right. I say, "I will see you in a couple of minutes." When the rocket explodes at 8:00 a.m. the entire city shakes. Many frightened runners pass us by in terror, but long before the bulls arrive. I start my stopwatch and know that in about two minutes, the entire herd will be on top of us. Down on the other end of calle Estafeta I can see camera flashes—the bulls have turned the corner and are on their way. Ari and I start running before we even see the bulls. We have practiced this timing over many mornings in Pamplona and know by the actions of the runners in the distance when to start. We might be able to do this with our eyes closed—using only our ears. Nevertheless, we sensibly do not try this.

Now at a full gallop, we see people all around us falling or dashing to the barricades or crashing into the crowds of runners shrinking to the sides of the running course. We slap their grabbing hands off our shirts and leap their fallen forms. We watch bodies uncontrollably slide as runners tumble and heads hit the cobblestones with a beautiful thud. There is screaming all around us from onlookers, many of whom suddenly realize that this is no merry-go-round. At every step, at every turn, at every moment, the bulls are *this close* to killing runners all along the streets. It is a miracle that dozens do not die every morning. Many will survive by luck, despite stupidity, or by skill. Those watching from the balconies, seeing each and every close call, and realizing how close the delightful morning is to becoming tragic, are often more terrorized afterward than the runners.

Then, there is no one in front of us in the middle of the street, and there are only bulls behind us. Casual runners have melted into the sidelines. It seems that for our fiftieth run, that old tricky Saint Fermín has arranged for a special present for us. The sea of humanity parts. Like it never does. Three of the bulls whisk past us (two to my left and one to my right), and three remain at our back. Their heads bob up and down as they run. The tiring bulls behind us are loping along while we run at full speed and ability to avoid being trampled or worse. Still the bulls close on us. We turn onto the Telefónica stretch of the course, and I know this is a special run. But there is no time to celebrate. I have to stay on my feet, and keep my wits, as even without the three bulls, the mass of runners behind me could kill me. Together Ari and I pass into the shade of the short tunnel leading to the bullring, with the bulls at our heels. If we had wanted to (and we didn't), we could have run into the bullring arm in arm. We did burst in to cheering and celebrations, and peeled off to the left to pass the bulls on to the professional handlers. Probably less than 250 people in the stands actually knew us, and no one was cheering for us specifically, but it did not matter. It felt like holding Lord Stanley's Cup over my head with tears in my eyes after a Game 7 victory, only better.

We shook hands with some friends, and I grabbed Ari to climb out of the bullring. When we finally made it outside, we stood under the huge, ancient trees that surround Pamplona's glorious Plaza de Toros. I said "Ari, how about fifty more?" He replied, "Not a problem," as if there was no doubt about it. When we get there, we'll do fifty more and then fifty more. We walked up calle Espoz y Mina to the Plaza del Castillo and Bar Txoko and whispered to a couple of friends that we just hit our fiftieth run. We kept it quiet, though by nature we are actually babblers, but it is just not in style in Pamplona. Nevertheless, the word was quickly passed around. Pretty soon we had sore backs from all the congratulations, and it drew out impressive stories from our fellow runners, many of whom have run hundreds of times since starting as boys. Then our close friend Bob Lombardo brought famed Pamplona bull runner Julen Madina Ayerbe over, and he invited us to the "Runners Only" breakfast. As recounted later in this book, I witnessed Julen's horrifying 2004 goring. This invitation was a very touching gesture from our Pamplona family. We had heard about this breakfast, held on the final day of the fiesta for many years. We knew that invited English-speaking, Spanish, and Basque runners whose bull-running credentials cannot be challenged and whose contributions to the Pamplona fiesta are unsullied gathered together to celebrate their last morning in the sun and to start the impatient wait for the next summer. We knew about this breakfast, and honestly, we wanted in. But even this quiet wish bordered on defiling the spirit of bull running. You aspire for nothing other than a

beautiful, brave run. You don't look to become "considered" anything. You don't lust for compliments or praise. There is no "elite"
versus "amateur" status in running with the bulls. There are no
professionals. There are no "experts," and if you find someone la-
beling themselves as an expert bull runner, you know someone
who will soon be taught a lesson by Saint Fermín. Yet we know
who the overall beautiful runners are, and we know the cobblestoned street legends of Pamplona. They probably know it, but
rightfully, would never admit it.

With this stunning invitation, we walked with a couple of the
other guys over to Caso Paco on calle Lindachiquia and down into
its belowground dining room, and we were blown away by who
was sitting around that table. We had no right to sit at this table
with these runners; there are consistently a hundred better runners than Ari and me. But we were touched by the sentiment. We
try to run bravely, and everyone knows we love the fiesta. I hope
that we can carry the fiesta banner high in the air the rest of our
lives. Not only were some of the superb runners of the modern era
there, but also many of the brothers who are the standard-bearers
and guardians of our beloved fiesta; those who embody the spirit
of Saint Fermín himself, who benevolently steer newcomers toward an understanding that the running of the bulls is more
than a drunken, madcap zip with some tame rodeo bulls. Rick Mu-
sica (the next "mayor" of Pamplona) was there, along with Robert
Kiely (my favorite American Irishman, even though he is a Boston Bruins fan), and El Bomber (the kindest soul on earth), and Jim
Hollander (the famed fiesta photographer). I nudged Ari as we
found our seats. Joe Distler and Larry Belcher were walking in to
sit for the breakfast. Joe is about the most famous living American
bull runner on earth, and Larry (a Texan rodeo cowboy and professor) is perhaps my favorite person with whom to just talk
about the world. He is as interesting as anyone you'll ever meet.
Joe started running in 1967 and has run over three hundred
times. He is the Iron Man of Pamplona. We sheepishly said hello.

Clearly, we should have been ushered into some junior achievers room or at least to the children's table.

We sat with Angus Ritchie (from Glasgow, Scotland), who runs the corner as wildly and bravely as anyone ever, and Alexander Fiske-Harrison (from London), a brilliant writer and actor who graduated from Eton and Oxford. Gus and 'Xander were born on different sides of the railroad tracks, to put it gently. Here in Pamplona at this breakfast it did not matter; it is the greatest social experiment on earth. We are all bull-running brothers, and equal in every way. A perfect morning. It was the best eggs and ham I'd ever eaten. Breakfast always tastes better with a side of bulls.

We go to Pamplona together every summer and survive it. Well, almost. *We love Pamplona.* It rules our eyes-wide-open dreams. But those who think that this is a man-meets-bull, man-runs-hysterically-in-opposite-direction story has missed 99 percent of the tale. Each bull festival is its own Epic of Gilgamesh. No fiesta is the same, and none is better than another. They spectacularly stand alone. Please, I beg you: You must absolutely and unconditionally experience Pamplona yourself. Arrive alone or with someone you love. If you have to, come with someone you love— but who still annoys you a little bit, and who apparently reenacts the Battle of Trafalgar in your hotel room bathtub every morning; or who turns on his Garmin nüvi in the middle of the night over the ocean and wakes you up to show you what direction you are flying. "Dude, it is east. We are flying east. When we are coming home, we fly west. It does not change."

You must go and come back year after year to have the full experience. Every year is an independent masterpiece. I'll explain. On the morning of July 11, 2013, I was having a great fiesta, without any inkling that things were about to unravel. You can see that even with some minor bumps, we were really enjoying ourselves.

We had arrived on the sixth, walked down and saw the bulls

in their pens, and had dinner at La Cocina de Alex Múgica and I had the cod. We tracked down friends in the Plaza Consistorial and went to the fireworks.

On the seventh, we ran, and then wallowed on the beach in San Sebastián, and I came down with the most horrific case of gastroenteritis on the drive back to the hotel. Because we had a manual rental car, and Ari still cannot master the stick shift, I had to drive and we had to stop every couple of miles for me to dry-heave.

On the eighth, we ran even though I was still sick, and I was viciously knocked over trying to run into the ring, and I soiled myself. Remember, I was sick. In the afternoon, after changing clothes, we drove out to the Monasterio de Leyre and took a nice hike in the hills and ate a picnic lunch while I continued to recover. For dinner, I had the biggest bloody steak they could rustle up for me at Asador Olaverri and the red peppers in garlic and oil. We both had a junket for dessert. I was declared completely well by Dr. Ari.

On the ninth, we ran, and a steer died when it ran into the wall in the bullring. It was one of the worst things I have ever witnessed. It tripped and hit its head, and it was gone just like that. Photos of my run with the bulls were in the newspaper and all over the Internet later that day, and I got about a thousand emails. In the afternoon, we had lunch in Zarautz at Aiten-Etxe. I had the black lobster, of course. We rented a cabana and watched the crystal-blue waves roll in for hours. We discussed the nuances of language translation with some local teens when I asked them whether they knew where I could buy "a Coke," and not "some coke." For dinner, I had the Iberian ham and hake at Rodero, many hugs and kisses with friends, and some kind of French toast concoction for dessert that made me dizzy.

On the tenth, I ran with the herd into the bullring, and we had lunch at the world-famous Mugaritz in Errenteria, and the meal lasted well over four hours. It felt like four minutes. We sat on the veranda for dessert, leaning back and sated and relaxed, and tiny birds flitted about in the trees and we precariously approached having a perfect day. Then, we drove back to the beach in Zarautz and swam until past dusk. Well, I swam. Ari waded. We hiked up into the hills and explored some future hiking paths in the failing light, and watched some locals play Basque pelota in Getaria. We had Burger King back in Pamplona around 10:30 p.m. before the fireworks, and reveled in the irony of our lunch and dinner choices for the day.

In between all this, we sat and stood with friends old and new, and laughed at stories old and new. We went to the fireworks, rested in the shade, and debated whether to have ham or *lomo* with our eggs. We nursed coffees, got lost, and talked about hockey with bona fide Canadians. We translated drunken French into English. We were having a wonderful time.

Then there was the eleventh. We were supposed to join friends for enormous steaks at Asador Epeleta after the running of the bulls. Supposed to. In the morning run, three of the steers came first with a solo brown-and-black bull, and then four bulls (two black, one brown, one white) loped past my left shoulder as I fought for space with another runner in green who fell against the brown bull and spun around from the impact and kept running. I was amazed he stayed on his feet. The horns of the white bull and then the brown brushed my shirt. I was so happy. Forward and to my right, a police officer on the barricades was yelling and motioning with his fingers that all the bulls had passed by. I was quickly reviewing the count of bulls that had run by me and beginning to doubt his conviction as to the number of bulls and whether we were done or not, and then someone clipped me from behind in the enclosed tunnel that leads into the bullring. My ankle snapped as I fell forward, and if I think about the sound it made too long I still become nauseated. It was loud.

The entrance to the bullring, euphemistically referred to as "narrow," was the perfectly wrong place to fall. A street full of bulls and thousands of panicked runners are tunneled into a place hardly wider than my wingspan. As I fell, I knew I was too far back to crawl under the little protective slots at the base of either wall. I also could hear the distinctive sounds bull hooves make on the cobblestones, and more importantly, the sustained screaming the crowd makes when the bulls or, in this case, a lone bull approaches. Hah, but there was little satisfaction that I was right and the police officer was wrong. I rolled against the wall in the fetal position, or as far into the fetal position as I could roll at forty-three years old, and covered my head. Runner after runner after runner jumped me and kicked me and shaved the back of my head with their sneakered feet. As I was lying against the wall, I could not peek to see what was happening behind me. Oddly, I was not scared, but upset we might miss lunch. A bullring minder in a green beret was slapping the wall with his hand from his protective wall nook to get my attention, and I could sense two things. First, there was a gap in the runners, and maybe I could get to my feet without being plastered from behind. Second, I could smell the bull. They stink.

Like a great, lumbering awakening beast I rose to my feet. I knew the injury was not a mere sprain. If it were a scene in a movie the slow-motion effect would be unnecessary, because I was already in slow mo. I steadied myself against the wall with my right hand. Then, I could see why there was a gap in the runners. Another white bull with blood dripping from its horns and malice in its heart had turned around while running and was holding the waves of lads behind me at bay. The minder with the beret was coming unhinged shrieking for me to flee. He was slapping his beret against the wall now. He looked like he was preparing to watch me die right there. I fled and limped into the bullring and to the right on my compound fractured ankle (a vicious, horrible break). I leaned against the wall, and reached down and could feel two tiny nubs poking through the skin, and my fingers came back covered in blood. Now the Red Cross workers were shouting at me to crawl over the wall, but I could not get my right leg to cooperate. As I was about to tell them, "Don't worry, the *encierro* is over," I saw the objects of their alarm. Two bulls had refused to be tucked away under the bullring and were running counterclockwise around the ring right against the wall. They would gut me in a moment. I had nowhere to go as a senior citizen Basque woman leapt over the wall (surprisingly spry and selfless) and shielded me with her body. The bulls miraculously passed by us without interest. Not so much as a sniff. This anonymous Basque woman and several emergency workers carried me on a triage stretcher into the bullring operating room. As they did, I could feel thousands of eyes and hushed voices as I passed by the crowd. Friends stood with ashen faces, and some ran alongside asking if I needed anything. In one of the great thrills of my life, I gave them all two thumbs-up from my back and could hear a great rolling cheer as I passed into the tunnel under the bullring. In the bullring infirmary, I spent most of my time comforting a young man who had been struck in the eye by the horn of a bull. Bones sticking out of my leg seemed tame by comparison. Later came the fun ride to the hospital.

You'd think I would recall this as a bad fiesta. No way. It's my *Starry Night;* my Apollo and Daphne. Fiesta endures, man. I sat in that miserably hot, Soviet-era maternity hospital (the nurses offered the baloney explanation that rooms in a maternity hospital should not have air-conditioning because "it's bad for babies") for three days and nights and another long morning and listened to the fiesta outside my window in breathless pain. I could only hear the fireworks in the distance. My fiesta ended four excruciating days early, and our post-fiesta trip to Corsica (a childhood dream) was ruined. I had to get a catheter after surgery. Then, we did not even know I had also suffered a 5×7 inch third-degree burn on my calf from the exothermic reaction that occurs when water is added to calcium sulfate (plaster of Paris). My cast burned me cruelly. I had to have a skin graft when I got home, and the wound took nearly six months just to close up (a year later, it was still not completely healed). Fiesta was still great. I love the look on people's faces when they ask, "So, you're not going back anymore, right?" Of course I am.

In the hospital, I made a ton of new friends, I got interviewed in French, and Ari and I added about a hundred new stories to our repertoire. I got a plate and seven screws and a washer in my ankle. I got a seven-inch scar instead of the tattoo of a bull that so many of our friends have gotten. They brought me a really good breakfast in bed each day. Ari had to dote on me after the surgery and carry my bags at the airport. That was great. I got to park closer to the county courthouse for several months afterward. I got a really cool scooter to tool around in. I might just break my ankle every summer.

2

The Running of the Bulls
(this is what it is)

"I go to Spain in the summertime."
—JAKE BARNES, IN *THE SUN ALSO RISES,* 1926

When Ari and I were kids, every week a Martin Brower semi delivered supplies and products to our store at the Echelon Mall. It was full of 50 lb. bags of sugar, frozen waffle potato fries, and 40 lb. boxes of frozen chicken, among everything else needed for the store to operate. Often Dad ordered too much of something, and it was nearly impossible to stow away. For instance, he'd mean to buy one box of 32 oz. cups. However, he'd write "32" in the line instead of "1," because he was thinking about "32 oz." cups. Putting them away was like playing bizarre Tetris with giant boxes of cups or napkins or pie tins in our small storeroom. During holiday seasons, we sometimes got two trucks in a week because we didn't have enough room to store everything we needed during the busiest times of the year. Somehow Dad convinced Ari and me that it was a privilege to unload the truck, and that no one else had the qualifications for this special task. For the largest trucks, he'd let us pick out a female assistant from the store. My now wife was frequently the then "female assistant" chosen back in our teenage years. She would help us unload the truck and shelve stock away. We treated it as a serious selection process, as we wanted to pick someone we liked and someone who could work hard. I realize now that Dad is still schooling me all these years later. He let us pick out a girl to show off for. By showing off, we unloaded the truck faster. Darn him. We strutted around on truck day like Donald Trump, Ari's favorite historical character. In reality, it was bitter, hard work. We had to unload the truck and then wheel everything inside through the back halls of the mall, and then put it away. The back hallway to get to the store was at least two hundred yards and involved three right-hand turns and a left. We always had two carts, but one was always busted. The truck was always running late because of weather or traffic or because the kids at the delivery before us were lazy. Around Christmas 1989, the truck was hours and hours late. We sat around waiting and generally annoying Dad. Finally, he agreed to let us leave the store to wander around the mall and get dinner. Instead of dinner, we went straight upstairs to the arcade by the hobby store and the mall ministry. The day manager knew us pretty well from eating in the store. When he saw us, he reached into his pocket and handed us the key for unlocking the games to play them for free. A state of nirvana is a term often thrown around too loosely. We approached nirvana with that key and could visually observe the ideal condition of rest, harmony, stability, and joy. Literally, a rainbow emanated from the key. We played a single game of S.T.U.N. Runner. The room then filled with fog, and we both felt an icy grip on our shoulders. Dad found us, and retrieved us, as the truck had just arrived. At least that's how I remember it happening. A couple of weeks later the arcade closed for good, and we never saw the key again.

The fiesta de San Fermín starts at noon every July 6 with the *chupinazo*. The day explodes, as famously described by Ernest Hemingway, and there is no other way to describe it. After the *chupinazo*, the fiesta is beautiful and perfect.

At noon, the mayor and other officials step out on the balcony of the Ayuntamiento (the town hall) in the Plaza Consistorial and declare the fiesta open for business. This is the most dangerous event of the entire fiesta. The crowd is extremely large—the largest crowd of the fiesta, usually—and teeming, immature, anxious, and often cruel. This event is regularly marred by youthful thoughtlessness and tourists who fail to understand the fiesta. After the fiesta opens, a large food fight occurs with wine and staining bags of saffron (some yellow faces last for days) and flour and eggs and other foodstuffs. Mostly wine. For years, the amount of broken glass left behind was stunning. Bloodied feet and faces were not uncommon. Glass is now banned. This is a surging and pushing and relentless crowd, and we usually avoid this event entirely. The police can act poorly during the opening and strain an already stressed event. In 2010, police unreasonably refused to allow Basques to unfurl the Basque flag (the *ikurriña*), which started a pretty violent exchange. From the balcony, someone threw a large bottle, which struck José Carlos Arranz, a high school biology teacher from Madrid, in the head, causing irreparable brain injuries. It took three years to catch and convict the culprit, who was sentenced to multiple years in prison. José is still learning to speak again. All glass and capped plastic bottles were subsequently banned from the plaza during the opening ceremonies. Those pining for a bullfighting ban would better spend their energies banning the throwing of bottles. Such incidents are grossly the exception.

In 2011 in *Time* magazine, Michael Stipe wrote of Patti Smith, "[I]nnocence, utopian ideals, beauty and revolt are enlightenment's guiding stars in the human journey." I tore out the page! Fiesta is more or less the only thing in my life that compels me to launch into lectures concerning these concepts: innocence, utopia, beauty, and revolt. Innocence? The fiesta has not lost its simple farmer-and-herder-from-the-hills vibe. Utopia? No event better exemplifies citizens of various cultures and backgrounds getting together without conflict over anything. Beauty? If something or someone doesn't take your breath away during San Fermín, you haven't been conscious. And, my favorite is Revolt. Fiesta is satisfyingly

anarchistic. While "regulated," it is ungoverned. It's nice to be re-
minded that the state, in its political sense, isn't always necessary.
Those who call for the European Union (EU) to "ban" the *encierro*
or feria cannot stand, at a base level, to see that their beloved governing agent has failed to extend its bony fingers to the minutiae
of the entertainment of a few Navarrans, Spanish, and Basques
in rural northern Spain. Funny thing, though: With all its pag-
eantry, music, laughing, singing, merriment, dancing, fireworks,
eating, and general charming "fiesta-ess-ness," death itself lurks
around every corner during the fiesta. And it has really long horns.

The running of the bulls occurs in Pamplona, Spain, each
morning at 8:00 a.m. between July 7 and July 14. That means there
are eight runs per fiesta. This is not a well-known fact. Very commonly, international media report only the first run, and nothing
more, unless someone dies or an American is injured. I predict that
when an American girl is seriously injured or killed in Pamplona,
we will see the most serious efforts to end the *encierro* or, at the
very least, radically change it. Many of us run every day. It is quite
exhausting to endure the entire fiesta, and running with the bulls
eight times.

The running is known as the *encierro* in Spanish, which literally means "the enclosing." A religious fiesta has occurred yearly
in Pamplona since 1196. Seeking better weather, the city moved
the start of the fiesta from October 10 to July 6 in 1591. This is
funny to us, because Pamplona can have fantastic weather in July
and deadly weather in July. We have experienced temperatures
approaching 120 degrees Fahrenheit, or 49 degrees Celsius, whatever that is. People die from the heat. In Pamplona, it's a good bet
that the heat has killed more revelers than the bulls during our
time in the city. In comparison, at night, we have seen our breath;
once, we were forced to build an igloo. Here's the general weather
rule: If I leave my San Fermín sweatshirt at home, it will be freezing
during the fiesta.

Many other Spanish and Latin American cities have similar
fiestas. They are just not as well known. For instance, the lovely

coastal town of Denia has an *encierro* where the bulls run into the ocean instead of a bullring. It's known as Bous a la Mar, that is, Bulls of the Sea. Other cities have a fiesta de San Fermín, but *sin los toros.* Many local youths are putting their *encierro* photographs from other towns on social media, so it is much easier today to educate yourself about other fiestas, which have been kept secret for centuries (not on purpose; those towns just don't care if foreigners visit). Now, we're forced to endure fantasic stories from friends about fiestas we can't attend in little towns with names we can't pronounce.

The fiesta de San Fermín ends at midnight on July 14 with the Pobre de Mí (literally, "poor me") ceremony. The *encierro* is but a small part of the entire celebration. The running lasts under five minutes (one hopes) in a day jammed with events. In fact, there is an astonishingly organized "official" program of activities, which is matched only by the "unofficial" daily events that occur during the fiesta.

It's easy to forget that the fiesta is, at its heart, a religious celebration. For a while, the city's website read, *"Setting religion to one side,* the bull run is the central event of the fiesta of San Fermín." Tourists set aside religion. The local citizens do not: They are going to church, getting babies blessed, and making penance during the fiesta. It is the primary focus among friends and family. There is plenty of time during the fiesta for forced, soulful begging, searching, and bargaining prayer. If you run the *encierro,* you'll find the words yourself. This isn't a book about religious doctrine, but it won't kill you to take a moment to reflect on the true meaning of the week while not under duress of the bulls.

I am not a Roman Catholic, but you don't have to be in line for the next papal opening to be touched by the conviction and sincerity of the Pamplona citizens. These are Roman Catholics from a bygone era, and perhaps memories of the Franco terror years enhance their devotion. Many found religion in the United States during our civil war also.

Pamplona is located in northern Spain and is the seat of the

Navarre government. This region was traditionally known as the Nafarroako Erresuma, or the Kingdom of Navarre. Now, it's the Chartered Community of Navarre, or the Nafarroako Foru Erkidegoa. In English, it's Navarre. In Spanish, it's Navarra. In Basque, it's Nafarroa. In this book, I will use the English. Basques keep this confusing on purpose. Japanese is an easier language to casually pick up. In fact, during the winter, after all the tourists are gone, I think the locals of Pamplona must gather for seminars and lectures with professional PowerPoint presentations on how to keep foreigners bewildered. This is the southern frontier of the Basque Country, and many living in Pamplona do not consider themselves Spanish but Basque or Navarran. Don't just ask someone if they speak "Spanish." Of course they do. They probably also speak French, English, and Basque. Along with some people living in southern France, many desire to form their own separate Basque Country, or at least maintain some degree of autonomy, or maintain more autonomy than Madrid will allow. Their movement is largely sympathetic to us, even when their methods are untoward. Under Generalissimo Franco, their language and culture were suppressed, and the Navarran and Basque people were strongly persecuted. They are proud and fascinating and worthy of respect. They are tough and industrious and long-suffering. However, even today, neighbors and families are bitterly split on how to proceed in the region. Innumerable numbers of their people are political prisoners—some fairly, and some wrongly. Any legal action to bar people from speaking their mind, or banning them from simply unfurling their flag, is reptilian. This, though, is not a political book. We're just trying to have some fun. A good friend tells me they used to chant and sing during fiesta before my time when times were tenser "¡Fiesta si, politica no!" I might refer to the Basque people and culture a lot in this book, and I am sincerely fascinated by them, but it should not be taken as a slight to anyone that lives in or around Pamplona. This includes Navarrans, Spaniards, Pamplonicans, Basques, or whatever. We are not taking sides.

Ari and I love you all. Now, we can all spend our time better teaching the French modern hygiene.

That said, *and setting religion aside,* the primary event of the fiesta de San Fermín is the afternoon bullfight, not the *encierro.* Originally, people came to town for the fiesta and the bullfights. The *encierro* serves a practical purpose—getting the bulls to the bullring from their paddock down by the river.

On each morning between July 7 and July 14, it is necessary to move the bulls from their temporary corral to the bullring. Why? Because the bullring was built so far from the river—about a half-mile away. The corrals were built near the train tracks or the river for delivery of the bulls from their *ganadería,* the ranch or farm that raised the individual breed of *toro bravo,* or bulls used in bullfights in Spain. Neither the river nor the train passes by the bullring.

In 1899, the *encierro* was shortened when the city decided to build a mini-paddock across the river. Now the bulls are placed in the main corral when they arrive in Pamplona (by truck these days) and moved nightly in batches to the bottom of calle Santo Domingo. Each night, there is the "little *encierro,*" or *encierrillo,* during which the bulls for the next day's fight are tiptoed over the bridge from their temporary holding place into the corral. This is a solemn and serious event, where revelry and foolishness are not tolerated, with prejudice. If you go, you'd best be quiet.

For the morning *encierro,* revelers start gathering at the Plaza Consistorial, in front of the Ayuntamiento, between 6:00 and 6:30 a.m. This is key. If you want to run with the bulls, you must be out in front of the Ayuntamiento de Pamplona before 7:30 a.m. at the absolute latest. The Pamplona city website states, "All participants should congregate on the Cuesta de Santo Domingo, between the military hospital and the plaza. There is a doorway in the Plaza del Mercado which will be closed at 7:30 a.m." This is so unhelpful, and since it is Spain, the "rule" is not always enforced exactly to these terms. Best bet: Make sure you can see the town hall clock in the Plaza Consistorial. You will recognize the building for a number of reasons. First, it's the only big, fancy building in the Plaza Consistorial. Second, it's the only building with a clock. Third, it has two giant statues of Hercules wielding clubs flanking statues of Prudence and Justice, with a statue of Fame blowing her bugle on the pinnacle of the building. A recurring theme in this book, but everyone can play in the brass section of the orchestra in Pamplona.

The authorities close off the entire running course at or around 7:30 a.m., except for the area in front of the town hall. This limits the number of runners. The permitted space changes yearly and daily. But if you can see the clock on the top of the building, you'll always be safe. Some locals step out of their store or homes into the street at the last minute. You can't. Pamplona is a town full of tourists during the fiesta. False rumors start and fly easily. Don't fall for any garbage about where you need to be and when you need to be there to make it into the course for the morning run. You must start the day in front of the Ayuntamiento de Pamplona in the Plaza Consistorial. You must—you must. Don't listen to the stupid rumors started by overconfident Americans, drunken Brits, Aussies, their girlfriends, or their progeny. Every day we talk with someone who "heard" you could start somewhere else in the streets, and at 7:59 a.m., they are removed from the running course by the police, and they completely lose their chance to run. Latecomers become early watchers.

We talk every day of the fiesta to people who were tossed off the course moments before the running, and on their only day in the city. The police will not care about your sad story, and you'd be better off not trying. The police also will wait until the last possible second to let you know what you planned to do won't fly. Tear this page out of the book and put it into your pocket and don't listen to anyone else.

On the busiest days of the fiesta—the first couple of days, the weekends, and the weekend nearest Bastille Day—you should be out in front of the Ayuntamiento by 6:30 a.m. Otherwise, you need to be out in the Plaza Consistorial before 7:30 a.m. On the weekend nearest Bastille Day, the city becomes thick with Frenchmen. It's palpable. Bastille Day is the French national holiday celebrated on July 14. In France, it is formally called La Fête nationale, which is loosely translated as "Let's Go to Pamplona."

A little before 8:00 a.m., the police allow the crowd to disperse throughout the running course. If you are not on the course already, you will not be permitted to cross the wooden barriers. Sometimes they give the runners ten minutes, sometimes two. It is consistently inconsistent. This is your opportunity to go to your chosen "spot" to start your run. The course is over a half-mile long, and the bulls run almost as fast as cheetahs. At twelve years old, my son Sam boldly claimed I'd made this up. Cheetahs run at a speed of about 45 mph. *Toros bravos* run about 35 mph. In the street, the difference is negligible. However, I'd feel much better with six cheetahs in the street. I might even try to pet one. You cannot run the entire course. Anyone who says he has or will is lying. Work out your plan beforehand, and expect those plans to go the way of mice and men. Yet a plan takes away from the panic of the morning, and at least knowing whether you will run on the left or right to start, and where you will meet up with friends and family afterward, helps.

If at all possible, you should walk the *entire course* before your first run. Start at the beginning and walk all the way to the bullring. You cannot do this the day of your first run. Ari and I walk the course every year as soon as we arrive in Pamplona, and again halfway through the fiesta. We look for any changes, slick spots, damaged cobblestones, road patches, or new sewer grates. Sewers grates are the bane of bull runners.

Often, first-time runners seek out potential safe doorways. They start out with a plan to hang from the wooden barriers or escape early by gently climbing between the railings before seeing bulls. This is not right, and don't waste your time doing it. This is the running of the bulls, not the standing in the doorway of the bulls. There is no safe doorway, and often bulls catch standers flush. Really, everyone tries for the same doorway anyway. We've all had to seek higher ground to escape a charging bull, but no one should *start out* on the barriers. The police and other officials will vigorously push you back into the fray should you try to climb the barriers; they are for emergencies (and real emergencies!). And, climbing only draws the attention of the bulls. Running hard, and straight down the middle, is really the safest option. Usually, those who get gored are not running. Some think they can start the run hanging from a ledge or a lamppost or a drainpipe. You shouldn't, but more importantly you cannot. The police will yank you down. Then the crowds will cast aspersions.

Take a moment to reflect on the dignity of the animal you are running with in the early morning of the fiesta. The goal here is to run with the bulls. You are joining their herd. This is not the "touching of the bulls" or "smacking of the bulls." The goal is not to touch the horns. Those who brag about touching the horns or smacking the bulls completely miss the purpose of the running. This isn't some rite of passage to manhood. It isn't a contest to see who can act like a jerk.

To truly run with these bulls requires an understanding of the history and tradition of these God's wonderful beasts. You aren't running from them; you are running with them. Since birth, these bulls have known each other and have instinctively joined as a herd, as brothers. Watch the bulls in the paddock—they comically bicker with each other, too! Look! The taller bull is much more handsome! It is their natural urge to stay together. Today's sunrise is most likely their last. If you run with honor, respect, and dignity, if you run right in front of or alongside the herd, you will join—for just a moment—these brothers who imminently face a noble, brave, bloody, and (controversial) public end. Once in a lifetime, a bull fights so grandly, and his torero fights so bravely, that the bull is left to leave the ring alive, never to fight again. I have never seen this, but it's said that grown men cry like babies. I have seen bulls merely recognized in the ring for their uncommon bravery, but not pardoned. Just thinking about it gives me goose bumps. The children's book *Little Egret and Toro* addresses this concept better than anything. Written by Robert Vavra but illustrated by Philadelphia's own John Fulton, it solemnly considers the merit of showing mercy to the bravest of *los toros bravos*.

Running in the *encierro* is serious business. Dignified and moral running and safety are not actually always matters of common sense. A plan to stand still and let everyone and the bulls run past you is no plan at all. Frankly, this is what we did on our first trip to Pamplona. We were, as in many areas of life, without a clue. However, standing still was very dangerous to us, and to our fellow runners.

These safety issues and rules are outlined more in chapter 5. But, for instance, new tourists to Pamplona often circulate the rumor that the goal is to touch the bull. This violates one of the few rules of the *encierro*. It also violates the spirit of the event. You may even see locals doing it or talking about it. That doesn't make it right. In Philadelphia, you might see a local vomiting in the street during the Mummers Parade. You wouldn't copy him, right? A local idiot acting rude isn't carte blanche moral authority to mimic. However, keep in mind that there is a difference between you or me touching the bull and an experienced Navarran ranch hand doing so.

The *encierro* deserves respect, or at least some reverence. This started way before us and will continue long after we're gone, unless the EU gets its way. I doubt it ever will. Regardless, it's not about you or me. Running the right way is important.

To get a sense of the history of the *encierro*, consider that in 1776 the city installed the iconic wooden barriers defining the modern running route. The course was adjusted in 1856 and again in 1922, when Pamplona christened the new Plaza de Toros. Instead of branching right to the old bullring, the course veered left to the new plaza. Navarrans were running long before those years. This is, and has been for a while, an historical event. So, safety aside, cobblestones in the morning with *los toros bravos* is no place for drunks and louts and morons. And it's no place for people touching the bulls.

Among other goals, it is our ambition to pass on to our fellow American travelers a higher regard (a respect) for the *encierro*.

The official sanctioned *encierro* has always taken place at the "same solar time." The bulls ran at 6:00 a.m. until 1924, and at 7:00 a.m. until 1973, and have been running at 8:00 a.m. since 1974, due to legislated changes to true time, and not an altering of the earth's orbit around the sun or anything like that.

Minutes prior to the run, to ask for his protection, runners sing to Saint Fermín waving a newspaper in their hands in front of a niche located at the base of the hill on calle Santo Domingo. The song is sung three times (at 7:55 a.m., 7:57 a.m., and 7:59 a.m.).

At 8:00 a.m., the paddock doors are opened, and a rocket announces that the first bull has left the corral. How will you know if it's *the rocket*? You'll know. Potentially, you could be up to a half-mile away, so it is natural to ask whether you will hear it. You will hear it. You may find yourself asking, "Was that it?" If so, then rest assured that wasn't it. The rocket is loud and jarring, and the scariest noise you'll ever hear.

A second rocket announces that all bulls have left the corral. We carefully count the seconds in between, because bulls running together are much less likely to engage in mischief. If there is a long time between rockets, it's likely the bulls have become separated, and danger is afoot. A long interval between the first and second rocket, barring some foul-up at the paddock with matches and the like, means the bulls are separated. They will lose the instinct to make the decisions they would normally make in a herd. Look at the faces of the local runners—if they turn green and leave the streets, *leave the streets*.

In total, four rockets are launched every morning. Your safety depends to a large extent on the rockets being launched properly and on time. Things do not always go as planned. Fuses are long or short, it's windy, matches are wet, the lighter is empty, the guy lighting the rockets was out late, or someone forgot the rockets are all among the excuses for delayed launches. If you've ever tried to light a candle in less than optimal circumstances, you know why keeping time by rocket launches is not the preferred mode of keeping time. Things go awry. However, in theory, the first rocket is launched when the clock on the church strikes 8:00 a.m. The gates of the corral are then opened. The second rocket announces that the entire herd has left the corral, the third that the bulls and the oxen are in the bullring, and the fourth rocket indicates that the entire herd has entered the corral at the bullring. For a good reason, a train conductor uses his pocket watch, and not rockets in the distance, to tell time. You get the idea: Keep your wits about you, as the rockets are not entirely timely, and in fact are comically impractical.

People for the Ethical Treatment of Animals (PETA) and the like claim that the bulls are "forced" to run and that they are shocked, or someone tortured them into leaving the paddock. Nope, the doors are opened, and the bulls run off. They want to run.

From the paddock, the bulls follow a fast but meandering course throughout the city. It is commonly broken into eight distinct segments:

Calle Santo Domingo. Between the corral and Plaza Consistorial is the fastest and most dangerous area of the run. This stretch is about three hundred yards long, on a rising slope with a slight left. It is a steep slope and the bulls tend to group together, except when they don't. The bulls run hard through this section, as they have an instinct to press on hastily when running uphill. Some *mozos* (a term of endearment for runners in Pamplona, which loosely means "lads") run toward the bulls in this section, which in my opinion is not reflective of the traditions of the *encierro*—I think it always creates a risk of breaking up the herd at this critical point (if the bulls get separated here, mayhem is sure to follow). Others disagree. Notable Pamplona citizen Carmelo Butini Etxarte believes that the act of the runners charging toward the herd helps keep the bulls together. Nevertheless, much of the course here is hemmed in by sheer walls, and there is nowhere to hide. The street along calle Santo Domingo is always slippery, and there are dangerous curbs. We've seen some runners take terrible falls off and up onto those curbs.

There are several manhole covers, which are like ice. At the top of the hill, it is not uncommon for the bulls to stumble or fall as they enter the Plaza Consistorial. This section of the run is for very experienced runners only. Truthfully, we rarely run here—not for any rational reason. *It's just that your run is over so fast.*

July 12, 2008—This was the first morning we had ever awoken to pouring rain in Pamplona. Back then, Ari and I had a *brilliant* plan for a rainy morning. We would run calle Santo Domingo, the most dangerous stretch on the bull-running course. I did not believe then that the bulls would step up on the sidewalk, and there is a small portion of this run with sidewalks on either side of the street. Bulls, like many large animals, look to avoid hazards like steps and holes. With the rain, we were very concerned about slipping if we really pursued a vigorous run. So, we waltzed down calle Santo Domingo and talked it up with some older Basque gentlemen until the bulls arrived. The lead bull took just a couple dainty steps at a full gallop and, bang—he was on the sidewalk. I remember thinking, "Maybe he wants to buy a newspaper." We scattered. A runner near us slipped running off the sidewalk and smacked his head flush on the curb, opening up his skull. We don't go on the sidewalk anymore.

Plaza Consistorial. This is where your morning should have started—in front of the Ayuntamiento de Pamplona. From calle Santo Domingo the bulls make a slight left into the Plaza Consistorial, run through the plaza for about forty yards, and then make a slight left onto calle Mercaderes. The entrance to the plaza is a colossal bottleneck. Then, Plaza Consistorial itself is the widest part of the running course, and is surrounded by wooden barriers on both sides. It is almost square, or a squashed trapezoid. It is the least crowded area of the course, usually. I love running the two left-hand turns with the bulls here a couple of times each fiesta. There are several wet drain covers in the plaza, and there is always slippery trash left behind by those waiting for the morning run. Crushed plastic cups are the worst. The left onto calle Mercaderes is among the most iconic of Pamplona; as the bulls approach, the sun rises over the mountains and buildings from the east. Sometimes it can be quite blinding.

Calle Mercaderes. From Plaza Consistorial, the bulls make a slight left onto calle Mercaderes. Between the Plaza Consistorial and the hard right onto calle Estafeta, the course is wide, with storefronts on the left and wooden barriers on the right. This is about 75 yards long. At 8:00 a.m., the sun is just high enough in the sky to peek over the buildings at the end of calle Mercaderes, and I enjoy running there with the herd awash in sunbeams. If you have impeccable timing or remarkable luck and are photographed with the horns, the herd, and the sunbeams together, well, then, you've had a pretty good morning. It is possible to start running hard, when you see the bulls in the distance, at the bottleneck at the top of calle Santo Domingo and run through to the hard right onto calle Estafeta—through Plaza Consistorial and down calle Mercaderes. Assuredly, the bulls will overtake you somewhere in there. And you will be sucking wind. Recently, Dennis Eóghan Clancey has owned this part of the course in the mornings. A graduate of West Point and of the U.S. Army Special Forces, Dennis is a filmmaker and a brilliant runner. He runs the entire plaza in front of the herd, and often all of calle Mercaderes, and then often around the bend. These are unusually spectacular, athletic, and brave runs. I have watched his untamed momentum flip him onto the back of a bull, and then watched him casually slide backward off the running bull, land, and keep on running beside it. When we saw him after the run, he coolly did not even mention it.

Behind calle Mercaderes is the old town market. It is the best place for picnic and bullfight provisions in the town. To the best of my understanding, its hours are random, and guards are posted around town to warn the market when we get nearby so it can shutter its doors. Inside, when we do get inside, we buy cheese and pastry worth dying for.

Bend of Calle Estafeta. At the end of calle Mercaderes, the road turns right onto calle Estafeta. It is a little more than a 90-degree right-hand turn. This is the most dangerous single spot of the running course. You will hear some call it "Hamburger Corner" or "Dead Man's Curve." Such references are considered crass and lowbrow, and they are frowned upon in Pamplona. It's the bend, or *la curva*. Experienced runners try to dance around the turn with the bulls. However, by the bend the bulls are running at a good clip, and on many mornings they slip and fall and crash into the wooden barrier on the outside of the bend when trying to make the hard turn (except when they don't). The city has tried everything to make this area less slippery, including etching the corner cobblestones *with acid*. Nothing works. This is the prime place where the bulls get separated from each other. This is also a place for the most experienced runners. A rare runner actually runs around the curve with the herd. Conventional wisdom is that the turn should be taken on the inside; however, many, many, many other people have the same idea every morning of the fiesta. It can get very crowded. The bend is the best place for a bull to fall on you. Immediately after the herd passes, a gate is closed to prevent the bulls from coming back up the street. If you are behind the herd, you might not be able to get through. A friend broke his leg in 2013 when the gate slammed closed on him. You can get hurt in Pamplona many ways.

Right now, there is no one better than Angus Alexander Ritchie (Gus) from Glasgow, Scotland, running the corner from calle Mercaderes as the herd turns right onto calle Estafeta. *Absolutely no one*. We met him in 2011 and talked with him for over an hour. We actually understand some of the words he uses, but we still sometimes require the "English"-to-English translator. He is charmingly boyish (even though he is two years older than me), and tough as nails, and disarming. In the corner, Gus does not wait for the bulls to gather at the turn to step into the herd. He finds a bull on calle Mercaderes, gets in front, and runs with the whole herd around the bend. The bulls don't breathe on his pants, they step on his pants. In fact, they rummage through his pockets. He is no bigger than Ari. He does not use grace or athleticism in his run, but grit and backbone and sheer determination. He is a daring and spectacular runner, and always on the horns. He wears a yellow jersey from the Partick Thistle Football Club, which plays futball (whatever that is) in Glasgow. Daily, he is photographed in the corner with the herd. His pictures are used in Pamplona promotional materials around the world. He falls, and is horrifyingly splayed out on the cobblestones all the time. He is covered in scabs and wounds and bruises by the last morning of the fiesta, and relentlessly comes back for more. In 2014 he showed up on the cobblestones with his entire head spray-painted red, but no one could remember how it happened, including Gus. Even as the fiesta ended, the paint was still wearing off. These things happen to him often, and are endearing. A fiesta without Gus will be a sad fiesta.

Gus loves hiking and is shameless (we've all seen him nude, and more than once, too). He is famous around the world. In Dublin, Ari was explaining to total strangers while we waited in line for steamed burgers past midnight why his leg was bandaged, and someone asked, "Do you know that guy that runs in the Partick Thistle kit?" During the fiesta, my wife finds pictures of him online and emails them to me. Not of me or Ari, just him.

Calle Estafeta. This is the longest part of the running course (320 yards), and you normally would not notice that there is a 2 percent incline—that is, unless you were running from *toros bravos*. This is also one of the main street settings of the fiesta—the section of the run usually shown briefly once or twice on American television. Along calle Estafeta, the course is hemmed in almost exclusively by storefronts and the occasional wooden barrier at street intersections. The street is shadowed by balconies and bunting and cheering onlookers. This is the best part of the course to get out and stay in front of the bulls for a long time. While crowded, the seas part when the herd approaches. Every year, some young buck gets out in front and runs forever with the herd, and makes the afternoon newspapers. It is physically impossible to run the entirety of calle Estafeta. Midway down the street, after the herd passes, another gate is closed.

Telefónica. At the end of calle Estafeta, the ancient cobblestones end, and the course is covered with Home Depot–type paver stones. This is the Telefónica, and the least slippery part of the course, even in the rain (which is rare). It is bordered by wooden barriers only. This street section starts in front of the old Telephone Exchange and is about 100 yards long. You cannot run the entire length with the herd. This stretch leads right into the bullring. There is a slight left from calle Estafeta onto the Telefónica, and there's a swinging left into the stretch leading to the bullring. The bulls rarely have trouble making these turns, and in fact speed up on the decline into the corral. There are many, many runners gored along the Telefónica. Other than "the bend," this is the best area for the bulls to become separated. This is where Daniel Jimeno Romero died in 2009, when a bull turned and gored him against the barrier. The wooden barriers funnel everyone quickly downhill into the bullring. I have fallen multiple times on the Telefónica, because I am going at a good speed and trip over myself or fallen runners. I find it hard to keep my balance running downhill with the herd and the crowd. The Telefónica is the favorite place of the *diviños* (the divine: the most famed, experienced runners). At the end of the pavers, another gate is closed when the bulls pass. This is the most dangerous gate to get caught on the wrong side of, because the crowd often continues to surge from behind. A friend got his arm caught in the closing gate trying to squeeze into the bullring in 2012.

The Callejón. This is the three-meter-wide tunnel leading to
the ring. *Callejón* means "alley" in Spanish. Running through
here with a bull or the herd is the holy grail of the *encierro*. It takes
some timing and a lot of bravado and luck. Before going to Pamplona for the first time, Ari and I were inspired by a photograph
of finance professor Gary Gray, shown bursting from the Callejón
in his blue trucker hat with the herd in tow. This alley is narrow,
and the herd and multitudes of runners must pass through. As
such, dangerous human pileups are not uncommon here. Locally,
these are ominously referred to as *montónes*, literally "mountains." In
July 1922, the herd jumped and climbed over just such a pile, leaving over 100 wounded. We saw our first pileup on July 12, 2004
(one of the worst ever), when we witnessed the bulls horrifyingly
goring the pile. If you fall in the alley, there are few options. There
is a large gap at the bottom of the wall to roll under to safety. In
fact, there are Red Cross workers in the little rooms behind the
walls to help drag you underneath. In 2012 I fell here and was
pulled under the wall immediately. I had never been under there
and was grateful for their quick hands. It was like fiesta rapture.
From here, do not try to run into the bullring after the bulls have
entered.

In 2010, a twenty-eight-year-old Bill Hillmann walked up to
Ari and me after the morning run while I was still catching my
breath. He was wearing white baseball pants (dirtied by the bullring sand), his now patented blue-striped, long-sleeved, No. 9
rugby jersey, and his now even more patented newsboy cap. We
immediately liked him. Bill is from Chicago (and still lives there)
and has a fantastically goofy smile, which makes his eyes twinkle
and rise when he does, which is often. He leaned in, offered his
firm handshake, and said, "It's such a privilege to run with guys
like you." I looked around like someone was joking with us, but he
continued to thank us and seemed more than genuine. When he'd
left, Ari said, "Who was that?"

"Never saw him before," I answered.

I had no idea, but we'd just made a lifelong friend. After the fiesta ended, Ari and I were looking at our fiesta pictures in the Madrid airport lounge, and Ari kept saying over and over, "Hey, it's that guy." Bill reached out to me at home online, and we started to become Pamplona family. Bill's actually been running with the bulls in Pamplona since 2006. He's just a little taller than Ari, but actually athletic. He was a 2002 Chicago Golden Gloves champion. He runs the dangerous Callejón daily and makes the tricky transition from the ancient cobblestones to the modern pavers, and finds the horns every morning.

Then, in July 2011, as Bill burst past me in the Callejón with the whole herd in tow, I had a moment of clarity. It was like watching Gale Sayers run the Callejón. When I was in middle school, my mother gave me a compilation of the best writings of Red Smith, the Pulitzer Prize–winning sportswriter. I underlined the heck out of it, including this phrase about Gale Sayers: ". . . there was a magic about him . . ." Red Smith would have loved to watch Bill Hillmann run with the bulls in Pamplona. He's a sawdust throwback. Sayers's and Hillmann's feet don't seem to touch the grass or the cobblestones. As a running back, Sayers distinguished himself by charging through the lines—he didn't run around or seek refuge. Gale Sayers subtly altered his running route without tripping, faltering, or slowing pace. Watching Bill is the same: He doesn't dodge the bulls or flee; he *moves* past them. He uses quickness and angles. He starts running before knowing how the bulls have formed, and adjusts accordingly when they arrive at his heels. They breathe on his pants every morning of the fiesta. They whisper in his ear. After his 2011 fiesta, Bill became pretty famous, and he did a great job being (acting?) embarrassed about the attention. He had no need to. Sometimes my wife asks me on the telephone if Bill is okay before asking if I am. He's that kind.

Bullring. Immediately upon entering the bullring, you should peel to the left or right and not run up the middle. The middle is left free to allow the bulls to run through, and for the *dobladores*, ring workers who help direct traffic. Do not panic when a herd of *cabestros* (oxen) runs through the ring afterward. These are sent in case any of the bulls try going the wrong way.

The post of the *doblador* ("guider") was invented in the 1930s to protect the bulls and the runners once each enters the bullring. Usually there are four *dobladores*. They are or were professionally employed fulltime in bullfighting and have considerable experience with the Pamplona *encierro*. They are experts. They are charged with getting the bulls entering the ring into their pens underneath the grandstand. They are the dudes with the capes—the ones who are supposed to have capes. Wannabe matadors who jump into the ring with capes, trying to make a name for themselves, are arrested! With each pass of the cape, a bull learns a little more about his ultimate goal—getting the matador. No one is allowed to make cape passes with the fighting bulls after the run. The *dobladores* drag their capes to get the bulls into their pens, and keep the *toros bravos* from running amok in the crowded ring. They are professionals, and you should respect their instructions and give them a wide berth to do their jobs. Don't get in their way. They have a thankless but dangerous job.

Again, these are the sections of the running course:

> calle Santo Domingo
> Ayuntamiento de Pamplona
> calle Mercaderes
> the bend
> calle Estafeta
> the Telefónica
> the Callejón
> bullring

I am sure you have noticed that I describe nearly every section as "the most dangerous" part of the course. That's because it's all true.

It's important to remember: You cannot run the entire course. A bull is faster than Carl Lewis. The route is over 900 yards. No one can run that distance at full sprint, even Ari in his "prime." Even at top human speed, the bulls are much, much faster than any person running. It is actually something you have to experience to understand.

To summarize then, shortly before 8:00 a.m. the police will allow those who gathered in front of city hall to spread out along the entire route. Pick a point on the course and wait. Start running hard in the middle of the street as the bulls approach *in the distance*. If you wait too long to run, they will pass you by before your brain can tell your feet to get on the move. When you are running down the center of the street, the bulls will quickly overtake you—"just" slide out from the front of the horns, and back away to the side of the street. You will just have to run with the bulls. This of course makes it sound much easier than it is. You should know that I felt nauseated as I wrote this, as my very soul is involuntarily recalling each hagridden moment with the bulls. Honestly, I try not to think about Pamplona before going to sleep at home, because I won't get to sleep or even be able to spit if needed.

Don't wait for them to pass you. Run when you see the bulls. Or, run when you are about to see them. This is the absolute hardest skill to master. You may have to run dozens of times before you really feel you are getting a notion of when to start running. Some runners use buddies as spotters on a balcony or at the entrance to the ring to flash hand signals when the bulls reach a certain point, and to indicate how they are grouped together. However, if you are relying on somebody like that (or you don't know the guy spotting), make sure you get it straight whether they are showing bulls that have passed or bulls that remain. For me, that lesson has also already been learned.

The effort to summon the courage to step into the middle of the cobblestones—against all instinct—is paralyzing. The urge is to linger on the sides. Because of the crowds, staying to the side is a bad idea, for two reasons. First, everyone else will be to the side also. Second, you have to fight through the throbbing morass of panicking runners to get to the center once you see the bulls.

Everyone makes the mistake of staying on the walls at least once. On our first run in Pamplona (July 9, 2004), Ari and I stood together in a doorway at the far end of calle Estafeta. We were so far behind the crowds that we *didn't even see* the bulls as they ran past. But we heard them thunder past. I think we were holding hands. I know my eyes were closed. This hardly counted as "running with the bulls." This is the absolute worst kind of "run." If it matters, we've gotten much better, even though this book tends to indicate otherwise.

It is hard to see if the bulls are coming, because of the crowds, and because it seems everyone is taller than the bulls coming from a distance away. Even Ari! There are hundreds, if not thousands, of people in your sightline. Some friends advise that they start running when everyone stops looking back over their shoulder. Older generations looked for the wash of camera flashes from balconies as the bulls approached, but modern photography is beginning to end this custom. Many people jump in place to see (an iconic and distinctive visual experience is all the *mozos* jumping in place after the rocket).

In 2011, someone with an apartment near the end of calle Estafeta wheeled out a flat screen onto their balcony so we could see the live-feed broadcast on the second floor (this has since been banned, because *everyone* started congregating in the same place). Knowing where the bulls are helps a runner judge when to start running. This changed the way I run and, because it gave me some certainty of the position of the bulls, increased my boldness. However, I prefer using the constant of time to judge when the bulls are approaching. From where we usually run on calle Telefónica, I watch my watch, which reminds me that the bulls won't be turning the corner for at least two minutes after the first rocket explodes. Except in 2011, when the bulls ran the fastest average *encierro* ever. I remember looking at my watch and murmuring, "Look at all those scared dopes. We won't see bulls for another 45 seconds. Uh-oh." Oops. I was nearly run down by what must have been hybrid beasts (part bull and part gazelle).

My height gives me something of an advantage over runners who are a great, great, great, great, great deal smaller—like, say, Ari. *I have no idea how he ever sees the bulls.* After the rocket, but before the bulls get to you, beware of the crowd surges that invariably occur. Tourists rushing and heaving past in a swivet do not necessarily mean the bulls are approaching. They pitch and swell like the tides. Rely on your own senses, and not the smirky premonitions of other random runners, such as Monsieur Jean Bonnot over there with the cigarette hanging from his lip.

In all this, count the bulls. Seriously, count the bulls. You absolutely must keep track of how many bulls are still in the street. However, keep in mind that the bulls are released from their corral with a couple of *cabestros*. How do I say this nicely? *Cabestros* are castrated bulls with bells. The term *cabestros* may be used interchangeably with "steers." They are friendly and happy. They know the way from the tiny corral to the bullring already. The steers help persuade the bulls to keep moving, and the bulls have been led around by steers on the hometown farm for much of their life. During the *encierro,* the bulls usually start following, but often surpass the steers while running the entire length of the course. The bulls do not have bells around their neck; the steers do. For reasons beyond my understanding, the number of bulls released is always the same; the number of steers is not. Six to eight steers are released. Normally it is six. For larger crowds, eight are sometimes used. Mostly, it is just to confuse me. Sometimes they are all run together but often they become separated, making your count of the number of actual bulls remaining important. The worst thing that can happen is to be caught celebrating your brilliant morning run thinking that six bulls have run past, when another bull (or, couple of bulls) appears and you've been really only counting steers passing by. Again, it is very difficult to count the bulls, as they are running fast, and chaos reigns.

In 2010, I ran Plaza Consistorial and almost the length of calle

Mercaderes from the Ayuntamiento to *la curva* with the entire herd, or what I thought was the entire herd. It was toward the end of the fiesta, and tourists had largely left town, and there were large open spaces in which to run. I folded into the herd, counted six bulls and six *cabestros*, moved aside, and started walking back toward Plaza Consistorial in the middle of the street to find Ari. A lone black bull, which had fallen on calle Santo Domingo, turned the corner. I realized that hardly anyone was in the street but me, and stood perfectly still, upright, in the middle. The bull whizzed by with a sonic whoosh on my right. Lesson learned. I would not wish to repeat this event. Never rely on me for the bull count, because I am terrible at it.

When running, if you hear the locals yelling *suelto,* you know there is a lone bull and danger approaching. A bull separated from the herd is more likely to attack, to become tired and afraid, and to cause damage to person, property, and pants. Ari compares a *suelto* to a pinball. Bouncing side to side. The *sueltos* are the most common bulls to inflict injuries on runners. *Sueltos* frequently turn around and run the wrong way on the course. This deadly serious topic is addressed more in chapter 5.

Pastores (herders) are charged with guiding the *suelto* back to the proper path. The *pastores* have been a traditional part of the *encierro* since the Middle Ages, when they were responsible for herding the bulls on foot from the pasture and then through the cobblestone streets of Pamplona.

Now, there are ten *pastores* every morning. They are all dressed in green shirts, with the title *pastores* emblazoned on the back. They carry a wicked willow stick for smacking runners and bulls alike. Each is assigned a section of the run of approximately 100 meters. They pass the herd down the line. The *pastores* run behind the bulls in an attempt to keep the herd together, to prevent the bulls from reversing course, and to keep revelers away from the *suelto.*

The *pastores* are professionals in handling cattle, and can make cutting short a charging bull look easy. It's not. We have found most of them are farmers or fishermen and not fulltime cowboys. While they may seem serious in the morning, they are good guys, and they put their life at risk for the safety of the bulls and the runners. Follow their instructions. If you act dumb, they will hit you with their willow stick, and you will know it happened. Never in your life will you say, "I *think* I got hit by the willow stick." They have many other jobs during the fiesta and work tirelessly to make things appear smooth. They are responsible for all bull-related aspects of the fiesta, including the late-night *encierrillo; las vaquillas* (the baby bulls described in chapter 7); the Fiesta Campera (amateur bullfights); and the *sorteo* and *apartado* (the process of assigning bulls to a specific matador explained in chapter 7).

In 2009, Ari was hit in the head by the willow stick as it ricocheted off a bull's hide. That was funny. In 2005, I was struck in the arm after getting too close to a *suelto*. That was not. The entire story, of the exciting morning a runner named Xabier and I had, is told later in the book. Run long enough, and you too will get hit. Afterwards, stop and talk, if you can, with the *pastores*—to inquire as to why you were hit, or if it was an accident. Discuss how you each could have better approached the situation. They really are great guys. Then, apply ice liberally.

Crowds are a major topic in Pamplona during San Fermín. During boom economic times, the city is packed. On busy weekends, runners are crammed into Plaza Consistorial. Many people frame the crowds as problematic (get me on the wrong day and I do, too), and pine for the days of Hemingway, when the streets were wide open for fantastic runs between the horns for entire city blocks. One of the primary unofficial activities of the fiesta of San Fermín is talking about how it "used to be." We've been going long enough now to be guilty. Likely, in the days of Hemingway everyone talked about the 1890s, when they talked about the 1300s. It's human nature. We've only been running since 2004, and we already have opinions on what is now better and worse about the fiesta.

Crowds are a serious danger during the *encierro*. Most of the

injuries I've suffered while running are primarily related to falling over other runners or being pushed by other runners. It is not
uncommon to hear an inexperienced runner talking about his
intention to push someone else into harm's way to avoid being
gored. Humans are not shields unless you are a Middle Eastern des-
pot. These statements are made gleefully and with foolish bravado.
After someone pries my kung fu grip from his neck, I enjoy calmly
reminding the dullard that civility is essential to the fabric of our
shared community, and that the frothed Navarrans and Basques
tend to beat such scum into wishing they had taken the bulls instead. If you push another runner into harm to protect yourself,
the locals might just murder you. Forewarned is forearmed.

Someone grabs me during almost every run. In moments of
panic, I've had people I know and trust—*friends*—grab onto my
sleeve, or the collar of my shirt from behind. It is just something you
have to prepare yourself for mentally, and you need to have a plan
for how to adjust. You just need to be prepared for the impact, and
the surprise. Now, I vigorously chop at any arms and hands that
find themselves on my person. In 2014, my son Sam was running in
front of me and I saw another runner clearly reach out to grab him.
My big right fist left a big red mark on his left cheek. I am a bigger
guy than most runners, and I can easily brush off the average
clingy Frenchman. If you are French and are reading this, any derogatory references in this book to the French are purely the result
of a bad translation. If you are not French, let's make fun of the
French together some time. Personally, I love France and have visited many, many times. Frenchmen, though? Yikes. Every fiesta, Ari
and I always find excuses to cross the border to the French beaches.
The Spanish, the Basques, and the British have serious ancient disputes with the French, some of which are still being mediated every
morning in the street. Loudly. Under our room window.

Fallen runners are a hazard when running, but *falling
runners*—clutching wildly as they plummet—are even more dangerous. Even a true saint couldn't resist dragging his own mother
down as he falls onto the cobblestones.

So, you know not to stand still or touch the bulls. You know to count the bulls. You know to run in the middle of the street, as fast as you can marshal. You know to run every day. You know what *suelto* means. You're worried about the crowds, and about the bulls. You know where to be in the morning, and that shortly before 8:00 a.m. you will be permitted to spread out over the course. So, where are you going to start? And where are we all meeting up afterward? Then, what are we having for breakfast?

3

Burnin' Daylight
(getting ready for Pamplona)

"Slap some bacon on a biscuit and let's go!
We're burnin' daylight!"

—JOHN WAYNE, 1972

When we were all working together at the family store, and when we were still sullen but tired teenagers, we put in long, hard hours with Dad, who rode us like a 1935 Stakhanovite. We did not awaken in the morning to an alarm clock—we'd have slept through it anyway. Instead, Dad opened the door and kicked the beds and said—every morning—"It's a beautiful day in the neighborhood." Except Dad wasn't reciting Mr. Rogers to be ironic or contrary. He really meant it—really thought it—and he said it every morning. Every morning. When it was time to leave, he'd say, "Saddle up," like John Wayne, as if we were driving 400 head of cattle to Bel Fuche. Except we had a 1983 Red Chevette (the "Emasculator," which smelled of chicken and peanut oil), and neither the heat nor the AC got running right until we got all the way to the Echelon Mall. Yet Dad somehow sold us that we were suburban cowboys, and that hard, dirty, miserable work meant something. That's how we got ready for the long day,

and we got ready early. Now, we've really got to get ready for this
fiesta.

On July 15, shortly after midnight and moments after the end of
the fiesta, we immediately form the *camarilla* committee to ensure
our return next year. On the walk back to the hotel room, we stop
and make our next year's hotel reservations at the front desk. We
begin plotting the details of our triumphant return as soon as we
get home. You must start planning your time in Pamplona for San
Fermín early.

Physical Preparedness

You have to prepare for the sprint and for the marathon. The morning run (the sprint)—especially if you run *day after day*—takes its
toll, but so does the long daily grind on the cobblestones (the marathon). I take an awful lot, an official sponsorship amount, of
Doan's Caplets to get me through the fiesta and dull the annual
San Fermín Lower Back Spasm. Even Ari gags an aspirin down
sometimes. Like a baby bird with a watermelon Jolly Rancher.

Running with the bulls does not require a six-month workout
regimen. No one on earth is in good enough "shape" to run with
the bulls. Pump all the iron you want, but you will still be made
of flesh and blood.

You do need to be able to run a good distance—say, fifty
yards—and potentially run it hard. Practice running corners. Coax
swiftness from your sinew, which is far more important than
speed. You have to be sturdy, and able to take a hit from the other
runners. Some arm strength to push back doesn't hurt. You have
to be willing to suffer some pushing and shoving in a crowd,
skinned hands and knees and elbows, and a hard fall to the un-
forgiving ground. You have to be able to recover from a smacking
thud on the ground. You have to be able to sensibly protect yourself. It helps if you like the taste of cobblestones.

Any "training" you do should focus on balance, running while looking over your shoulder, jumping fallen runners, and swift reactions. I prepare my knees and lower back for the daily cobblestone grind by shooting hoops with my boys in the driveway and running sprints in the street. I use a Derek Jeter Series SKLZ Reaction Ball (a six-sided high-bounce rubber ball designed to cause the ball to leap and bounce randomly) to encourage quick feet, rapid change of direction, and sharp hand-eye coordination. I exercise the eye muscles used for peripheral vision by pretending someone is sneaking up on me while I am sitting and waiting for my case to be called in court. I do.

Falls present a more regular dangerous foe than the *toro bravo*. I have suffered serious injuries from three falls.

First, on July 13, 2010, bulls from the El Pilar ranch ran. No one that morning knew much about them, because they had been used in Pamplona only once since 1980. Where the Telefónica stretch turns toward the bullring, I picked up that the herd was not in a group but running nearly in a line. I saw my friends Bill Hillmann and Gary Masi in front of me on the right side, and Farmer Bob (he is a local Basque farmer boy with a terrible mullet whom we call Farmer Bob because he won't tell us his name; he wears a green plaid shirt and purple pants *every day I have ever seen him*—even the Basques think he's unbalanced) aggressively took to the center of the street. Jose Manuel Pereira was dodging the second or third bull in the long line in his patented blue-and-white striped shirt. I was running full tilt and found myself between Bill Hillmann and Farmer Bob three across in the center of the street, and glanced over my shoulder to see that the herd was no longer in a line but *running six wide*. They were running fast, too. So, there was no room for error. While there is a never-ending debate as to what happened next, Farmer Bob and I tangled while fighting for free space, and I fell forward while running as fast as I could muster. My momentum caused me to slide about ten yards, and I rolled head over teakettle a couple times, and then the entire El Pilar herd danced over and on me, which I guess was better than on my grave. A bull and multiple runners kicked me in the head and stepped on my back and shoulders. All of the horns missed me (not for their trying), because I kept prone, and stayed down. Farmer Bob goose-stepped into the middle of the ring with the entire herd. I tore open my leg, my arm, and my shoulder, and I had hoofprints on my back and head. I suffered a concussion but was featured in mirific photos in the local papers. "Yes, that's me under the bulls," I told perfect strangers. I never really figured out how we ended up in San Sebastián that night. Truly, the cumulative wounds acquired from falling in the street throughout the fiesta are debilitating. Mirific? I love this word. It is used when phrases like "wonderful and amazing" are insufficient. I learned it by staying at the Hôtel Mirific Opéra on Avenue de Clichy in Paris, where the owners have a sense of irony. Even today, Farmer Bob remains elusive, although I feel like I've known him for over a decade. No one talks to him in the morning. Is he ETA (the formerly armed Basque nationalist and separatist group)? An otherwise wanted man? In 2013 I resolved to get to know him for real. Every morning I found him before the run and practically had to force him to shake my hand. He warmed up slightly by actually making eye contact. In 2014, I started giving him a hug every morning against his wishes, but he started to laugh a bit. I even asked his name, and he said "John" and was clearly lying as he walked away to avoid any further discussion. He is a brilliant runner who takes the running "anonymously" diktat just too far. At this writing, he may be the best, bravest bull runner in the world. He is on the horns every morning. He is fast and graceful and runs with his head thrown back. Nobody knows who he is. On the last day of the fiesta in 2014, I horse-collared him in the bullring and gave him my red neckerchief, the *pañuelo*. I had to force him to take it. Ari said, "I think he just smiled." Next year, we are going to buy him breakfast.

Second, on July 9, 2011, I was raring to go because we got to the fiesta late on the seventh, and I had already fallen on the eighth. That morning, as the herd approached, I got trapped against the fence on the right side of the Telefónica stretch, and as a bull passed by, its horn grazed my shirtsleeve, creating friction that actually melted it. Then (presumably in total shock) I was pushed over from behind. I broke my elbow (which I did not know at the time), and tore open my elbow (which I knew immediately), and rolled under the fencing by accident, where my angry emotions were captured in Ari's favorite fiesta picture (me sitting on my backside behind the fence). A serious staph infection formed in the elbow after several days of swimming in the Mediterranean a week later. The elbow blew up to ten times its normal size on the airplane, I had to be hospitalized back home, and the doctor even discussed the possibility of my losing my arm! There is some debate about whether I sought medical attention from the Red Cross workers after the fall. If I did, they would have cleaned the wound to prevent infection in Pamplona. No amount of scrubbing would have saved me from the dirty Mediterranean, even the clear blue waters in Nice, a week later. I don't remember what I did after the fall, or significant parts of the rest of that day. I know a naked guy got loose in the bullring afterward and was viciously tackled by three female police officers, which salvaged the morning.

Third, on July 11, 2013, as I recounted earlier, I broke my ankle falling in the Callejón when another runner collided with me from behind. As the fiesta approached in 2014, I was still recovering from that injury.

Clearly, no amount of cardio workouts in the winter would have prepared me for these falls.

If you are running multiple times during San Fermín, you will need some long-term stamina. When Ari and I run every day—on July 7, 8, 9, 10, 11, 12, 13, and 14—and stay out till all hours of the night, we swear we will never do it again. It is incapacitating and painful. We wouldn't have it any other way. So, in my late thirties and forties, I had to start preparing myself physically to prevent shin splints and the annual Pamplona assorted aches and pains.

Mental Preparedness

Getting mentally prepared for the fiesta is more important than the physical preparation. Come the weeks before the fiesta, we hash out and rehash the moment of truth to convince our bodies to follow the instructions from our brains rather than act on instinct. Instinct alone would keep me home in New Jersey.

At some point before leaving for Pamplona, I reflect on and deliberate the *encierro* in excruciating detail. I prepare myself at home so that I am prepared to focus, despite the millions of distractions, on the bulls.

There is no casual run with the bulls. You cannot say, "I am just going to take it easy this morning." We made that mistake one time only. July 12, 2004, was the last day of our first fiesta. Our plane was leaving for Granada at 12:20 p.m., so we figured we could run at 8:00 a.m. and have plenty of time to get cleaned up and drive to the airport. We thought we would just take an "easy, casual" run. We figured we could just stay on the sidelines and not get all sweaty and dirty. Wow, were we wrong. As ill-informed new runners, we did not know that the Jandilla breed of bulls running that morning was the most feared breed in Pamplona. That morning, they created what was among the most dangerous mornings in the last couple of decades, with eight runners gored and ten more suffering serious injuries, many related to a *montón* at the bullring entrance. Most of this happened at our feet. There is no casual morning running with bulls. In that chaotic war zone, buckets of adrenaline were released into our collective bloodstream. We spent the rest of the morning at the airport shivering as our bodies moved blood to the brain, heart, lungs, and major muscles as we waited for our flight.

It is so important to think things through. Do you have a plan? Do you have your mind prepared for the jar of the first rocket, the sound of the hooves on the cobblestones, and the shocking sight of the bulls in the street? The bulls are massive and frightening, and even the most experienced and noble runner knows it. You will not always follow the plan. For instance, on July 8, 2006, at the end of the Telefónica, a single black bull from Dolores Aguirre ranch (known in Spain for their "proud bearing") decided I was on the breakfast menu and chased after me on the right side for so long that I finally crossed though traffic to the left side and found he was still chasing me. I knew this was wrong, and planned ahead to never do it. First, crossing over the middle of the running course is suicidal. Never did it before or since. That I made it without being gored or run down by another runner was a miracle. Second, to celebrate my stupidity, the bull showed mercy and decided to just smack me across the face with his feces-covered tail (it was like a whip; it left marks) as he ran right by, and as I found myself turned around and running the wrong way.

What are you going to do if those around you in the street start panicking? Can you control your urge to panic? Have you re-hearsed what you will do if you fall down? Or if you're gored? How will you handle the sight of pooling blood? The smell of blood? An open torso? What about your own blood? What will you do if there is a pileup of fallen runners? Where will you be meeting friends and family after you run? Where's breakfast today? You know, the important stuff.

You should never run the *encierro* without walking the entire course. Use your common sense: What areas look the most dangerous or slippery? Where are the manhole covers? These you should avoid like a French armpit. Where are the curbs? Avoid them like a manhole cover.

You should never fall for the "logic" of the turns. Whether the bulls will take a turn tight or loose is impossible to predict. The general rule is that the bulls will run wide *except when they don't*. That's not a rule by which to guide your life.

Can you control the emotional urge to resist street rumors? False information blows through the Pamplona streets like it is grade school lunch with snow in the forecast. If an Australian twenty-two-year-old with the words "BUSABOUT" written in Sharpie on his forehead who lost his shirt three days ago tells you something he heard last night in the campground, he's probably wrong. However, a week into the fiesta, when you've gotten fifteen hours of sleep in five days, that guy starts to sound pretty reasoned. Resist his sage wisdom.

Mental preparation for running cannot be overemphasized; this includes educating yourself about the *encierro*. Hundreds and hundreds of people have asked us, moments before the run was to start, "Which way do the bulls come from?" If you are stepping out into the street with six of the most vicious animals on earth, and you don't know where they are coming from, you have not mentally prepared yourself for the *encierro*. As to the aforementioned question, the date is unknown to us, but Ari and I were going to run through Plaza Consistorial, and after the first rocket exploded, and the run was under way, a freaked-out but pushy new runner started asking us—begging us—for help. "Which way do the bulls come from?" he shrieked. "Is this dangerous?" he inquired. While we can block out most last-second inquiries, we felt pity and gave him the twelve-second tutoring. Distracted, as the bulls quickly fell upon us, Ari and I stepped out into the fray and—"clang"—we ran right into each other, knocking ourselves to the cobblestones. A million other people in Pamplona and I clonked heads with Ari.

Clothing

You need to put together your San Fermín kit, which should include white pants, a white shirt, a red scarf, and a red sash. A red-blooded American boy will have trouble finding white pants to buy in Pamplona, unless he is diminutive. You can buy the rest in Pamplona minutes after the airplane lands.

The *pañuelo* recalls Saint Fermín's beheading. The red sash is just for style. Both of these are available superfluously in Pamplona. What you learned from Bugs Bunny about red capes, etc., was wrong, though; bulls are color-blind.

The shirt and pants are allegedly white to reflect a religious uniform. Or, perhaps to recall the local butchers who originated the tradition of running. I believe they're white because the town is secretly owned by Procter & Gamble. They sell detergent, and lots of it. *You will get dirty* during San Fermín. Even Hemingway suggests only bringing a woman to Pamplona who does not mind getting wine spilled on her. I don't like wine splashed on my nice white pants, either.

An example of clothing getting dirty is needed for you to truly understand. In 2008, I bought a brand-new pair of white pants online. I had them fitted and cuffed by a seamstress. They were delivered to my office, and I drove them home. I ironed them and carefully packed them so they would not crease in the suitcase. I drove the suitcase from Philadelphia to JFK airport. I watched my bags travel down the carousel, and they connected through Madrid to Pamplona. I collected the luggage from baggage return. I put the suitcase in the trunk of the rental car and drove the pants to our hotel. I carried the bags up the hill from the parking lot to the hotel and through a crowd of revelers. I dragged the suitcase into the elevator and into our hotel room, opened it, and changed into my *brand-new white pants*. I opened our hotel room and stepped into the hall and into the elevator. I pressed the button for the lobby, and *as the doors opened*, someone spilled wine on my pants, mere minutes after the fiesta started. A lot of wine, too. Someone burned my shirt later that day.

Your white pants and white shirt will get wine-stained, burned by cigarettes, burned by little European cigars and big, fat bullfight cigars, burned by candles, *burned by fireworks*, blood-stained, mud-stained, urine-stained, petrol-stained, mayonnaise-stained, Gorgonzola-stained, grass-stained, "trash juice"–stained (you'll understand later), and excrement-stained. There will be pants you are unwilling to return to your suitcase. Other people are so dirty, you get dirty just bumping into them. We call these "Frenchmen."

Ari claims that the fiesta does not officially start until the fireworks set my shirt on fire. For me, the fiesta does not officially start until mystery blood appears on Ari's pants. As to our problems with petrol, in New Jersey, we are not allowed to fill our own tanks at gas stations. Thus we lack this skill set by legislative edict. Amusingly, several petrol stations in Pamplona use pumps that do not automatically shut off when you're filling the tank. If you are not careful, they fountain like tiny petrol derricks. Unless you are adapting Upton Sinclair's *Oil!* into a screenplay, you will want to avoid what is known in literary circles as "finding out the hard way." What is the best way to handle pumping gas in white pants? Carefully repeat this old apothegm: "Ari, I think it's your turn today." The cheese issue? The Restaurant San Fermín is hidden on calle San Nicolás and serves a simply lovely *chuleta* (bone-in beef steak) drenched in Gorgonzola. As to excrement, you will get it on you in Pamplona eventually. No one ever queries whether a bear wipes in the woods. That's because they don't, and neither do the bulls. They are filthy back there. More than once, Ari and I have hit the wrong end of the bull when it "stops short." If you run into the back end of a bull, you will be the "butt" of jokes for the rest of the day, and no one will want to stand near you, either.

On July 7, you wouldn't imagine sitting on the wet and muddy ground or cobblestones—you want to protect your pants. By the tenth, you'll be happy for enough space to sit in the middle of a puddle that's "just" muddy. By the fourteenth, broken glass on a urine-stained door stoop positively looks like a 1950s porch swing for courtin'. I have long felt that a chair salesman in Pamplona could be the richest man in the world.

In the city, there are fiesta t-shirts for sale everywhere, and the red *pañuelo* and sash. For the most part, we buy new every year and wear them till they disintegrate. Ari has worn the same sash for every run, and it's disgusting. Sometimes we have to just throw out sneakers, because we don't want to permanently damage our luggage, or shock our wives, or scare any bomb-sniffing dogs.

If the idea of getting a little dirty renders you positively Prufrockian (or *shilly-shally*, according to our British friends), this is the wrong fiesta for you.

As for shoes, bring a couple of options so you always have a dry pair. Your shoes will get wet during the fiesta. I bring a pair only for the *encierro*. Don't bring flip-flops or shoes with open toes. If you do, you are going to get hurt, potentially badly. There is glass everywhere, always. Use a waterproofing agent on your shoes before leaving for Pamplona—this is no joke.

Don't bring protective equipment, like a rugby helmet or elbow pads. You are not permitted to run with that type of gear.

Bring completely new and clean clothes for the first day after the fiesta—preferably with the store labels still on them. Hermetically seal them in a bag in your suitcase, and don't take the bag out until after the fiesta is over. Those new, clean clothes feel incredible on the fifteenth.

Weather

The climate of Pamplona and the surrounding Kingdom of Navarre is oceanic in the damper northwest, alpine in the northeast, and Mediterranean in the drier south. That means that if you find just the right spot in the city, you'll think you can see the ocean, the desert, the mountains, and Greece, all at the same time.

The summer in Pamplona is usually hot and dry, but it often gets seriously cold at night. It rarely rains during the fiesta, but when it does, you can always buy a 15-euro poncho that cost 2 cents to make. Sweatshirts and sweaters (red *and* white!) are sold everywhere, all the time, during the fiesta. But do not wear a new red sweatshirt over a white shirt, unless you like red fuzz all over. Again, learned the hard way.

Locals, who don't have to stuff their vacation clothes into a single fifty-pound suitcase, have a significant advantage in clothing for changing weather. In my imagination, they all have a full walk-in closet dedicated to the fiesta, with red sweaters and heavy white jeans and red raincoats. It must be heavenly.

Money

You will need enough money to last, and a hotel room or flat with a safe. During the fiesta, banks have weird hours (the first full day of the fiesta is a bank holiday every year), and usually are loath to cash or change anything but small amounts of Travelers Cheques. ATMs exist but are often empty or not functioning, especially on the weekends. Both banks and ATMs, when open and operational, have lines to stand in. The ATMs are in better shape, with smaller lines the farther you venture from the old town. Remember this when visiting Pamplona: You will need a lot of money.

Get a room with a safe, and if you cannot, never let your money or passport out of your sight. I carry the majority of my money and my passport in a pouch around my neck, if it's not in the safe. I leave only a few euros in my pockets. Getting ripped off during the fiesta is a definite possibility, and if Ari has to look like a dork reaching into his little pouch, so be it.

For major expenditures (hotels, restaurant meals, rental cars, *encierro* photographs), credit cards are de rigueur. They want identification usually. You will still need cash currency. If you are like me, you will need currency for café con leche, Red Bull, pastry, replacement funny hats, balloons, sodas (especially Fanta), orange juice, replacement sunglasses, a new harmonica, ice cream, fries, candy, tipping the sidewalk actors, tipping waiters, Aquarius, and its evil twin, Aquarius Naranja. Aquarius is a mineral drink. It originated in, and was first introduced in, Japan and Hawaii in 1983—as a grapefruit-flavored sports drink, a response to a competitor's brand of sports drink called Pocari Sweat, which, because of its name, is only sold in Japan, where products with revolting names are commonly sold. Aquarius was later introduced in Spain, and it became the official drink of the 1992 Summer Olympics in Barcelona. During the average fiesta, I easily drink forty-five to fifty cans just to stay coherent and upright. On the other hand, Aquarius Naranja is mixed in the toilet, and no responsible human would drink it.

Finally, in Europe it is not gelding to carry a change purse. In the United States, it is cause to be subjected to a social orchidec-tomy. However, in Europe, the dollar bill is replaced with a 1-euro and, my favorite, 2-euro coin. When you are making lots of small purchases with the large bills you received at the ATM, these coins accumulate quickly. So, if you see me opening my European change purse, let it ride. Just let it ride. Ari and I place anything less than a 50-centime coin in a Ziploc bag in the hotel room labeled "The Fiesta Highway Toll Fund." Toll collectors *love it* when you pay the toll with low denominations. I used to carry camera film canisters to hold my coins. Smart, right? They are hard to find now. It is possible that someone reading this book is young enough to not know that cameras once used film.

Read the News
Little details about the fiesta change every year. The city makes changes. The Casa de Misericordia, which runs the bullring, makes changes. Your hotel and favorite restaurants make changes. The *peñas*—social clubs—make changes. There are political changes. There are economic changes.

The best way to keep up-to-date on the changes is to consult with the local sources, which are plentiful online.

The absolute best source is the website sanfermin.com, where you should read everything. Every little bit. A local design com-pany called Kukuxumusu (in Basque, "kiss of the flea," of course) and their San Fermín website are now an essential part of the fi-esta experience, and the most helpful resource for local news. They provide updates on town events and the earliest access to the fi-esta schedule, and they reflect the whole fiesta vibe. They're funny and creative, and utterly helpful. Every year, they sponsor a Day of the Tourist. They have a never-ending vat of goofiness hidden somewhere. Visit their website. Buy their stuff. Their sense of hu-mor is decidedly blue. I am not responsible.

You will also want to review feriadeltoro.com and pamplona .net, which are the bullfight website and the city website, respec-tively.

As to pamplona.net, it is the city's "official" website. Like any government, they are hopelessly behind, always. So, the information, when posted, is helpful, but often not as much as when it first appears in August after the July fiesta. In 2011, they were using this brilliant slogan—"Pamplona me gusta!" which was written, apparently, by the Taco Bell Chihuahua.

The most important thing is to get hold of the fiesta program before the fiesta so you can map out what you absolutely cannot miss. Every year, around New Year's Day, I start checking online for the program, which does not come out until the summer. For years I have tried to mark on a calendar when the program is released in late May or June, but never remember to do so.

Learn Some Spanish Spanish

The first time we rented a car in Pamplona, we didn't pick it up at the airport but in the city. We stopped at our hotel front desk to ask for "walking directions" because we were "renting a car" from "Avis." We spoke respectable enough high school Spanish for the entire inquiry, except "Avis," which we pronounced as if it rhymed with "Davis" because the name of the multinational company is the same in every language. However, "Avis" is pronounced differently in Pamplona. It's pronounced as if it rhymes with "novice." The hotel clerk clearly had never heard of the car rental corporation "Avis" that rhymes with "Davis." He looked completely befuddled by our question, and brought out five or six of his friends from the back room to huddle. While we actually mimed the question to the clerk for fifteen minutes, a front-desk counterpart finally interjected by explaining that we probably meant we needed "walking directions" to "Avis," which he pronounced as if it rhymed with "novice." Moe slaps all around.

They do not speak the same Spanish in Spain you learned in your junior high Spanish class. It's Castilian. For a lark, just try *encantado* on a nice barman in Pamplona. Make sure you start in a defensive posture. Even worse, in Pamplona and Navarre, the language spoken is really a mixture of Basque and local colloquialisms, English TV catchphrases, French pop music, and formal Castilian, but with confusing accents and mixed with what I believe to be everyone imitating Jackie Stewart covering the Indy 500. But on helium. And fast. Good luck. The language barrier can present challenges. You can go an entire fiesta without knowing anything but English. Trying to fit in is nice, though.

X

Learn some of the local language. Pamplona's youth know more English than I know Basque or Spanish. As with any culture, a mere attempt at learning to talk as the locals do will open many doors. And remember—you are not really going to Spain. You are going to Navarre, which is technically an "autonomous community" in Spain. The official language is Basque (aka Euskara), while very few speak it fluently. Basque distinguishes between laminal and apical articulation for the alveolar fricatives and affricates. What does that mean? They use a lot of Xs, and almost everyone's name starts with *E*. For more reading, you can consult Michel Morvan's 1996 masterpiece *The Linguistic Origins of Basque*, which is written entirely in French. Just kidding, I would never read anything in French.

Here are some helpful terms.

Kaixo means "hello." *Agur* means "good-bye."

Gazta is "cheese," which comes up more than you'd think.

Jai alai or *pelota* is the Basque national game, and don't let some kid trick you onto the field of play. That ball really hurts.

Pintxos is the Basque version of Spanish tapas. It's pronounced "pin-chos." Don't call them "tapas" anywhere in Navarre. This is very serious. The "tx" is pronounced "ch," as in "Hey, Chuck. Why do Basques use so many Xs?"

Txapela is usually used to refer to the Basque beret, even though it literally means "hat." Hey, Rusty, these berets are superfluous here. If you care to don one, be ready for the attention of Pamplona's older ladies, who are cheek pinchers, or *pintxers* in Basque. The Basques wear these without comic intention. The *txapela* is actually given as an award in Basque culture in situations where a trophy would be presented in America. The Basque term for "champion" is *txapeldun,* which literally means "the one who has the hat." So, if someone presents you with a beret, treat it respectfully, even if you were raised in an anti-beret culture like me.

Txistu is the Basque flute. You will be humming the tunes you hear on the airplane ride home.

Bai is "yes." *Ez* is "no." *Mesedez* is "please."

"¿Bai ote?" is "Really?" which is my favorite Basque phrase to use in Pamplona. It's helpful for good-natured arguments. Also, I love *"¡¡Bizi gara!!"* ("We are alive!!"). The frequent street response is *"¡¡Bagarela!!"* ("So we are!!").

Problem with a drunk in the street? Try *"¡Barregarria da!"* for "He's funny!" Or, more direct is "I'm not interested!"—*"¡Ez daukat interesik!"*

"Egun on" is "Good morning," and *"Egun on, bai"* is the standard reply. This is great for the hotel doorman.

"¡Eup!" is the Basque version of "What's up!"

Most importantly, you can always lead with *"Gora Iruña,"* which is the equivalent of "Viva Pamplona."

Dinner Reservations

If you wait until you get to Pamplona to make dinner reservations, you will be shut out, or end up eating in a tent. If you are eating in a tent, you have missed the fiesta. If you wait until May for July reservations, you will likely be shut out. Pamplona and the entire Kingdom of Navarre have become a premier dining destination of the world. These are famous and world-renowned restaurants. You will need to call ahead. Do not just send an email—follow up by telephone. Try to make the reservations in the native languages.

During the fiesta, you cannot just pop in. We start making our dining reservations in March and April before July fiesta—if we didn't make them for the next year while paying the check.

The Rental Car

"Viva San Fermín" loosely translates into "unexplained front-end damage." Hah, get the insurance. And, learn to drive a stick.

While parking is horrid during the fiesta, a rental car is essential for dining in towns near Pamplona (like Lekunberri, Tafalla, and San Sebastián) and for getting out into the forest or mountains or the beach to cool down.

The worst time to find parking during the fiesta is late at night, before, during, and after the fireworks, and the worst time to drive is during the morning parades or anytime on July 6 after 11:00 a.m. until the end of the fiesta. Draw yourself a handy flowchart. Get the smallest car your group can handle, and put the calmest person in your party in charge of parking the rental. In 2008, we rented a giant van, and I nearly lost my mind parking and driving. The streets are narrow, and you have to get through crowds. Our hotel has an underground lot, which is amazing. There are many other lots throughout the city, and if we get stuck we usually go with the bus station underground lot. Never park in the El Corte Inglés underground lot during the fiesta, because it closes on Sundays and at night, and locks you out from getting to your car.

You may recall that people become intoxicated during the fiesta. As they ramble down the streets, they may be unwilling to get out of the way of your car immediately. Each and every person thinks he invented the joke on the spot. Yes, ha-ha! You got me! They even pretend to be the matador. How quaint, after twenty million other Frenchmen did it just this morning. While your initial urge may be to gun the compact Volkswagen Golf, don't. They will move after having their little giggle. Driving through the crowds can be stressful. Just chill and enjoy it.

Because it is a fiesta, it is almost impossible to return a rental car without damage. Frankly, I don't know why Avis continues to do business with us. Get the insurance.

So, while you've probably already seen the *60 Minutes* special, I've committed the following United Nations atrocities with our rental car during the fiesta:

Dropped the car rental keys down an elevator shaft;

Left the car in neutral so it ran down a hill and hit a tree;

Left the car in neutral so it ran down a hill and hit a bench;

Left the car in neutral while parking on a hillside (Ari is now officially in charge of reminding me about the emergency brake, because the car, with us as its contents, did roll backwards down a steep hill, and came within inches of vaulting off the cliff at the bottom. If he doesn't remind me now, all damages that accrue and our deaths thereafter are henceforth his legal and moral responsibility);

Left the car unlocked in the bus station underground parking lot, so bums slept in the car all night and stepped on Ari's pictures, and the car smelled like bums' BO the rest of the fiesta;

Abandoned the spare-tire equipment roadside while changing a flat on the AP-15 (the user's manual directions were only in German anyway, and one of us grew tired of Ari "trying" to translate because he had German in high school. While trying to solve the mystery of dislodging the spare tire from underneath the car, a sheep leapt from behind a rock and eventually forced us to drive away on the flat tire);

Racked up many, many, many, many, many unpaid speeding tickets (the tickets arrive via airmail months after the fiesta. It's actually a nice fiesta souvenir. They have a nice photograph of the rear bumper and license plate of the rental car going past some camera, probably returning from some beach. Don't ask how I know so much about this. To be helpful, the tickets are written entirely in Basque. So, they don't get paid. I am the Navarran scofflaw you read about);

Lost the parking lot ticket (a yearly event);

Demagnetized the parking lot ticket (a yearly event);

Allowed car to become surrounded by heard of giant angry cows, which would not be shooed away;

Burnt out the clutch and came to a coasting stop in a tollbooth;

Forgot where we parked (not limited to Pamplona or the fiesta, or anywhere in Spain, for that matter);

Broke the headlights while parking in underground garage;

> *Broke the taillights while parking in underground garage;*
> *Scratched and dented the passenger door while parking;*
> *Scratched and dented the driver's door while parking; and*
> *Backed into a mountain while making a K turn.*

In 2013 someone stole our giant magnet car mustache right off the rental car. They left the giant magnet Band-Aid. Who would do this?

Sadly, all of these are true, and the list is far from exhaustive. During the fiesta, you get tired and do stupid things, mostly with the rental car. Since Ari can't drive a stick shift, I am left to do all the driving. I am not sure whether he is patient with my foibles or privately amused. He takes a lot of notes, though.

Tourist Balconies

A lot of people ask us about balcony rentals. We have rented balconies for our families (women and children); however, we do not make it an annual practice.

Since we started visiting Pamplona, the number of online rental offers for balconies has increased a thousand percent. It is very expensive, and the balconies are crowded, and the urge to criticize this trend is strong. A Basque mother explained to me that she makes more money renting the balcony during the fiesta than at her year-round job—teaching school! So, it is hard to begrudge the locals making some money while louts from Old Sodbury, Gloucestershire, are urinating in the streets below.

There are several tour companies offering "Pamplona Packages" that originate from outside of Navarre or even outside of Spain. On their websites and in their media presentations, they make misleading claims about how hard it is to procure housing, or rent a balcony, or get tickets to the bullfight. Then they mark up their costs by several hundred percent, if not more. Tickets they bought for 20 euros should not cost a customer 750 euros. They rent the balconies from the locals for 100 euros and then charge 1,000 euros. Of course, we have been going to Pamplona long

enough to become personally acquainted with a few of the operators, and actually friends with others. I've caused a little fuss with
them more than once by expressing my disapproval, especially online to potential customers. I argue that there is nothing needed
to visit the fiesta beyond the normal skill set of the first-time traveler. I won't point to any company specifically in this book, but I
would encourage all our friends operating these entities to act
responsibly. Don't ruin someone's fiesta with multinational corporate concerns or profiteering. In 2013, the international travel
agency Thomas Cook announced it would no longer promote
packages for tourists to visit Pamplona due to pressure from various animal rights groups. This was funny because I have never
actually met a single person visiting Pamplona on a Thomas Cook
organized tour.

And there are plenty of places to see the running for free, or
nearly for free.

If you are going to watch and not run, getting down at course
level is the best option, and it is free. There you will meet other
actual people, and not just other tourists who couldn't afford a balcony rental. The course is surrounded by wooden railings. If
you decide to sit on the railings to watch, get there early (at least
6:00 a.m.), but sit *on the back railing*—not in the front row. Tons of
people sit on the front rail, thinking they have great seats. At
7:50 a.m., the cops will kick them off, as they have done every
morning for the last hundred years, and these people don't get to
see *anything*. The front railing and the space in between the railings are for emergency personnel. It should also go without saying that one cannot watch the running while standing inside the
running course.

My wife and children actually prefer watching the *encierro*
from inside the bullring, where La Pamplonesa—the Pamplona
Brass Band—plays music, and the entire run can be watched on
the large screens. Plus, they get the action of the runners and bulls
entering the ring, the crowd jeering the runners who are way too

far in front of the herd, and the dodging of the baby bulls after the *encierro* finishes. This costs only a couple of euros. It is never sold out.

You Never Will Know
During the fiesta, you never know what will happen to you. You can plan for everything and then something weird will happen.

July 14, 2009—On the final day of this otherwise spectacular fiesta, I ran into the bullring with the last bull of the fiesta from the Núñez del Cuvillo ranch. He fell where the course changes from pavers to sand, and then *kicked me in the leg* as I ran by while he was still lying on his side. Ari and I (limping) went to the *sorteo* and *apartado* that afternoon, and saw the same bull kick a cinderblock wall with his back left hoof and smash the block to pieces. I still made it to the top of Gibraltar two days later, and petted a Barbary ape, fulfilling a lifelong dream. Good advice: Don't get kicked by a bull, *and* some monkeys will accept the promise to buy them a Pepsi as a bribe and let you pet them. Yet there is no way I expected to get kicked by a fallen bull when I got out of bed that morning. The possibility had never remotely occurred to me. Be ready for anything during the fiesta.

Packing
There are some things you should buy at home and pack, because things are often not where they are "supposed" to be in Spain. In Spain, you get suntan lotion at the optometrist or the pharmacist. If you get in any kind of trouble in Spain, *the pharmacy is a good place to start for help*. They usually speak English, know their town better than a 1950s American mailman, and, if they cannot help you, will know where you should go. A Spanish pharmacist is leagues more helpful than someone at Walgreens in the USA. More than once a Navarran Florence Nightingale has helped me limp through a fiesta.

Earplugs—Pamplona during the fiesta is the wrong city to do your earplug shopping. You will need them, especially at night, and especially if Ari is watching the Tour de France on TV, or translating German MTV, or talking while I am trying to nap. A nice sleep mask doesn't hurt when you're taking the elusive afternoon nap, or if Ari is inconsiderately changing outside of the bathroom.

Penknife—someone will hand you a wheel of cheese at least once during San Fermín. They'll wonder what kind of man doesn't carry his own knife. It's handy for ribbons around pastry boxes. It's also the coolest way to eat fresh fruit while hiking.

Soap—you will be getting dirty, and the tiny hotel soap will not do. I bring my own soap dish so Ari doesn't get "confused" and use my soap, again. Trust me, this is serious business—your own USA-sized bar of soap may salvage your mental state over the course of the nine-day fiesta. If you are reading this and don't understand, you didn't get dirty enough in Pamplona.

Wound kit—if you are running, chances are you will suffer at least minor injuries. If you don't, you are probably doing something wrong. My lovely wife puts together an impressive medical bag for me, with varying sizes of bandages and Neosporin and scissors and blister pads. Nothing ruins the fireworks more than an oozing wound sticking to your white pants.

Shoe kit—your shoes will get demolished in Pamplona. I bring sneaker cleaner, a stiff brush, extra laces, and a tube of Super Glue, because when the trash juice hits your shoes they will start falling apart.

Trash bags—there will be things you do not want to put back into your suitcase unless they are wrapped in plastic.

Bathing suit—the beach beckons loudly. This ain't France—suits are required.

Poncho—you will need a poncho multiple times during San Fermín. Don't bring an expensive poncho, because it won't be making it back to the hotel room. Here's our best poncho joke: "Ari, should I bring a poncho?" Ari: "I don't see any arm in it."

Lighter—there will be multiple times when a nice lighter, and general knowledge of how to light a cigar or some fireworks, will ingratiate you with the local older gentlemen during the fiesta. Twice, my personal lighter has been used to light the evening fireworks bull. Twice!

Something to sit on—I carry an old, large handkerchief. Everything is filthy in Pamplona. When the ground is the cleanest option for sitting, you will look like a genius pulling out the handkerchief. Old Pamplonican housewives in the middle of their ninetieth fiesta congratulate me on my éclat as they smack themselves in the forehead.

Cell phone charger—this is really just to remind Ari, again. Ari says this only happened once. "Only once!" he says. He forgets his every year.

Upset stomach medication—if you do not feel sick to your stomach during the fiesta, again, you are doing something wrong. You will coincidently need something for your stomach the most when the stores are closed. The ham alone, which is aged perfectly and just too readily available, will upset your stomach sometimes.

In 1978, when I was little, my father brought home from work a Warner Bros. record with Sammy Davis Jr.'s rendition of *Plop Plop Fizz Fizz* for Alka-Seltzer. In the TV commercial, he said, "When my aching head and my stomach start to boogaloo, I get Alka-Seltzer and I take two." It's like he had the fiesta in mind. Your stomach, too, will do the boogaloo and more.

Photo album—a great way to safely transport pictures home. Ari also brings a poster tube, because he purchases the fiesta poster every year.

Hat and sunglasses—Pamplona is hot and sunny, and you may die without these. Local touts sell these everywhere, but they test positive for the highest concentration of lead of any hats in the world.

Iron—Spanish hotels rarely have one in the room. You can tell by how the Spanish tend to dress.

Hangers—most European hotel closets have those ridiculous wooden hangers that are permanently attached inside, with those clips for women's pants. If you need to spread things around to dry or quarantine from your own clothes, a few wire hangers from home come in handy. They can also be bent into swords for late-night hotel room swashbuckling.

Coin purse and money belt—Again, the San Fermín fiesta is the International Pick-Pocketing Olympics. And, on any trip to Europe, coins accrue faster than in the United States.

Miscellaneous—in 2014 I packed two monk costumes and an alligator squeeze toy. It just seemed like the right thing.

Notary kit—for memorializing resolution of room disputes over who gets the chair; who was supposed to bring the room key; who tracked dirt into the room; who left their stuff on my bed; who took forty-five minutes in the shower; etc. Ari retorts by complaining that I left dirty Q-tips on his bed in 2012. However, he thought they were real, and does not know I bought gag dirty Q-tips, left them on his "stuff" all week, and sat back on the bed closest to the window and watched him slowly come unhinged. "I found another one!" he'd yell, and then retch a bit. He won't know this until he reads this book.

Triage Laundry

During the San Fermín fiesta, the most memorable days usually end with the dirtiest clothing. In the middle of the night, your dirty pants wander the old city on their own, which is why they look so tired in the morning.

You cannot pack enough clean clothes to make it through the fiesta. You can resort to the hotel laundry, and abandon the chances of your daughter having that nice wedding, or you can set aside some time for laundry triage. At the beginning of the fiesta, you will care oh-so-much about trying to keep your clothing clean. By the end, you will wear anything that doesn't smell of vomit or Ari's cat.

In between, you will need to clean your clothing. We bring Tide To Go Pens and Shout Wipes and a little bottle of Febreze. I actually feel sorry for Hemingway, who had to forge through the fiesta without Febreze. Really, there is not enough Febreze on this earth to clean up the fiesta. That requires fire hoses, which are used to clean the city every morning. For larger personal cleaning efforts, we fill the tub with the hottest possible water and mix in some laundry soap we packed. I use the plastic end of my toothbrush (or the bristle end of Ari's toothbrush if he was dumb enough to leave it out in the open) as an agitator and stir. We squeeze-dry in the bathroom, roll the items up tight in towels, and hang the laundry throughout the room. Since Pamplona is hot and dry, clothes dry fairly quickly when spread around the room. We set aside some time every fiesta to bitterly argue and finger-point over who is hogging the best drying spaces. And why Ari dripped water all over the carpet. For the first time, in 2014 we rented a flat with a washing machine and dryer. I don't know if we can go back to the old ways.

Some prep at home doesn't hurt, either. I always spray my shoes and hat with waterproofing and stain repellent before leaving for Spain.

But please, keep it in the room. Ari once tried drying his ridiculous lime green swimsuit outside the hotel room window, and it was somehow "lost." He has been falsely accusing me ever since of nudging it over the balcony to its deserved end. Really, I didn't.

Getting Through to the End

Actually, if you figure out how to do this, let me know.

Some discipline is necessary to make sure you can run the entire fiesta marathon. I have a couple of suggestions, which have worked with varying degrees of success.

> *Drink lots and lots, and lots, of water. Many people succumb to dehydration every year in Pamplona. If you have trouble with this like I do, bring some rehydration salts. This is critical: We've had friends lose precious fiesta days in the hospital getting fluids.*
>
> *Don't eat the steak every night for dinner which is a lesson I discovered the hard way.*
>
> *Don't eat the ham every night for dinner. Imagine that:* ham in Spain. *I did this in 2006 (on a senseless dare), and the effects lingered until the following Easter.*
>
> *Don't eat a giant plate of beans every night at dinner, which is what we call the Ari-Sangüesa Bean Fiasco of 2008.*
>
> *Force yourself to get some sleep* in a bed. *A bench is not a bed.*
>
> *Use Red Bull intelligently, and legally. My record is twelve in twenty-four hours. Not smart at all.*
>
> *Meet new people and talk to them. Write down their email addresses.*
>
> *Sing words to the songs you hear, even if you have to make up your own, to whatever nonsense they are singing about, again. (Are they still singing? Come on, it's 3:00 a.m. and we are trying to sleep.)*
>
> *Do not miss the fireworks. They are life-sustaining.*
>
> *Eat real meals, with salad and vegetables.*

Escape the city heat at least a couple of times.

Don't let Ari hog the hotel room closet.

Don't use a tour guide. You do not need a tour guide for this fiesta unless you are the kind of person who takes his butler to a party.

Schedule some actual quiet time—take a hike, dip your feet in the river, lie down in a field—but not a pasture. If you don't know how to tell a field from a pasture, use your nose.

Swear you'll never do it all again.

Finally, we find that scheduling a period for convalescence after the fiesta is necessary. If you jump on the airplane and fly back home to start work, you probably will die. In *The Sun Also Rises,* even Jake went to San Sebastián, in chapter 19. Hemingway writes, "Even on a hot day San Sebastián has a certain early morning quality." San Sebastián is a great place to recover from the fiesta. Barcelona and the beach towns to its north, along with Ibiza, Cádiz, Nice, Biarritz, and Saint-Jean-de-Luz, are all good places to lick your wounds. You may already know this, but I am the Side Trip King, the complete Barry Shalowitz, if you will.

4

Etxea
(history of the San Fermín fiesta)

Ez zara eroriko
Arbola maitea.

—"GERNIKAKO ARBOLA," 1853

*Our time working together with Dad defines my life with Ari today.
This is our favorite "store story": Back then, shift leaders had an asterisk next to their name on the schedule. They wore white shirts
and a red tie instead of a red polo. Except when we were working,
there was no asterisk, and we only wore red polo shirts. We'd say,
"Dad, who's in charge of the shift?" He'd say, "I am," which we knew
was ludicrous because he'd be off "marketing" or "schmoozing" or
whatever it is that he did all day, and if things weren't perfect when
he returned, we'd answer for it. "Why haven't you started people taking breaks?" "Why isn't anyone splitting chicken?" "Why is the trash
overflowing?" "Are we out of nuggets . . . again?" So, we had all the
responsibility, but none of the express authority. Even when he
went on vacation and actually left us in charge, he refused to christen
us officially as "in charge." He would even post a sign reminding everyone at the store that Ari and I did not have the authority to fire
employees while he was away, which we did anyway. It seemed like*

a challenge. So, eventually Ari and I found a box of white shirts in the garage, and old blue ties but no red ties. We decided to wear the old blue ties. We hid in the bedroom until it was too late to send us back to change clothes, and came out and announced to him that we were now "blue-chip crew leaders," which was Ari's awesome idea. Dad just shrugged and said, "Get in the car." After that, we strutted around using our new fake title, and other employees starting asking for blue ties, which Dad very rarely gave out (I can think of only one other, to Scott Keating, an employee that became a very close friend). Years later I asked Dad about it. I said, "Were you just ignoring us or teaching us a life lesson? Don't wait until someone tells you to take the initiative? Seize it on your own? Take responsibility without prompting?" He slyly said, "I guess you'll never know."

Etxea is literally "house" in Basque. What it really means is "history." The chapter epigraph is in Basque and says, "You will not fall, dear tree." This is from a song that is the unofficial anthem of the Basques and celebrates their famous tree in Guernica and Basque freedom. The Spanish, Navarrans, and Basques have a very sobering history. The French are never sober, at least not that I can tell. This chapter focuses on less serious matters, including the Pamplona fiesta.

History of the Fiesta

In 75 BC, the Roman general Pompey encamped with his army on a high hill, where the city cathedral stands even today. To him, it looked like a good place for a city, and he named it Pompaelo, even though the ancient Basques lived there already and had their own name for the hill. Pamplona later fell into the hands of the Visigoths and the Muslims and, even later, in modern times, to chunky and drunk British girls.

Tradition tells us that Honesto, a priest born in Nîmes, France, arrived from Rome in Roman-controlled Pamplona, as sent by Saturnin, who was later martyred by being tied to a bull and has been forever but confusingly known as Saint Cernin. Honesto came to evangelize the town, which was fully stocked with heathens and idol worshipers. He met Roman senator Firmo and his family (at the Hotel Yoldi, I presume), and each was converted to Christianity. Senator Firmo was already the governor of the area and served two Roman emperors, Diocletian and Maximian. Christianity then flourished in Pamplona.

Fermín, the son of Senator Firmo, was taught the tenets of Christianity by Honesto, and at thirty-one, Fermín left to preach the Gospel in Gaul, and if you spend a day there you will know that Pamplona still has trouble with the French today. Moving from city to city, Fermín arrived finally in Amiens, a city stocked with French pagans, but where he succeeded in achieving a great many conversions (still a rookie record!) in only forty days, and where he was imprisoned by said Frenchmen. On September 25, 303, he suffered martyrdom by beheading at the hands of the remaining pagans. His body, which was buried in secret by some Christians, was found, suspiciously and amazingly enough, centuries later, on January 13, 615, but disguised as old dirt that putatively still looked a little like Fermín. I have a friend who investigates miracles for the Catholic Church. He explains that it is well within the powers of the Creator of the universe to preserve a martyr's remains for some centuries, a point that is well taken.

When Fermín's remains were finally brought back to Pamplona in 1196, the city decided to mark the occasion with an annual event. Saint Fermín, or San Fermín, is now the "co-patron" saint of Navarre, along with St. Francis Xavier, who is the patron saint of bootmakers, wine traders, and bakers. The springtime boot and baker fiesta is far less popular than the summer San Fermín fiesta. Xavier was a missionary to India, but I've never heard anyone even mention the poor guy once during the fiesta. The Javierada is an annual pilgrimage from Pamplona to the Basilica of St. Francis Xavier in Dyersville, Iowa, which is probably why he's a little less popular than San Fermín. This is not a joke.

Over the centuries, the fiesta, the ancient annual fair, the running of the bulls, and the subsequent bullfights have all melded together. The celebrations in the saint's honor used to take place on the tenth of October, but as early as 1591 the celebration was transferred to the seventh of July, when better (hot) weather could be "guaranteed."

In the early years the fiesta lasted two days. It opened with a speech and had musicians, tournaments, theatrical events, and bullfights. In the years that followed other events were incorporated—for example, fireworks and dances—and the fiesta was extended by a number of days.

Seventeenth- and eighteenth-century written chronicles describe "religious acts" along with musicians, dancers, carnival giants, tournaments, acrobats, bulls, and the bull runs. Writings of this period record the presence of people from "other lands" whose shows "made the city more amusing," an unmistakable ancient reference to Australians. During the nineteenth century there were "fairground curios" and attractions as notable as the woman cannonball, the unbreakable pencil, exotic animals, and wax figures. Now, crowds line up around the block during the fiesta to see the only living Sasquatch in captivity, or as I know it, Ari's Hairy Back.

Giant History

Every day at 9:30 a.m. during the fiesta, the giants depart the bus station to meander through the city, often leaving crying children in their wake. Good times. Pamplona times.

It was already an ancient tradition. It started well before Columbus sailed.

During the procession of San Fermín in 1276, three giants—Peru Suziales, Mari Suziales (his wife), and their friend Jusef Lukurari (aka "The Usurer," a personification of the popular repulsion against the Jews "at that time")—were paraded dancing through the streets. Even in 1926, in *The Sun Also Rises*, Robert Cohn, who Hemingway constantly reminds the reader is Jewish, is stereotypically portrayed as a feminized and complaining whiner, leading Bill to sarcastically suggest to Jake, in chapter 10, "Haven't you got some more Jewish friends you could bring along?" There is still more than a whiff of this in Europe and around the world.

Later, in 1607, Joanes de Azcona, who is popularly considered the father of the modern parade, carted out the giants with a bona fide minstrel to accompany the march. An ancient receipt from 1620 evidences that a carpenter named Joan de Torrobas was hired to mend the giants, and was handsomely paid an entire "88 reales," whatever that is. It probably was just enough to buy his fiesta pictures at Foto Auma.

While today they march after breakfast, the giants used to parade in the evenings after the bullfights, but covered with fireworks and before being tossed into the bonfire. Pamplona phased out the nightly bonfire to make it the safe fiesta it is today!

Over time, the giants became more ornate, and permanent, and then they were kept away from the bonfire and were involved in more religious processions. The Parade of the Giants continued until July 10, 1780, when King Carlos III banned the use of "dancing giants" in any religious processions inside or outside all churches within the entire kingdom. This stopped the San Fermín celebrations, and giants belonging to the town hall disappeared without any further trace. The church's giants were put in storage and forgotten until 1813, when they were discovered by a carpenter who revived the old tradition. The citywide response was so enthusiastic that the town hall started anew, and gradually rebuilt their collection of giants. The giants presently in use date from 1860 and were made by Tadeo Amorena, a Pamplona painter. Each stands over thirteen feet tall.

During the fiesta, the giants and their posse parade and dance through the city from 9:30 a.m. to 2:00 p.m. This event should never be missed, especially if you are bringing children to Pamplona. The daily route is published in the city newspapers, so while close up it appears to meander, it is organized. Often, the parade route has planned stops for people in less fortunate settings who cannot get out and about, like homes for the elderly. It is really quite touching.

The two-story-tall giants (the kings and queens of Europe, Asia, Africa, and the Americas) are followed by thousands of children. While the event is steeped in history, the parade is used as a tool to wean local children off their pacifiers. No kidding—the Pamplona children pick their favorite giant, and hang their pacifier on it for good during breaks in the parade.

The giants dance, sway, and spin to Basque *jotas*, polkas, and waltzes, while a band plays traditional songs on the *dulzaina*, which is Basque for "that annoying squeaky oboe." Every song ends with "ta da." Sing along. It is an honor to be picked to carry a giant, but an exhausting honor in the morning and afternoon heat to carry the giants through the city. We've enjoyed getting to know the local characters entrusted with the giants, which weigh around 130 pounds. The Pamplonicans are hardly heavier. Most of them would rather lose a limb than lose the privilege of carrying the giants. Many of them use their character's name as their middle name in social media.

The Parade of Giants is accompanied by the Zaldikos (the pretend horses and riders) and the so-called Royal Entourage, which includes the Cabezudos (the Big Heads): the mayor, his councilor, a grandmother, and two Japanese figures, of course.

Intermingling with this crew are the famous and beloved Kilikis, who act as informal bodyguards for the kings and queens in the streets of Pamplona. These alone are worth the trip to the fiesta. Each has its own distinct and amusingly offensive personality: Caravinagre (Señor Vinegar—or "Vinegar Face," of the perpetual frown), Verrugón (Giant Wart Nose), El Barbas (The Beard), Coletas (Pig Tail), Patata (Señor Potato), and, of course, Napoleón. No fiesta event would be complete without mocking the French. If I could be one of the Kilikis, I'd be Napoleón.

The Kilikis and Zaldikos (together known as the "terrors") are literally used to "terrorize" the children of the fiesta, by chasing and smacking them with a sheepskin filled with foam on a rope and stick, aka a truncheon. I enjoy witnessing an annual fiesta tradition: when the Kilikis mistake Ari for a Basque child and whack him upside the head. Many children carry their own "weapon" to respond in kind. Others cry in real terror. Usually, local children wear their *pañuelico* (a children's-sized *pañuelo*) with the name of their favorite Kilikis, or a miniature outfit of their father's *peña*.

The Kilikis will bonk you, too. Here's the general rule: If you want them to hit you, they won't. If you are talking and not paying attention, you will be getting smacked upside the head. Amusingly, if one of the terrors breaks your glasses, and they might, there is a guy with insurance forms (not kidding), and the city will replace them! He follows the terrors with a form to complete. Local toddlers run in terror from the guards. And I mean screaming and crying. Fathers push their kids into harm's way with giant smiles. *Nothing* says family togetherness like dragging "X Junior" out to get his head smacked by the scary puppet. It's not uncommon to catch a parent with tears in his eyes recalling his own childhood dread. I absolutely love it.

Along the parade route, you will find few tourists. You can step right out in the street and join the parade. My children, and my wife and I, love this daily parade, and if you don't, you don't have a soul. Hopefully one of the terrors will beat one into you. Aptly put, the fiesta could survive without the bulls, but not without the Parade of the Giants. The giants joined the World's Fair in October 1965 in New York City. The slogan of the International Fair was "Peace Through Understanding." The fair asked that the giants representing the Americas, which are black, remain in the bus station in Pamplona. The giants marched in New York without the American giants, but the citizens of Pamplona never got over what they saw as an unfair slight, and never sent the giants outside the city again. However, to be just, it was 1965 in New York City.

Every July 14, at the end of the final parade, children from all over Pamplona gather to watch the giants and their friends being put away until the next summer in the ceremony *Despedida de los Gigantes* (Farewell to the Giants). It looks like moving day. It is an oddly emotive event. Don't mock my tears.

Encierro Fences

Pamplona is surrounded by walls. These medieval walls still wrap around the city for about three miles and include bastions, gates, demilunes, ravelins, and forts, which we gaily learned about at the Interpretation Centre of the Fortifications of Pamplona. It's an afternoon we'll never get back!

Every fiesta, someone falls off the walls, presumably while "stone-cold sober." Internationally, this is treated as a tragic accident, while in Pamplona they write, "¿Qué hacías tan cerca del borde?" on the tombstone (What were you doing so close to the edge?).

You can even eat pastry cooked in the old huge ovens that have rested against the old Roman walls since Roman times (including the famous Churrería La Mañueta, on calle La Mañueta).

As a medieval city, Pamplona surrounded itself with walls to defend against invaders (which included Muslims and Charlemagne). When the Kingdom of Navarre became beholden to the Crown of Castile in 1515, the walled city was used as an advance post of the Spanish crown against France.

The *encierro* course is also surrounded by walls in the form of wooden barriers.

In medieval times, the bulls were led on foot from the countryside into Pamplona because in medieval times, no one had bothered to invent trucks or a railway. As the bulls arrived in the city at dawn, they were herded at running pace. I once read that the bulls were pushed to run in order "to not disturb the locals." In Pamplona, the countryside trotting delivery method survived the intervention of the steam railway and common sense, thankfully. Given the impossibility of barring the fun, or "prohibiting it due to its popularity," the city government accepted it, *nolens volens*, and adopted the *encierro* as a formal event in 1867.

For centuries, the original path of the *encierro* started farther around the corner at calle Santo Domingo (to the bridge over the Arga River) and ended in the Plaza del Castillo, where a temporary bullring was constructed yearly. In 1844, a "modern" Pamplona bullring was completed, but it was poorly constructed, and abandoned in 1849. Another was built in 1852. All of this resulted in an alteration of the running route to its neoteric course, and the bulls were brought up calle Estafeta for the first time in 1856. In 1922, the "more modern" bullring was opened, altering the course yet again. A new tier of seating was added there in 1967. I believe it would not be a bad idea to extend the modern run back to the old starting point at the river. This will not happen, ever, unless the bulls get into better shape. In 2013 we spoke with a ranch hand who told us they do have the bulls run around the ranch to improve their cardio. A run of this length would leave many bulls gassed by the end of the course, and with an added turn, it's more likely that they would get separated. Both changes would stand to make the fiesta more dangerous. Yet it would help with the modern crowds, because there would be more wiggle room.

In those olden days there were no fences for the bull runs, which meant that the bulls escaped into the city streets. Imagine the stories CNN would run if that happened today. The modern barricades were added to the party in July 1776 while, simultaneously, the Declaration of Independence was being read in the streets of Boston and Philadelphia. Even into the late 1930s there was only a single barrier, from which bulls escaped routinely. If Pamplona ever sees fit to reduce the tourist hordes, they could always go back to the single-barrier system. Many would stay in bed rather than risk that mayhem.

Among the more fascinating ways to pass the time during the fiesta is to watch the brigade of dedicated city workers assemble and disassemble the barriers. They wrestle with this monstrosity daily and efficiently. The running course includes over 1,800 boards, 40 gates, 590 posts, 200 palisades, 2,000 bolts, and thousands of shims. I have no idea what a palisade is (see chapter 5). Some portions of the fences stay up during the entire fiesta. But large sections must be removed and reinstalled every day to ease street traffic. Immediately after the last run on the fourteenth, the barriers are completely removed within the hour. They even solder the post holes closed. It's almost too sad to watch. A good fiesta souvenir is a discarded barrier shim that has soaked up the trappings of an entire fiesta. Keep it away from open flames and wounds.

Again, now there are two sets of barriers. The inside fence is for the media and emergency personnel. The outside barrier is for sore viewing fundaments. Those seeking to watch the morning run must sit on the "rear" barrier. During the rest of the day, sit where you want, and you will learn how to climb over, climb through, sit on, and fall off the barriers.

Hemingway

In the twentieth century the fiesta reached the ridiculous height of its popularity with the Hemingway novel *The Sun Also Rises*, also called "Fiesta" in Europe. I guess the American title is too erudite for the average European. In France, it's called "Book!" In Canada, it's just "Eh?"

Ernest Hemingway was born in Oak Park, Illinois, in 1899 and committed suicide in Ketchum, Idaho, in July 1961, with tickets for the San Fermín bullfights in his nightstand. Days before his suicide, he had personally called the Hotel La Perla in Pamplona to cancel his room reservations for Room 217 for that year. In all seriousness, after you visit Pamplona, you will understand how chapfallen such a call must have left him. It's a call I never want to make.

Beginning in 1926, Ernest Hemingway's writings encouraged people from all over the world and across generations to come and take part in the fiesta in Pamplona.

The things that happened could only have happened during a fiesta. Everything became quite unreal finally and it seemed as though nothing could have any consequences. It seemed out of place to think of consequences during the fiesta.

It is still fun to imagine rolling through town with Hemingway or Orson Welles, and many of the early twentieth-century sites they made famous remain, including Bar Txoko, Hotel La Perla, Café Iruña, Plaza del Castillo, and the Hotel Yoldi. Most of those places are pretty awesome today, even with just Ari.

While a fiesta fixture, Hemingway only attended nine times: 1923, 1924, 1925, 1926, 1927, 1929, 1931, and, after the Spanish civil war and World War II, in 1953 and 1959 (he also briefly visited the city in 1956, but not during the fiesta). At this writing, this author has been to eleven fiestas and has run in seventy more *encierros* than Hemingway. However, my influence over the fiesta is more stunted. Much, much, much, much more stunted. Nevertheless.

While older generations were forced to endure visits from Hemingway, Orson Welles, James A. Michener (the famed author of *The Drifters* and *Iberia* was almost killed standing in a doorway on calle Santo Domingo in 1970), Arthur Miller, John Fulton, and Ava Gardner, in recent times we've benefitted from the enlightened presence of Dennis Rodman (2004), Joshua Jackson (four-time runner) from *Dawson's Creek*, Rosario Dawson (2008), Rick Steves (2010), and Tara Reid (2005). Even NFL coach Rex Ryan hung on the wooden barriers (2013). Wow, old people sure had it rough. I can't imagine the horror of sitting around Café Iruña in the late afternoon and having to endure yet another story about Rita Hayworth or Marlene Dietrich from Orson Welles. We did get James Franco in 2008, and he was already a pretty big star then. He's welcome back anytime. In 2014, after being dared by a local photographer, I licked Charlie Sheen's limousine window as it slowly drove through a crowd in the Plaza del Castillo.

Actually, Joshua Jackson ran on the horns, and appeared to be an all-around good guy. We sat near him in the bullring while he and actress Leonor Varela filmed a scene for the movie *Americano*. He even politely rolled his eyes when we yelled, "Hey Pacey Hey Pacey Hey Pacey Hey Pacey Hey Pacey Hey Pacey Hey Pacey Hey Pacey" at him for three hours. *Rosario Dawson ran like a pro.* Very impressive. Tara Reid? I recall thinking, I've never personally seen a drunker person in my life.

There's a Hemingway statue at the end of the bar in Café Iruña, and another in the front of the bullring, which was unveiled in July 1968. It is usually decorated with a *pañuelo* during the fiesta, but often blocked by fencing or a poorly parked media truck.

In every media interview I've ever given on Pamplona, every journalist asks what part Hemingway took in starting our annual fiesta tradition. He took very little part, and similarly Ari and I have no particularly interesting story about how we started calling on the fiesta. I believe we decided to go to Pamplona for the first time after seeing a special on the *encierro* on ESPN, unfortunately. That is the blot on my escutcheon. We've been working on a more romantic back story for several years. We welcome suggestions. I certainly am an admirer of Hemingway's novels (even though the popular trend is to criticize), and even more so celebrate the (possibly exaggerated) persona of his masculine, outdoors, and action-packed life. Unfortunately, machismo is a lost art in America. Hemingway is certainly a fascinating, but deeply flawed, American icon. He was a bully, a bore, and an anti-Semite, and he mistreated his children and the women in his life—that is, those he purported to love. These malefic characteristics certainly are not compulsory features of the machismo man. You can be macho and not a bigot or abusive. Run with the bulls, and love your wife. Raise and care for your children. These are not hard concepts to embrace while remaining "macho." This is not modern political correctness run amok.

Hemingway apologists make quick efforts to manage the author's prolific use of anti-Semitic slurs as "regrettable" but a common part of those times. Were Hemingway's writings mirroring his own personal views, too? There is some evidence they were, and if so, his anti-Semitism then and now was flat wrong. Certainly there is no argument that he used these offensive words in the same clever fashion as Mark Twain, who was not a bigot.

Nevertheless, Hemingway remains a focal point of the fiesta for many Americans, and during the fiesta it is easy to reconjure the days of the "moveable feast." Many of the sites made famous during his time are still standing. The fun part is that none of it is a museum. You can do exactly what Hemingway did then now.

Bar Txoko: this is in the Plaza del Castillo, and there are thousands of photographs of Hemingway with celebrities, friends, locals, and hangers-on here at the corner of calle Espoz y Mina in the Plaza del Castillo. English-speaking revelers still congregate here daily, as do we. A very good American friend bumped into and knocked completely over a bookcase *filled* with dishes and silverware here in 2012. He remains anonymous here to save him from the embarrassment, and because he is simply gigantic.

Bar Milano: this is complicated. In *The Sun Also Rises*, Hemingway called it Bar Milano, but it was really Café Bar Torino. Now, it's the Windsor Pub. It is still a central gathering place for Americans. Degenerate, appalling, but good tipping Americans.

Hotel la Perla: the Gran Hotel La Perla is still located in a corner of the Plaza del Castillo. Poor Hemingway did not stay here, but Rich Hemingway later did. Modernity and snobbery have ruined this site, but you can stay in Hemingway's alleged old room 217 (which is now 201) and watch the chaos on the streets below. Bring your wallet. Charlie Sheen stays here now, and it is debated whether the hotel is telling the truth about the "Hemingway room."

Café Iruña: this opened in 1888 and its fiesta electricity still illuminates the city. With its Belle Époque mirrored decorations, this was Hemingway's favorite spot. It is internationally famous, and overrun with tourists if you don't hustle to it after the running every morning. Having the luxury of returning yearly, we've gotten to know the waitstaff (some of the toughest guys you'll ever meet) really well, and we are big tippers, which helps us get a table and our breakfast should we be physically or emotionally unable to hustle. Usually that's the case. There is a life-sized bronze statue of Hemingway at the bar, and he is always ready to listen to your literary knowledge.

Hotel Yoldi: on Avenida San Ignacio, Hemingway famously visited his bullfighter friend Antonio Ordóñez in the hotel. Discussed at length later in this book, it is worth a visit even without the Hemingway lore.

Social Clubs

San Fermín and Pamplona would not be recognizable without the musical parades of the social clubs, or *peñas,* that march, sing, and dance, and commandeer the streets at all hours of the night. If you are trying to get somewhere quickly (like dinner), it is always better to walk with, and not against, those clangorous bands that clog the cobblestoned *calles,* but welcome everyone from everywhere, from noon on the sixth until well after midnight on the fourteenth.

Peñas were traditionally males-only clubs (but no longer) and are the basic organization of the pure anarchy of the fiesta de San Fermín. The oldest *peña,* La Única, was formed in 1903. If the fiesta is a nuclear explosion, the *peña* is the atom. You think, "How could such a tiny guy make such a big mess?"—and I am referring to the Basques, of course. Founded for the "purpose of providing a structure for its members" during the days of the fiesta, their activities are primarily focused on gastronomic and sporting events, and politics.

Through their *peña,* local Pamplona boys and girls celebrate San Fermín and other notable holidays together as with brothers and sisters. They dine together and attend the bullfights together.

They are an intermediary between the citizenry and the local government, and their members attend meetings at the town hall during the year and serve on committees that decide which events will take place each year. In 2010, they protested budget cutbacks by skipping the Sunday night feria. By coincidence, Spain beat

Holland 1–0 in the World Cup later that night, on what was one of the more interesting nights I've spent in Spain. The streets were utterly empty during the match. We called it the World Cup Rapture. Most people in Pamplona were rooting for Spain, but more than a few of the holdout Basques were openly cheering for Holland. After the go-ahead goal, a fire was started in record-breaking time in the Plaza del Castillo. At the conclusion of the win, we experienced a most surreal Spanish moment, in addition to the thousands of wine bottles that went flying overhead. Ask anyone who was there what song started playing immediately after the clock ran out on the win. Anyone in Pamplona that night will remember: In 2010 they of course loudly played "Money for Nothing" by Dire Straits from 1985.

After several years in Pamplona, we were surprised to learn that only around five thousand people make up the different clubs. During the fiesta, it seems like everyone is a member. There are sixteen *peñas* in Pamplona (there is a mysterious seventeenth that is barred from official status by the portentously named "Federation of the Peñas"), but there are now foreign clubs throughout the world, albeit a small number, including our "completely fictitious" Philadelphia Peña and Taurino Club.

Most of the clubs are located on calle Jarauta, which is never a bad place to visit during the fiesta. Each of the *peñas* can be identified by its "uniform."

They are:

> *La Única, formed in 1903. Members wear a green* pañuelo, *waistband, and espadrille bows, and a blue-and-white check shirt.*
>
> *Muthiko Alaiak, formed in 1931. They wear a collarless blue-and-white checked shirt.*
>
> *El Bullicio Pamplonés, formed in 1932, wear typical San Fermín clothing, with the society's shield on the* pañuelo.
>
> *La Jarana, formed in 1940, wear a blue-and-white checked shirt and a blue* pañuelo *and waistband.*

Oberena, formed in 1941, wear typical San Fermín clothing, with the peña's shield on the pañuelo.

Aldapa, formed in 1947, wear no special shirt. They are tremendous musicians.

Anaitasuna, formed in 1949, wear a shirt with the shield embroidered on the pocket and San Fermín on red pañuelos.

Los de Bronce, formed in 1950, wear a blue-and-white, large-check shirt and official shield on the pañuelo. The members of this peña wear no waistband, making them the smartest peña in Pamplona.

Irrintzi, formed in 1951, wear black shirts and love to walk in the mountains.

Alegría de Iruña, formed in 1953, wear a green shirt with red collar, cuffs, and pockets. Very cool.

Armonía Txantreana, formed in 1956, wear a red pañuelo with their shield embroidered.

El Charco S.D.C.R, formed in 1974, wear a blue pañuelo and sash.

Donibane, formed in 1977, wear a blue shirt with green shield on the pocket.

Rotxapea, formed in 1978, wear a blue shirt. This is one of the peñas with the youngest membership and one of the first to accept women.

7 de Julio San Fermín, formed in 1979, wear a black-and-white checked shirt, decorated with the shield.

Sanduzelai (aka San Jorge), formed in 1980, wear a black-and-white checked shirt.

You have not experienced the San Fermín fiesta until you've sat with a *peña* for a bullfight. You have not gotten dirty until you've sat with a *peña* for a bullfight. It is inconceivable that the *peñas* will not welcome you and treat you like family in their area at the bullfights. Bring a poncho.

Most amusing is the nightly *peña* march out of the bullring at around 8:30 p.m. They march back into the night with what is left of their brass bands, singing, and dancing. They personify ragged-ness, and it's hard to believe that they'll be right back out at it the next afternoon. If you join in, please enjoy the flour fights, the din, and the hours-long walk to go a couple hundred yards back to their club.

Runner History

Run long enough and you will have your own Pamplona history. There's always someone at or nearing the end of a glorious running career. They pass on knowledge of the right vs. wrong way to run, and the secrets needed to survive annually. For us, that was Joe Moskaluk. Papa Joe was born in 1941, served in the United States Army, was a butcher in his own shop in Kinderhook, New York, and played Santa Claus annually in his adopted hometown of Gallatin, Tennessee. He had massive white muttonchops and of-ten wore floral shirts while running. Others joined in just to honor him. On our first morning ever in the streets of Pamplona in 2004, he approached Ari and me and offered his friendship and asked for nothing in return. Joe talked to us not to hear the sound of his own voice but because of his remarkable love of the Pamplona fi-esta. In that hour before the *encierro* started he educated us about the fiesta exponentially more than we've learned on our own since. After that we sought him out in front of the Ayuntamiento every morning, and loved our time with him. In 2007 or 2008 he fell hard during the run, and it was simply amazing to see the throngs—out of sheer love—pushing each other aside to help him to his feet. He started in 1985 and retired from running in 2008 in his late sixties, and died suddenly in March 2012. Everyone in Pamplona misses him. He was a true-life Pamplona history-making legend.

Montónes, Records, and *Cornadas*

For me, even scarier than a bull goring (*cornada*) are runner pile-ups (*montónes*), which occur when runners fall, and the runners following from behind fall on top like lemmings on the pile. If you run long enough, you'll experience a miniature *montón*, but spend a moment before each run praying that you won't experience a real one. Both Ari and I have escaped smaller pileups with minor injuries, but each was scarier than anything. The crushing weight on your chest, and that sickening panic of not being able to breathe, even momentarily, is nothing but execrable. I think I'd rather take the horn. I know I would. There have been twenty-five large, ugsome pileups in the last hundred years of the fiesta, with in excess of seven hundred serious injuries. The most infamous pileups usually occur at the entrance to the bullring. For instance: July 7, 1922 (100 injured); July 7, 1943 (24 injured); July 9, 1975 (1 dead, 116 injured); and July 8, 1977 (1 dead and 35 injured). More than a few men who were running on the date of the deaths in 1975 and 1977 are still regular runners during San Fermín today.

On July 13, 2013, there was some sort of mismanagement with the door to the bullring when a couple of police officers tried to get off the course without climbing over the wall, and panicked runners started entering the ring (long before the bulls arrived), and ran behind the door to the right, benightedly thinking it had been opened for them. The door was forced open by the runners, closing half of the entrance to the bullring, and hundreds piled up and locked themselves together at the feet of the closed door. When the bulls arrived, led by our good friend Owain Hoskins, I feared the worst as I watched on TV (I was laid up with my broken ankle in the hospital). Owain spectacularly leaped onto the top of the pile and crawled across for his life. Amazingly, the bulls sensed that something was wrong and they did not move to gore the huge wall of runners. If they had, dozens would have likely died over the many minutes it took to undo the pile. One bull even lay down, and photographs made it appear that he was reading a discarded newspaper in the street. In the end, two runners suffered very serious injuries related to asphyxia; however, at the time of this writing, both were rumored to be on their way to a near-full recovery. This had the makings to be the darkest day in fiesta history. Somehow a monstrous tragedy was avoided. Just watching friends arrive at the wall of people one by one and wondering if any were on the bottom was awful. We are very, very afraid of *montónes*. Very.

Since we started running there have been three very serious *montónes* (July 12, 2004; July 13, 2008; and the aforementioned July 13, 2013). As to the first, Ari and I were in the middle of it but escaped without a scratch. However, our friend Julen Madina, an extraordinary and legendary runner, suffered a terrible goring. He was gored five times in the entryway to the bullring, where a group of runners had fallen into a pile and were attacked by one of the bulls. He "retired" from running after 2012 when his baby was born but still ran in 2013. The lure is irresistible.

In modern times, each run is timed (presumably accurately), and that is valuable information. In general, the longer the run lasts, the more significant the horrible carnage. The average run time is three to four minutes. In 2011, several runs were well under three minutes, which was shockingly fast. Those bulls regularly reached the Telefónica stretch under two minutes after the rocket. Every day I was down there with my watch, insisting that the bulls could not have already reached us. In fact, the bulls ran so fast that year it was a common complaint that even experienced runners were not able to stay in front of the horns for a meaningful amount of time.

On July 13, 2011, the bulls of the El Pilar ranch ran the entire route in two minutes and eleven seconds. Covering the entire course this fast in a car would be impressive. Fortunately, it was not a crowded day, and I was able to run into the ring with the herd with almost no one near me. I will always remember the guy in front of me falling and his pants ripping off, though.

The longest recorded run in fiesta history, on July 11, 1959, lasted an astounding thirty minutes. The *pastores* just could not get the entire herd into the bullring. Finally, a dog had to be used to nip a Miura bull into the ring. (What other breed? It takes only a fiesta or two to understand why: They are the largest and most dangerous in the world, and while they are majestic, they tend to cause zany mornings.) If you see a dog on the running course, you can assume the worst. Go ahead and cry out like a baby, and flee for safety.

There have been fifteen official deaths in the *encierro* in the modern fiesta. Another died (injured in 1910) the following calendar year from infection, and is not regarded as dying from bulls. Several deaths were caused by runners who were foolishly up to no good, and at least one had the misfortune of being near some idiots. Some were expert runners, and others were random victims, meaning that they were doing nothing that was different from what the rest of us were doing. We used to say, "What do you mean? It's been more than a decade since someone died!" Now, it's been only a couple of years. The worst days in fiesta history were July 10, 1947, and July 13, 1980, when the bulls Semillero (*ganadería* Urquijo) and Antioquío (*ganadería* Guardiola) each killed two runners.

Every time you step on the cobblestones for an *encierro*, you put your life at risk. Anyone who discounts the peril is a self-important, arrogant balatron. (In 1988 I saw William F. Buckley Jr. call Michael Dukakis a "balatron" on *Firing Line*. I had to look it up; it means "buffoon.") Every year, a few days before the fiesta, some English-speaking clown will look into a TV camera and tell millions of potential visitors that the *encierro* is really not that dangerous. They are either idiots or liars.

Such an argument is easily dismissed with this list of those who died in the streets of Pamplona. Some died in a hospital, and even months later. Some were gone forever before the Red Cross workers got to their dead body.

The list is painful to review.

July 13, 1924—Esteban Domeño, 22, from Sangüesa, was gored on calle Telefónica. His tragic death was witnessed by Ernest Hemingway and memorialized in *The Sun Also Rises*. Domeño had turned to mount the fence to avoid the bull, but found the crowd too dense, and he was left in the open.

July 8, 1927—Santiago Zufía, 34, from Pamplona, died from a goring near the entrance to the bullring, after *another runner* taunted the bulls with a stick. The bull missed the taunting runner and killed Zufía. He initially struggled to his feet, and then fell dead into the arms of those who came to his aid.

July 10, 1935—Gonzalo Bustinduy, 29, a Mexican citizen living in San Sebastián, was killed in the bullring while enticing a bull to pass under his jacket like a cape. He was part of a larger group of people taunting the bulls from behind.

July 10, 1947—Casimiro Heredia, from Pamplona, on calle Estafeta, and Julián Zabalza, from Estella, in the bullring, were both killed by Semillero, a particularly agile and ferocious bull. Zabalza was killed when he left his girlfriend and sister and climbed into the arena from his safe seat to look for the *suelto* back through the entrance of the ring. Heredia was viciously gored from behind. After delivering the mortal blow, the bull returned and tossed Heredia around like a ragdoll.

July 9, 1961—Vicente Urrizola, 32, from Pamplona, was gored and died at the peak of the hill on calle Santo Domingo. His goring and death went famously unnoticed in the media for almost thirty hours afterward.

July 12, 1969—Hilario Pardo, 45, from Murchante, was gored twice by the same bull in a sudden flash of the horns and died at the peak of the hill on calle Santo Domingo.

July 12, 1974—Juan Ignacio Eraso, 18, from Txantrea, was gored on calle Telefónica after not accounting for all six bulls.

July 9, 1975—Gregorio Górriz, from Arazuri, suffered a mortal goring when a bull darted to avoid a *montón* at the entrance to the bullring.

July 8, 1977—José Joaquín Esparza Sarasíbar, from Pamplona, died at the tender age of seventeen at the bottom of a human blockade right at the entrance to the ring. The pile started with assorted inexperienced runners tripping over and over each other long before the bulls arrived. When they did, the bulls plunged their horns into the pile—repeatedly—to clear a way, without success. Then, the herd turned around to return from where they had come. Confusion reigned, with several of the gates being opened and closed in an attempt to get the bulls safely away from the pile. The entire debacle lasted six minutes, and left a teenager dead. We have friends who were caught in the *montón*, and friends who were caught with the bulls between the gates. Everyone with whom we have ever discussed this astonishing event struggles to convey its terrifying nature.

July 13, 1980—José Antonio Sánchez, 26, from Cintruénigo, was gored in the Plaza Consistorial and dragged along the street to *la curva,* and Vicente Risco, 29, from Badajoz, was gored at the bullring. The *encierro* lasted over ten minutes, and both runners were killed by a bull named Antioquio.

July 13, 1995—Matthew Peter Tassio, 22, from Illinois, died from a goring in front of the Plaza Consistorial. He was running in flip-flops.

July 8, 2003—Fermín Etxeberri, 63, an expert runner from Pamplona, died from a serious head wound suffered when the herd knocked him over on calle Mercaderes. He hung on to life until September 24, 2003, before finally succumbing to his injuries.

July 10, 2009—Daniel Jimeno Romero, 27, from Alcala de Henares, died while trying to regain his feet or slip under the barrier on the calle Telefónica stretch. Both Ari and I witnessed his goring, and Ari was mere inches away. We knew Daniel as a friend in Pamplona. We had just shared a good laugh with him a day or two before.

Every time you step out to meet the bulls you must be ready to defend your life, and this Pamplona history cannot be ignored.

5

Charlie Don't Surf
(philosophy of running)

"I can swim."

—ARYEH L. DEUTSCH, EVERY JULY

He can't swim at all. He says he "prefers" not to go into water that is over his head. He says he doesn't want to lose his glasses. He says he does not like the way floating "feels." In twenty-five years he has never admitted to me that he cannot swim; at the same time, no one anywhere has ever seen him swim. Before I leave this world, I would like him to just once look me in the eye and say, "You are right. I cannot swim." I swear I will fall over dead. He can't swim and we live near the Atlantic Ocean off the coast of New Jersey. We spend half the summer there.

Anything below Barnegat Bay, New Jersey, is the "shore" (not the ocean or the beach) and belongs to us living in southern New Jersey. Anyone who lives above that and calls on our beaches is a Benny, a derogatory moniker, which stands for Bayonne-Elizabeth-Newark-and-New York. The term refers to the fat, rude, shiny, greasy, loud, summer Italian American tourists from northern New Jersey and New York. When I was a kid, the derogatory term was *shoobie,* which was an old reference to tourists that came in from Philadelphia, and brought their lunch in a shoebox. Now, the term is just used to mock people that wear their sneakers in the sand. Both a Benny and a Shoobie bring noise, trash, and traffic, and a greasy residue to our beautiful shore. Both smoke on the sand and listen to Yankees games. Can you imagine our horror? The idiots on *Jersey Shore* are from New York and they are barely staying in their own neighborhood in Seaside Heights. New Yorkers try to argue that the term Benny actually is short for "Benjamin Franklins," that is, slang for the hundred-dollar bills they flash around. Ugh.

Matt Warshaw is my favorite surfing philosopher. He says that "surfing . . . turns not a skill into an art, but an inexplicable and useless urge into a vital way of life," and that "surfing . . . generates laughter at its very suggestion." I believe the same goes for the *encierro:* art, way of life, and laughter, except it is usually nervous laughter, and from my mother. In surfing communities, you will often see "NO KOOKS" carved into or tagged onto anything that doesn't move near beaches dominated by locals. In surfing, a kook is a know-it-all who's clueless. It's someone who dresses up like a surfer but with the leash on his wrist, or around his neck.

Kooks drop in on another's wave, paddle right out to the peak on another's beach, and ditch their board. They get in the way. Surfers hate them. So, with all due respect, in the streets of Pamplona don't be kooks. We run with the Pamplonicans, the Navarrans, the Basques, the Spanish, and our American brothers. We run with citizens of the entire world: England, Ireland, Scotland, Wales, Canada, Australia, Japan, Haiti, Mexico, Norway, Sweden, and everywhere in between. *Even some French-type persons.* Clearly, the locals and the bulls own the streets. But after a while, as you go to Pamplona year after year, you get to know the runners who run every day and every year—not the tourists or the people undergoing midlife crises. For many, running with the bulls is no lark but a way of life. There are those of us who, for the rest of our days, will pursue the horns every time they open that gate in Pamplona. We have a lot of emotion invested, and have a birthright claim to our space on the cobblestones. We have a right to demand that new runners observe the rules and respect those who came before. We do, and so should you. Our safety and our sensibilities depend on it. This might appear to completely conflict with the sense that the *encierro* is a completely democratic tradition. It doesn't. I believe in my pursuit of happiness and the pursuit of happiness for everyone. *Governing dynamics, gentlemen.* Anyone and everyone can run. Anyone and everyone can conduct himself in a way that offers a modicum of safety to all of the runners.

The *encierro* easily compares to surfing. With surfing, you take the wave the ocean provides. It may not be the perfect wave, it may be, and you might still get slammed into the coral. Or you might sit all morning waiting for a wave. You may see the perfect wave and blow it. In Pamplona, you might get trapped in the crowd, or trip, and end up running behind the herd. With the *encierro,* the traditional expression is that you "take what the saint gives you," and in your moment of danger, you ask him to "throw me a cape." In his moment of danger, a matador in the ring needs something to distract *el toro* from ripping him to shreds. A well-timed wave of the cape from a member of his *cuadrilla* usually fills the bill.

You cannot force a good wave, and you cannot force a good run. For both, you have to be ready when the circumstances are just right to allow the opportunity to be seized.

We especially don't like cobblestone kooks during San Fermín. In the morning, there are plenty of idiots in the streets. They are full of bravado, ignorance, alcohol, and bad advice. More than one Australian has spent the morning trying to tell me that the goal of the *encierro* is to touch the bulls *or grab the horns, which is insanity with a funny accent.* American media is nearly always wrong. The Internet is spilling with bad advice from British and Australians for large groups traveling en masse. If you are in a tour group with matching t-shirts and the word "party" appears anywhere, you are a kook, and you're traveling with a bunch more. If the tour website touts jumping from the fountain in Navarrería Square *as a major event of the fiesta*, you will be traveling with kooks, and lots of them.

I especially love our Australian fiesta brethren. But, they've got to get it under control soon. In 2011, an Australian thrill seeker continued to taunt a massive fighting bull inside the bullring despite clear and repeated directions not to do so. This tourist, in jean shorts, started waving his arms in the air, running and jumping behind a dark-brown bull named Esquillo, who turned toward him, lowered its head, and drilled a sharp left horn into his right thigh, tossing him across the ground and then pushing its head into the man's back. The horn pierced his right femoral artery. Australian newspapers described him as "the victim," which is ludicrous considering our friends who had to rush in and rescue this dope. He almost died, but because he was such an idiot, the city levied a big fine on him anyway.

The *encierro* and the fiesta are so impossibly important to us that we desire greatly to influence and encourage American travelers and visitors to Pamplona to be the right kind of runner. As to the British girls and Australians, no one can control them.

The right kind of runner runs anonymously, and in such a fashion as to respect the herd, which includes both bulls and brother runners. The right kind of runner does not celebrate the self, or glorify the violence of the day in any fashion. He doesn't ask, "Did you see me out there?" right after the run. He doesn't wear funny outfits in the *encierro*.

There are many, many types of bad runners. There is only one kind of right runner. Follow the rules. Act respectfully. Stay sober. Don't use brother runners as shields. Run, don't stand. Don't cower. Keep your hands to yourself.

Some safety issues are not actually matters of common sense, but each bears repeating. For instance, new runners often plan to hang from the wooden barriers or escape early by gently climbing between the railings before seeing bulls. Police and other officials will vigorously push you back into the fray.

The *encierro* is mind-bogglingly dangerous, and the giant crowds make it even more so. Many runs in the streets are needed before you really get a feel for how to run. Equally, the event commands respect, or at least some reverence. This started way before us and will continue long after we're gone. It's not about you or me.

Remember, to get a sense of the history, the city installed the iconic barriers in 1776 and defined the modern running route. The Navarrans and Basques were running long before that year. This is, and has been for a while, an historical event. So, safety aside, cobblestones in the morning with *toro bravos* is no place for drunks and louts and morons.

Among other goals, it is our ambition to pass on to our fellow American travelers the regard (respect) for the *encierro*. Here are some important things to take to heart before running.

Don't Bring Your Camera

You cannot run with the bulls safely while toting a camera. Cameras and video equipment are not permitted in the running course. It would be safer to carry a loaded gun in your pocket than a camera in your hands or around your neck when running with the bulls. Do not strap one to your hat or head. After 7:30 a.m., sometimes earlier and sometimes later, police will usually remove—by force, if necessary—potential runners from the street course who are showing or using cameras. Then you will be telling everyone at home how you "almost" ran with the bulls. At the beginning of the fiesta, and on weekends, and on crowded days, you can count on the police to walk among the crowd looking for cameras. Leave your camera in the hotel room, or with your girlfriend or your mother.

Also, any cell phone being flashed around may be interpreted as a camera. Leave your cell phone deep and hidden in your pocket if you absolutely have to carry it 24/7. You'd be better off not bringing anything you care about, except your own body, into the running. Sooner or later, everything, including your own body, will be broken. In the moment of truth, your mind may decide it is more important to protect your Leica M7 or, as in the case of Ari, his Motorola Razr, in case we travel back to 2003. Ari owned a Motorola Razr longer than anyone else in history.

Even if you're standing in the streets in the morning, and *someone asks you to take a picture* (with his camera) of Dougie Brimson and the Blades Business Crew before the run, don't do it. If the police see you with Dougie's camera, they won't care that you were doing a favor—you will be gone, and the boys with Sheffield United F.C. will not have much by way of condolences for you afterward.

Again, if they see you with a camera (and they are looking), police will remove you from the course. People with cameras tend to be stupid, or slow, or lacking common sense as to the serious nature of the run. More importantly, cameras are forbidden—it's the rule. You might disagree with the rule, but you might be watching the run from a bar because of your higher principles on camera use during the *encierro*.

Why is this camera issue such a big deal? Amateur photographers run backward, they run slow, they fall, they hinder and they obstruct the run. Camera work is "unsuitable for the smooth running of the *encierro*," according to the city's official rules on the running.

Because a camera is a dangerous object in the running, seasoned runners may also remove you from your camera. More than a few shutterbugs have gotten pushed around or punched out, or worse. In 2008, a junior paparazzo lost several teeth when he *stopped in front of me* to take a shot of himself with a dullard smile—all the while, the Fuente Ymbro breed was breathing down my neck. I ran through him and then went back to help him find his front incisors. And I'm nice about the cameras compared to grizzled locals. Running with the bulls is no place for a "selfie," a word that should be loathed anyway. In 2014, an international manhunt occurred for a runner who snapped a selfie with the entire herd behind him. If you held me down and tickled me to force me to answer, I'd admit it was a pretty awesome photograph. However, the police do not agree.

Let me give some general advice about the police in Pamplona during San Fermín. The police in Pamplona are mostly good people. There are exceptions, as in any community in the world. Early in the morning, with throngs of drunken louts, and over-worked, the police are not always in the best of moods. They don't negotiate, or speak English, or understand the International Hand Gestures for "but this is my only chance to run with the bulls." They will remove you from the streets if you flout the rules, and they might smack you in the head or throw you around.

There are three main branches of police in Spain: the Civil Guard and the National Police, which are run from Madrid, and the local Municipal Police. In Pamplona, the regional "Chartered Police of Navarre" are known as the Policía Foral. In addition, there are regional police forces in some autonomous communities, such as the Ertzaintza in the Basque Country. The local police have blue uniforms. The Policía Foral wear red-and-black uniforms and tall black leather boots. For those from the United States, the National Police allow you to hark back to quainter times, when the police could bash your head in with a baton because "you ain't from around here, are you?" The leather boots are there to ease the pain when they kick you in the head. Sometimes they carry automatic rifles and have mounted guns on the back of armored jeeps. If either version of the police asks you to do something (their favor-ite: "mueve hacia atrás," or "move back"), you can attempt to discuss the Magna Carta, The Hague, or your other rights, or do it. They are quick to the baton and quick to the pepper spray and quick to the knee in your back with your face mashed into the cobblestones. During the fiesta, and probably during the rest of the year, they suffer little debate. We have gotten to know officers from each kind of police force over the years. Individually, they are mostly good people to talk with. As a group, like any police force anywhere, they have the capacity to do some nasty stuff. In Pamplona, they are tired and on edge. Comport yourself accordingly.

In 2009, police tried to remove a nice gentleman with a camera from the course, but by pulling his head over the top barrier, and his feet under the lower. It did not work, but it did not stop them from trying repeatedly.

Don't Climb the Fences

Contrary to popular belief, the wooden fence barriers are not for your protection. They are to protect everyone else from the bulls. The workers who install them are real craftsmen, and the barriers themselves are a work of art. They are made of fir trees from forests in the Roncal Valley, constructed by local carpenters, and are around seven feet tall. Each of the thousands of pieces is numbered. Each post is placed in a preexisting hole in the cobblestones that has a steel lid welded to it the rest of the year. The posts are not square but a foot thick at their widest point. There are three levels of notches that go completely through the post where boards are inserted from both sides and bolted in. The boards are eight inches tall but only three inches thick, and just enough apart from each other to allow the average middle-aged American to crawl through. Then there are some sections where the boards are so close together nothing can fit between; in Pamplona these are referred to as the "palisades." Around twenty boards are replaced each year due to damage, from either rot or tourist malice. Ari and I have witnessed bulls striking the fencing so hard trying to gore runners that the wood has cracked. It makes a memorable, if not frightening, sound. Those boards are bigger and stronger than your bones.

The barriers are a beloved part of the fiesta, and we love receiving photos via email from friends in Pamplona when the annual fence installation starts, and it is always sad to watch the workers take them down after the final run on the fourteenth. We've spent many hours climbing over, under, sitting upon, falling off, and leaning on those fences. Mostly leaning. My favorite section to sit on is near the bullring to watch the parade into and out of the afternoon feria.

During the running of the bulls, it is forbidden to climb on or over the fences. Every day of every fiesta, some "brave soul" explains to us his intention to be sitting on the wall when the bulls run by. First, that's lame. Second, the police will not let you. In between the two sets of fences, the police and emergency personnel wait to help you in a real emergency. *A real emergency.* A bull running by is not considered an emergency, and the police will actively keep you away from the fences unless something really goes wrong. If something is really going wrong, you will not have time to climb the fence.

There is room to roll under the fence, but that cannot be your plan. You cannot plan to run, slow down, bend down, lie down, and roll under the fence. You will be crushed.

In 2011, a bull from the Dolores Aguirre Ybarra ranch ran into a runner, and that runner flew through the air and hit me from behind. I then fell (the first of two falls in 2011) near the right-hand fence running into the bullring. From the impact, my body rolled under the fence to safety in lieu of getting trampled. I did not roll under the fence on purpose. That was an emergency. In other words, I did not set out to roll under.

As to climbing the fences, to safely run with the bulls, you will have to be running so fast you will not be able to stop and mount the barriers safely. If you try to stop you will be overrun by the crowd from behind. Climbing the barriers is only for those who absolutely have to seek refuge but have already slowed down or stopped for some reason.

People do still climb the fences. At the moment of truth, these "climbers" channel the spirit of Sir Edmund Hillary. Bringing their own Sherpa, they climb a door or barrier or gate or lamppost at the first scent of hoof. Friends, this is not running with the bulls. This is watching others run with the bulls slightly below a balcony.

Don't Touch the Bull

Don't touch the bulls. It is disrespectful. The goal of the morning run is to join the herd, and not to touch the bull. You never know when touching a bull will cause it to lose interest in staying with its brothers. Distracting the bull from the herd invariably results in injury to others, and possibly death. The rolled-up newspaper is to gauge distance and, in the hands of experienced runners, to help herd any *suelto* toward the bullring. It is not for smacking the bull. The goal of the *encierro* is not to smack the bull from behind with the newspaper.

While you may see even the Pamplonicans, the Navarrans, the Basques, or the Spanish breaking this rule, it is still a jerk move. They will deal with their own people. The idea of the *encierro* is to join the herd—to run as brothers—in the streets. In Pamplona, you will face the daily onslaught of slightly drunken Brits bragging of their intentions to touch the bull. The *encierro* means "the enclosing" and not "the smacking."

The famous San Fermín photographer Jim Hollander says that running is to "pay homage" to the bulls. Nothing so erudite comes from typical media reports. That means respect the herd. In seventy runs I have touched the bull one time on purpose (the bulls have touched me more than once, but that is an issue for their own book). A bull was running to my right and the crowd pushed me into it. I used my hand to steady myself for a moment. That's it. You should never do anything more.

Fear the *Suelto*

There's what you do in a moment of panic, and then there's what you do when you hear someone yell *suelto*. In general, *suelto* means loose or untied. For instance, "el perro está suelto en el jardín" (the dog is loose in the garden). Or "el asesino anda suelto" (the murderer is on the loose). In the context of the *encierro*, it means "loose bull" or "lone bull." It means that a bull has become separated from the herd and has become exponentially more dangerous. In a "vanilla" *encierro* you can avoid trouble (really, no *encierro* is vanilla).

When the herd gets split up, a *suelto* finds you. A *suelto* is likely to turn back up the streets, run the wrong way, or to pinball down the street from side to side goring runners. It may choose a single runner and gore him over and over. In *The Sun Also Rises*, Hemingway writes, in chapter 13, "They're only dangerous when they're alone. . . ."

From the time they are born, bulls rarely see men off of horses. They certainly never get close to men. Early in their life, after being separated from their mothers at their first birthday, the bulls suffer the humiliation of the branding. This is the *herradero*. The calves are separated from their mothers in the fall, and according to the lore already have the arrogance of kings with a thousand years of fighting blood in their veins. They don't like to be touched. Six men are needed to wrestle the young bull to the ground, and the *ganadería* emblem is branded onto the hip. Since 1850, the bulls also get a double-digit number on their ribs. This number identifies him with his mother's fighting characteristics. The branding leaves the bull boiling in a rage, and Spanish tradition cites this event as the reason it is so willing to fight at age four.

On a bull's second birthday, it endures the *tienta*, or surgeon's probe. The bull ranch has a big lunch, and folks dress up, and the bulls are herded to the small bullring on the ranch. A ranch hand, armed with a lance, waits on the edge of the ring on horseback when a bull enters. He does not act overtly to attract the bull. Either the bull attacks the lance or doesn't. If he attacks it and does not draw back from the pain of the point, the ranch owner yells out *"toro,"* and the bull continues to be groomed to become a *toro bravo*. That day, he gets his name in the official *toro bravo* registry, with the requisite information about his mother and father, whether he snorted, bluffed, and how hard he fought to get to the horse. If he doesn't attack and wanders around the ring listlessly, the owner calls out *"buey,"* and the bull is *castrated on the spot*. It is career day, but for bulls. A little advice for the bulls—get a good night's sleep before your birthday party.

On the morning of the run in Pamplona, the bulls are at least four years old, they haven't seen a cape in three years, and if a bull doesn't have the instinct to stay with his herd, or he gets separated from tripping or getting disoriented (or sliding into the wall at *la curva*), those adolescent feelings may boil up, and *el toro bravo*—alone with men and noise for the first time—may seek to exact his revenge. That's a *suelto*.

Sueltos are unpredictable and mean. They spin around and dart at speeds I cannot properly impart to you in writing. The phrase "turned on a dime" is insufficient to describe their swiftness. Unless you grew up on a farm in Spain, your brain (like mine) lacks the instinct and learned knowledge to truly comprehend the quickness with which a lone bull will find you in a crowd of thousands. The bull may stop responding to the willow stick and the *cabestros*. Dogs may have to be released to get the bull back running to the bullring. Until you have serious experience out on the cobblestones, do not toy with or taunt or approach or tickle or whisper or pass notes in study hall to a lone bull. Run away, and let the experts handle it. You might think it funny or brave to jump in close to a *suelto*, and you may distract it in such a fashion that it ends up killing someone. Our friend Bill Hillmann was gored in 2014 when he joined in Navarran efforts to lead a *suelto* back into running toward the bullring.

I must admit that I love the *suelto*. These bulls take something already exciting and turn the dial to 11. In 2011, we left Pamplona without a single good *suelto*, and actually complained about it on the beach later in the trip. This was arrogant and silly, because a *suelto* is much more likely to flash its horns and ruin the fiesta. As an aside, *suelta* actually means "loose girl." As a father of two sons, they are to be feared also.

Don't Ignore the *Pastores*

The gentlemen with green shirts running with the bulls with the word *"pastores"* over their shoulders are not to be trifled with. *Pastores* have herded the bulls through the streets of the city since the Middle Ages. On the cobblestones, they are in charge. Respect

them during the run; thank them profusely afterward. Run enough
and a *pastor will save your miserable life* one morning. Some of them
have been at it for almost fifty years or more. Their only tool is a
long willow stick, which is used to keep the bulls running forward,
as they smack the ground hard (it makes a distinctive sound). *Pastores* are also in charge of keeping runners away from *suelto* bulls,
and will not hesitate to smack you with the willow sticks. You will
remember that sting for the rest of your life.

The *pastores* are experts in handling cattle. They know how to
cut short a charging *toro bravo*. Some work on ranches, but some
ride a desk, or are farmers or fishermen the rest of the year.

In the bullring, the *pastores* pass the bulls off to the *dobladores*,
who lead the bulls into their paddock under the ring with their
capes. They really don't appreciate anyone interfering with their efforts. So, don't. If you do, jail or a serious fine, or street justice,
may follow. When you run into the bullring, you should (and must)
immediately move to the left or right. Ignoring the directions of
the *pastores* or *dobladores* is simply unimaginable.

On a good morning, the running lasts about three minutes.
Then, we're drinking coffee by 8:05 a.m. and exaggerating how
close we got (the bull's breath is steamy hot). On bad mornings, the
herd breaks up and the bulls stop to examine the sights.

On Monday, July 11, 2005, Ari and I decided to start our run
about three-quarters of the way down calle Estafeta, with the intention of making a long run into the bullring with the herd. We
did not make it. The large crowds had left Pamplona, and we were
looking forward to a "carefree run," even though the breed that
morning was the Jandilla, a notoriously dangerous bull. We sta-
tioned ourselves near the bar Mesón Pirineo, near the side gates
into the Plaza del Castillo but on the left, facing the ring. We figured that a large portion of the crowd would start near the beginning or near the end and that, as we folded into the herd, the crowd
would thin for the turns into the bullring.

It ended up as an excruciatingly long run (5:33). Two bulls

charged past us as we started our run, and then there was a large gap, followed by two more bulls and a white speckled bull that flew past. With that, the crowd seemed to dissipate, and Ari and I lost count of the bulls.

Suddenly, a black *suelto* appeared, and a runner named Xabier (who later became our friend after he was released from the hospital) stumbled and caught the bull's attention. He was repeatedly gored on the ground. However, because he did not try to stand, he did not expose his underbelly, or his neck, and did not give the bull a good target. Ari saw Xabier bang his head on a pipe on the front of the building as he slipped and fell. He saw him gored in the leg, but when he was wheeled into the ambulance later, he gave the thumbs-up and everyone applauded. During the goring, the *pastores* began repeatedly whipping the bull with their willow sticks, but it had almost no effect. The bull concentrated on Xabier until it didn't want to anymore. It then turned and found me standing and staring at what was happening to Xabier. Poor Xabier? It was almost poor me. I had to shimmy up a downspout, and the bull stood and watched me for what seemed over a minute. Ari says it was less than a microsecond. A friend (even watching the video, there is a debate as to which friend) tugged at the bull's tail to distract him away from me. The bull started down the course, and I then climbed down. At that moment, I mistakenly got between a *pastor* and the bull, and was struck viciously with the willow stick, which left my white shirt bloodied: not with my blood but a bull's. I wore it proudly the whole day, and crowed to anyone expressing even minor interest. A photograph of the entire incident ended up on a tourist magnet sold in shops along calle Estafeta.

With the skillful help of the minders with their capes, this lone bull was finally led to the pens, to our relief. But I bought every magnet I could find, and suspect they put me on it specifically to drive up that year's souvenir sales. I have some in stock if you are interested.

Don't Fall. And if You Must, Don't Get Up.

The most dangerous element of the *encierro*, other than the horns, is tripping. It may seem obvious sitting here reading a book, but you have to remind yourself to keep on your feet once the bulls make an appearance. Among the odder experiences in Pamplona is falling and realizing you have fallen on top of a friend. On July 12, 2014, I fell on Jose Manuel Pereira, and I knew it was him right away because of his blue-and-white striped shirt. I did not gently come to rest, either. I crash-landed on his back. Jose serves as a *pastor* in *encierros* in other towns. He is a mesmerizing runner, but like me he finds himself on the ground more than occasionally while running Telefónica. After the bulls were gone I set out to find him, to make sure I hadn't hurt him. Oh, he had a fine time telling everyone he would rather the bull fall on him next time, hah-hah.

You can be seriously injured in a fall, especially if you hit your head, or if you are trampled. If you fall, cover your head. This is the big one. The most important advice I can impart is, if you fall, do not get up. Do not get up! If you fall, remember that everyone behind you is still running. If you try to stand up, you will be crushed. More importantly, a rising runner attracts the bull to try to gore you, and it will try to gore you; and your exposed abdomen is a perfect soft target.

Some people stay on their feet over hundreds of runs over a decade or more. I've tripped well over a dozen times. I've been pushed over, too. The crowds surge and people panic. My big feet get caught up all the time. If you fall, curl up into the fetal position while covering your head until someone *clearly* tells you all the bulls are past. Try it at home on the living room floor. Having a bull step on you is better than having it gore you as you get up. The instinct to stand is unbearable. But it is a death wish.

On July 13, 1995, American Matthew Peter Tassio stood up after falling and was gored to death. Matthew came to Pamplona on a lark, wholly lacking knowledge of even the basic rules for running, and wearing only flip-flops, with his sweater tied around his waist. He was unprepared. To me, this media account of Tassio's death is chilling:

> Matthew Tassio was among the scurrying runners in front of the bull. The young man slipped to the ground and struggled to get up again. But no sooner did he get to his feet than he fell once more as other runners dashed past. He began to lift himself once more to his feet when "Castellano" came charging up behind him and ripped into him with his terrible horns at full speed and with all the weight of its 575 kilograms. The goring was mortal from the first, the horns ripped into his stomach and cut through the aorta vein. The young man tried to crawl away to avoid the onrushing pack of bulls coming behind. He struggled as best he could toward the safety of the corral on the right, where a Red Cross unit was standing by. He was quickly rushed to hospital. The goring had caused severe anemia and he lost 90% of his blood even before he reached the hospital. Eight minutes after the goring he was in the Hospital de Navarra—a remarkably fast time. But even so, he arrived unconscious and in a deplorable state. Despite the efforts made by the doctors to revive him, he passed away a few moments after his admission to the hospital.

The bull tossed this grown man twenty-three feet in the air. Sit back and take that in before you think this is not dangerous. A rising runner attracts a bull already looking at the ground. It is the cardinal rule of the *encierro*. If you go down, stay down. In comparison, our friend Xabier survived an otherwise bloody Monday in Pamplona because he stayed prostrate on the ground.

Don't Forget the Count

In boxing, they count to ten. In baseball, it's balls and strikes. In Pamplona, it's six bulls. The bulls run the *encierro* with (normally) six *cabestros*. On farms, *cabestros* are generally used for dragging loads and pulling the plow. But some of these castrated bulls are instead trained to herd the wild bulls like sheepdogs. They have a big clinking bell on their neck, and because the bulls have been around them since birth, they instinctively follow the *cabestros*. These are the *cabestros* you will see in Pamplona and in most bull-fighting settings. It's really something to behold—the angry bulls will fold right in and follow and run with the oxen under calm circumstances. In a panic, the bulls may ignore the *cabestros*.

The City of Pamplona has amusing advice about the *cabestros:* "Bulls and oxen. It is easy to distinguish between the two. The oxen are larger, bonier, older and shaven. They have bells around their necks."

They are much larger, and they do have bells. You will be able to recall the sound the bells make for the rest of your life. But, bonier and older? That's not easy to judge with the herd bearing down on you. And, shaven? Well, I just have no idea what they are talking about. I try to get close, but never close enough to tell which of the animals is unshaven.

Counting the herd—six bulls and six (or more) *cabestros*—is an important skill to cultivate. You never want to think the herd has passed by and let up, only to find a straggler. Only a tourist starts to celebrate the day without being absolutely sure all the bulls have run by and are not coming back.

Don't Stop Running; Stop Running

The hardest part is starting and finishing. Inexperienced runners stop running too early, or are still running long after the *encierro* is over. Too many people plan their "escape route" and don't focus on getting into the running. Your escape route should be down the center of the street with the bulls. On the sidelines, with the crowds, it's hard to see the bulls coming, and if you are late, they are gone before you know what happened. If you stop running too early, you are going to get crushed from behind. Don't hang around—run. Some people stand around on the sidelines and prefer to watch when they should be running. These guys are often to blame for a *montón*, and that's when runners get injured. Just like driving, run defensively but not too defensively. Stopping along the route during the run is stupid—it's like stopping in the middle of the Autobahn. You should never lay hands on any other runner. More than once, someone has tried to drag me down. Someone pushed Ari over in 2008 and he cracked a rib (allegedly). Think about your fellow man. The run has to move forward.

However, when the *encierro* is complete, please stop running. You will see them, too: runners who are out to lunch even before breakfast and running down the streets with fear in their eyes long after all the bulls have been tucked away in the bullring.

Don't Forget the Rules

A couple of years back, the Pamplona City Hall published the *encierro* rules, which include the following.

It is forbidden:

> to run behind the bulls *[they turn around oh so fast]*;
> to run in the opposite direction to the *encierro*;
> to incite the bulls;
> to run under the influence of alcohol;
> to run under 18 years of age;
> to hide in corners, dead ends, or doorways;
> to carry anything while running; and
> to leave open the doors of the houses along the course.

These are all absolutely right, even though you wouldn't think you would have to remind the locals to shut their doors along the route. These are like unwritten rules accepted by locals on any surfing beach. This is just how things are done, and we have no reason to claim ignorance. There are tourists appearing in Pamplona every day of the *encierro* who get it in their mind that this list of prohibitions are the actual goals of running with the bulls. In 2014, new city ordinances permitted police to enforce these rules of their own volition and in the moment by assessing giant fines, from 200 to 60,000 euros. If you do not have cash on hand they will walk you to the nearest ATM. I am almost tempted to find out what you have to do to get fined 60,000 euros. Steal a bull?

Don't Vex a Perfect Woman Nobly Planned

This section starts with a quote from "She Was a Phantom of Delight," by William Wordsworth, 1804. Running with the bulls is among the last truly democratic activities. We've run with bus drivers, university professors, famous actors, famous farmers, comics, waiters, bad waiters, terrible authors, matadors, a guy who claimed responsibility for chicken wings at Pizza Hut, marines, Pacey from Dawson's Creek, and, not kidding: a count. Nearly all are welcome. Everyone is equal in the glistening, sun-streaked streets and in between the horns. You needn't fill out any forms or stand in any line. There is no permission slip or waiver. There is no qualification round. And only your mother can tell you that you can't run. And we are all brothers. So, is there room for sisters, too? Yes and no.

Ah, women. Ernest Hemingway famously wrote that you should not bring your own woman to Pamplona. In general, I think he just wanted to spend his time with women others brought to the fiesta. His posthumous daughter-in-law, the charming Valerie Hemingway, writes, in *Running with the Bulls: My Years with the Hemingways,* about his pretty petty treatment of those he did bring. For instance, in 1959, Ernest and Antonio Ordóñez "captured" a couple of midwestern coeds and paraded around with them in front of Mary, Ernest's fourth wife, who was in attendance for the fiesta. In his time, it was incomprehensible that a woman would want to run in the *encierro.* In fact, it was illegal until 1974.

Now, it is absolutely the most common question I am asked. "Should my wife and/or girlfriend and/or sister and/or grandmother run?" I would never, never, never, never let my sister, wife, or daughter or granddaughter run the *encierro.* My grandmother can make up her own mind. The rest of them, I would physically restrain. I know it is hard to have an honest and open discussion on this issue without running afoul of equality and gender concerns. Here's my attempt. ·

Some women are strong and athletic enough. Most aren't. Just like men. There, I said it.

In 2005, a slight, newlywed couple from Japan ran holding hands through the Callejón on the right and into the bullring. They were photographed with foolish smiles and with the bulls bearing down on them (in every newspaper in Europe), and apparently ignorant of the danger they created—danger to themselves and others. It was funny at the time, but when I see the photo now, it makes my stomach turn. They were literally inches from being massacred. It is just incomprehensible to me that a husband would put his young bride in the way of such harm. Neither of them should have run.

In 2007, moments before the run, a fifty-year-old university professor from Chicago introduced herself, and she ran safely and honorably. She was dressed appropriately, was fit, and was prepared. She was as tall as and as strong as the average tiny Spaniard (honestly, some are giants; mostly, they're just little dudes). It was still an uncommon sight only a few years ago.

In 2010, large groups of British girls on "holiday" ran together in flip-flops and tiny shorts and tank tops. Many were injured in falls, but that's really their business. Most disturbingly, they were dangerous to everyone else. They were physically unprepared, and frivolous in their attitude. Seriously, flip-flops? Down the stretch into the Callejón their bodies were strewn around the paver stones like some harebrained reenactment of Pickett's Charge. Countless runners fell over them while they drunkenly shrieked and laughed. Idiots, all of them. Confession. Many of my best 2010 *encierro* pictures had these same women in the same frame as my self-professed gallant runs. So they were doing something right, I confess. This is my least favorite comment from friends: "It doesn't look that bad. Look, there are some women running, too."

Honestly, for every girl in tiny shorts, there are 1,000 male counterparts drunk, or dopes running with their cameras. They are dangerous to everyone, too. Most of us have no qualms planting them on the cobblestones. I wonder what kind of trouble we will have when someone does that to Daddy's darling from Tinkerbush Lane, Oxfordshire (Crotch Crescent, Oxfordshire? Scratchy Bottom, Dorset?) 'cause she's acting like a fool. I hope we receive fair treatment.

You will hardly ever see a Pamplonican, a Navarran, a Basque, or a Spanish woman running. For them, it's a closed discussion. The most famous exception to this rule is Tania Alonso Villar, who is from Spain, and runs in Pamplona and in other *encierros*. She is a braver runner than most everyone. Almost exclusively, this is a United States, New Zealand, United Kingdom, Canadian, or Australian question. It is just a matter of time before an English-speaking woman is killed, which will result in near-deafening international calls to end the "barbaric" *encierro*. Some EU countries, having solved all their own problems, salivate at the notion of shutting down bullfighting and the Pamplona *encierro*. A dead British girl in hot pants and heels is just what they need.

So, if you are female, and as strong and athletic as a small Spanish guy, and dressed appropriately and sober and rested, you should run. Otherwise, don't. Same with guys.

Not on My Watch

I have two sons, Samuel and Jackson. For many years, when they were both younger, when I was asked in media interviews whether I would "let" my sons run in Pamplona, I would say, "Not on my watch!" Everyone would laugh, and I could say it because they were young, and it was not yet even an issue to consider. In 2014, Samuel came to Pamplona with Ari and me for the first time without his mother, and it was agreed upon at home that he was not going to run. It was his first fiesta since he was ten years old. He was just coming to hang out with us and get a feel for the *encierro* and the entire fiesta. We made plans for him to sit with some friends with daughters his age in the mornings. That would keep him busy. Heartfelt promises were made to family back home. He wouldn't run. He was going to carry our luggage up to the room; selflessly guard parking spaces; clean the bathroom; answer to "laddie" and "nipper" while running errands. He would listen patiently while we waxed poetic about the fiesta. Light ironing. But he would not be running with the bulls. *That would be crazy.* So, on July 5, we baked in the sun and challenged the surf in our much-favored purlieu, Biarritz, and had dinner at Arzak in San Sebastián, where we lingered until we were the last guests. Juan Mari and Elena walked us to our car. On the sixth, Sam convinced us to make a rare appearance at the *chupinazo*, which we survived unscathed, miraculously, at the absolute front of the crowd with our Canadian friends Jack Denault and Craig MacPherson. We wore monk robes and passed out inflatable neon electric guitars. Of course we did; it was the fiesta, and no one even blinked. Jack, a recent transplant to Los Angeles with his lovely bride, Victoria, also brought a *giant* inflatable Stanley Cup to celebrate the 2012–13 Los Angeles Kings championship. No one knew what it was. Jack is a shameless, hopeless hockey bandwagoner but a brave and selfless bull runner. He's met many famous athletes, musicians, and actors, and he is a terrific storyteller. He and Sam immediately clicked while talking in the hours before the fiesta started. Someone showed up dressed as Jim Carrey in *The Mask* and was a dead ringer. We debated the World Cup with strangers but new friends now and suffered through a patronizing lecture from a Swede about how the United States was still an "immature country." Ari had 20 euros and his red watch stolen from his back pocket (he also groused for the rest of the fiesta about losing his New Jersey driver's license during the *chupinazo*, and then found it on his kitchen table upon his arrival back home). The rockets launched and announced the start of the fiesta. Ashes floated down onto our faces, the crowd surged back and forth with thousands and thousands of camera flashes, and we cried out from the joy exploding in our hearts. We helped each other tie our *pañuelos* around our necks, and Sam was hooked. Absolutely and forever. We drank

coffee at Café Iruña and watched a hobo dressed like Captain
America sing and dance Basque *jotas*. "Usually," I told Sam,
"he's dressed like a cow." And, as we slowly walked back to wash
off the wine before we were stained pink for the week, or blinded
from the stinging remnants, I could tell we were going to have a
hard time keeping Sam out of the streets in the morning for the first
run. When we got to our flat on calle Descalzos, about a dozen
masked men were spray-painting ETA slogans, like "Freedom for
Basque Prisoners and Exiles," and posting large handbills with
wheat paste on our street. At the same time, the *peña* Donibane had
strung a volleyball net across the street and about a hundred
people were playing. A few stories up above street level, caged ca-
naries were singing on balconies. Someone was serving chorizo
in the street. This was all happening outside our door minutes
after the fiesta started. Sam's eyes approached saucer size. Later
in the day we all walked the *encierro* course together and looked
for ruts and new possible slippery spots.

The next morning the alarm woke us, and Sam said, "I want
to run." I derisively mocked him with a tone of parental responsibility, saying, "That's sweet. Not the first day." We walked down
calle Hilarión Eslava and through Plaza San Francisco and around
onto calle Nueva. At the bend to Plaza Consistorial, the din of the
crowd forming for the first *encierro* was unmistakable and un-
bridled. From behind me I could hear Sam say, "Oh yes, I want
to run," but he was dismissed with a "maybe tomorrow" as I waved
my hand over my shoulder. We then fought through the crowds
and climbed through the barriers into Plaza de Santiago, and his
negotiations started.

"I'll run today and then tomorrow I will . . . ."

"Let's just get it over with today and then for the rest of the
trip you don't have to . . . ."

"I have an idea. I'll just . . . ."

"I know what I'm doing because . . . ."

"Trust me. . . ."

I felt like American infantry advancing into withering fire at

Omaha Beach. Clearly, Sam was going to run, and no earthly force could stop him. I had about an hour to emotionally prepare for having him in the streets with me. Running with your brother is one thing; with your son is quite another. In the coming days (he ran every one of them in 2014), I found the urge to look after him overwhelming even when it interfered with concentrating on the quality of my own run, or even on the bulls, which, by the way, is pretty important. When the time came that morning on July 7, 2014, we all walked uphill to the Ayuntamiento and waited with friends, watching the clock tower. This was also my first run since breaking my ankle in 2013, and I was looking to regain my own fanfaronade after thinking about this morning for an entire year. We all wore white shirts with a yellow scorpion on the back, just like Ryan Gosling in the movie *Drive*. First, it was just cool to have a scorpion on our shirts. Second, it was an ideogram for the fable of "The Scorpion and the Frog," which I use when asked why we would return to run again. We could not blame Pamplona or other runners for the serious injuries Ari and I suffered in 2012 and 2013. It's the nature of the fiesta.

> *A scorpion and a frog meet on the bank of a stream and the scorpion asks the frog to carry him across on its back. The frog asks, "How do I know you won't sting me?" The scorpion says, "Because if I do, I will die too." The frog is satisfied, and they set out, but in midstream, the scorpion stings the frog. The frog feels the onset of paralysis and starts to sink, knowing they both will drown, but has just enough time to gasp "Why?" Replies the scorpion: "It's my nature . . ."*

As the waiting for the *encierro* grew more solemn, I could not help but reflect upon the nature of running with the bulls. Injuries are not uncommon, maybe even expected. This made the approach to running with Sam all the more agonizing. When they arrived, the bulls were in a straight line on the left side of the plaza, and Sam exploded off with them around the corner and down calle Mercaderes and disappeared. It took him forever to return to our agreed-upon meeting place, the red Gutierrez sign. When he did, he sheepishly reported, "No one told me when I'm supposed to stop running," and we had a good laugh at his expense all day.

Then he showed up in pictures in the newspaper on his first day ever running in Pamplona and all over the place online with a giant yellow scorpion on his back. Unavoidably, his mother saw him with the bulls before we could call to say he'd run despite the multitude of promises made otherwise. In the most passive-aggressive email in history, she tellingly wrote us: "Tell Sam the crease in his pants looks crooked."

American Television Changes Everything

"I said, 'I know, everybody funny, now you funny too.'" George Thorogood, 1977.

Since Ari and I starting running in Pamplona, there have been two primary American media incursions. In the early years, it was ESPN. Lately, it has been Esquire TV. Both are a pestilence. There's always someone shooting a documentary or making an independent movie about San Fermín. The Associated Press is always in the city, and you can always find a magazine or significant website looking to do an article. At home, Ari and I have been on local TV, in local newspapers, and on local radio. Those outlets are quaint—innocent. Friends and family might see them. A couple of people might recognize us on the boardwalk down the shore, or in the city. It has never hurt my law practice. Ari and I are always happy to help out with anyone's movie or article promoting Pamplona and its culture. Whenever Pamplona local newspapers or television stations can suffer through an interview with us, we will happily indulge them. There's nothing quite like seeing yourself on television or reading about yourself, especially when it relates to something you dearly love. It's natural. It's fun. But the large-market media outlets can ruin all of our Pamplona fun.

We have a couple of easy rules for small-market media:

1. We will not hoard media sources for ourselves. We give anyone who wants to interview us everyone's name and contact information that they could possibly be interested in, even if the media source ends up more interested in the other names.

2. We don't take money. It's our vacation and it will not become our job.

3. We will not miss a moment of our fiesta. We wait all year to get to Pamplona; I cannot imagine walking out on those things I love so much just to be on TV.

4. We will not become consumed by vanity. We get on TV because we go to Pamplona. We don't go to Pamplona to get on TV.

5. We will not be photographed or filmed together with Ari standing on a box so we are the same height. This actually almost happened once until I realized what they were trying to do. This is more like my rule and not "our" rule, necessarily.

We also have resolved to avoid being sucked into large American programming, like ESPN, because it changes a person. I found that I stopped acting like myself after the first big U.S. television exposure. I saw I could easily become more concerned about fame than the fiesta. No such thing should happen. In 2014, good friends—people we would consider to be our Pamplona family—to my horror abandoned normal social situations (*like having a nice breakfast*) in Pamplona to instead be on Esquire TV back home. They started acting funny. Some became absolutely consumed by their television persona. I found this soul-crushing. After the American cameras show up, great runners often start running for the camera instead of running for the sheer personal joy of running. The 2014 Esquire TV production was perhaps the most accurate and appropriate ever done. They wanted to give runners good advice and to explain the culture and history of the fiesta. Esquire TV was staffed by nice people. Yet I soon felt sorry for those who became addicted to getting interviewed every day instead of enjoying their time in Pamplona.

On the other hand, social media has improved upon Pamplona's fiesta. You can stay in contact year-round with the family you make in Pamplona. We get to know the family better and what is important to them the other 357 days of the year. We share photographs from running or dining or hiking. We also see pictures of their newborns, graduations, weddings, and holidays. It is a fascinating way to get to know another culture. We can even post embarrassing episodes such as Ari's horrible attempts at jumping to touch things slightly over his head. Those pictures are hysterical, but he will never know, suffering from his untreated "socmephobia," or "fear of Facebook."

Don't Be a Rick Reilly, Because Rick Reilly Is a Clumsy Ignoramus

Even though this happened several years ago, I am still irrationally irate. For kicks at parties, Ari will sidle up and say, "Peter, tell 'em about Rick Reilly," and watch me unhinge my lower jaw and convulse on the floor. Why? In 2010, Rick Reilly, a twitchy twit from ESPN who covers sideshow sports like the World Sauna Championship (where, in 2010, Vladimir Ladyzhenskiy died; Rick could barely contain himself) and writes cheesy books like *Sports from Hell*, came to Pamplona with his photographing spouse and used a baseball cap–mounted camera and swatted at the bulls from behind with a newspaper. Like a clown. The resulting article was universally excoriated in Pamplona. Rick Reilly was a very, very bad runner.

I love ESPN. I watch it daily—multiple times daily. Its inception is among the great moments of the twentieth century. However, I shudder when ESPN shows up in Pamplona to try covering the *encierro*. It apparently cannot resist the urge to gin up the bad news. It always butchers it, and presents misleading and exaggerated, if not false, information to viewers. Without exception, ESPN disreputably juices up the carnage and glorifies conflict and injuries.

People like Rick show up in Pamplona every year. "Rick Reillys" are senselessly oblivious that they aren't in Los Angeles, but demand everything be as it is at home. In Paris, they yell "Garçon" in restaurants, and in Spain they'll demand a menu in English. They take their "good jeans" to Japan and wear tank tops to the Vatican.

The actual Rick Reilly was far worse than his tourist namesake. First, he wore a camera on his head. Like Homer Simpson on *Bite Back with Kent Brockman and His Channel 6 Consumer Watchdog Unit* ("Homer and Apu," *The Simpsons*, Season 5.) Again, that was against the rules, and dangerous to his fellow runners. Rick Reilly with a camera was worse than the normal dope.

Second, he leapt at the bulls from behind and the side and swatted away with his newspaper—twice! That too was against the rules, and also dangerous to his fellow runners. A bull distracted like that makes the danger factor rise exponentially. It also shows a serious lack of respect for the bulls—runners are joining the herd for a last glorious run in the sunny morning, and not kicking a brother on the way to the gallows. Rick Reilly was smacking them on the hind quarters. Someone should smack him. In his column, he actually wrote, "Honor and bravery were mine!" in describing his dangerous and disrespectful behavior.

Third, he bragged about his courageousness in an ESPN column called "Welcome to Tramplona." What a jerk.

Fourth, he referred to *la curva* onto calle Estafeta as "Dead Man's Corner." Trying to interpret the fiesta like a NASCAR event is bad journalism. He falsely claimed that someone had died there in 2009, which was inaccurate reporting—emblematic of his entire column. It makes me wonder what else ESPN cannot cover accurately. No one but ESPN and the British call it "Dead

Man's Corner." It's uncouth. Running the corner is very serious business, and a trite or crass nickname is ridiculous.

In response, in the United States, the journalist Charles Robinson (then with Yahoo! and a serious runner in his own right) was openly critical of Rick Reilly's boorish behavior in Pamplona, and there was steady but ignorant online response that Rick was not dangerous to those around him. It is frightening to think that somebody will read Rick Reilly, believe it, and show up in the streets wearing sweatpants with his shirt tucked in and acting like him. Don't get me wrong. Rick Reilly is a colossal and total heel, but in response to his column, he found some measure of redemption by writing this: "I heard from a lot of people who thought the run and the subsequent bullfight each night, in which all six bulls are killed, was cruel and bloodthirsty. Maybe it is. But the Spanish people treat the bulls with such reverence. If you touch a horn on any bull during the run, you'll get the snot beat out of you by the locals. I saw it happen. If you taunt the baby bulls in the ring and don't treat them with honor, you'll get pummeled. Saw that happen, too. These bulls were raised for this specific purpose—the bullfight—in a country where bullfighting has been in their blood for 4,000 years. I just don't see how you can sit in Los Angeles and judge their culture." Well said, just not applied well in real life.

Don't Be Dennis Rodman, Because Dennis Rodman Is Bad, and Not in a Good Way

In the early aught years, Dennis Rodman had been seen "running" during San Fermín while advertising for a not-to-be-mentioned-here gambling website. The website failed. The whole thing was lame, and anyone excited to see Dennis Rodman anywhere deserves a good smack. He certainly is a poor representative of the United States in Pamplona. And those website folks were not getting their money's worth, because by the time the first bull left the paddock, Rodman had run into the bullring, climbed over the wall, left, had a drink, talked to some women, packed, and was halfway over the Atlantic. He never even saw a bull, let alone ran with them. So, if you have left the course before even seeing a bull, you are a Dennis Rodman. And, you have too many tattoos. And you married yourself in 1996.

Don't Be a Bad Runner

As Ari says, "Bad runners are bad runners." That's about as bookish as he gets. There are many subsets to this category.

"Champagne Poppers" nervously stand in the street and start running at the slightest sound—including, but not limited to, champagne corks being popped in the balconies along calle Estafeta. "Was that the rocket?" they shriek. Seriously, if you are that wound up, you should leave the streets.

"Flinchers Then Prayers" at least wait for the bulls, but they do not run. Instead, as the bulls pass, they stand still (maybe against the wall or in a doorway) and look away. Simultaneously, they pray they don't appear like this in that night's newspaper. Friends, this is not running with the bulls.

"Ouch, My Groin" runners instinctively cover their groin with their hands as the bulls pass. This is no joke: Watch any video of any *encierro* online and you'll see many runners assuming this stance. However, most doctors agree (as they replace your mangled hand with a hook) that in case of a groin goring, your hands will delay the explosion of your testicles for only about a second. So, you'll be a eunuch and a pirate.

Horribly, we've actually seen bulls tear apart the groin of matadors in the ring before. It's not pleasant. In 2009, El Cid had his groin area torn into, and the high-definition television programming repeatedly and carefully zoomed in on the goods on live TV. Assuredly, his mother was proud. Surprisingly, your groin is only third in the list of areas to protect. First, you'll want to protect your belly, which is where a bull is most likely to gore you. Second, you'll want to protect your skull, which is the least likely area to recover from getting smacked on the cobblestones.

The "Mascots" (try to) run in their Darth Vader mask or Superman cape, or some other costume. Every year, some moron tries to run naked. This is really an anti-costume. If you are contemplating this, trust me when I say your idea is far from original. Either way, thanks for that memory. In 2011, the police sent female officers to tackle, humiliate, cuff, and "perp-walk" one naked guy who put up a pretty good fight. Regardless, if you feel the need to wear an outfit, you are likely missing the message of the fiesta, which (for reasons I shouldn't need to explain) does not involve dressing up like Bart Simpson, Ella Fitzgerald, or Harry Potter. Perhaps you were looking for Brazil's Carnival, or perhaps you're a moron.

Honestly, calling attention to yourself is the last thing you should be doing in the streets. The herd deserves some dignity. There are plenty of chances to act like an idiot the rest of the day. And, wearing their own funny costumes, the local police are likely to pull you out of the crowd at the last second.

"Backpackers," ever fearing theft, attempt to run with their backpacks. They have no hotel room, they've slept on the street, and they're afraid someone is going to steal their precious possessions, which most people would describe as "litter," and then truthfully, steal anyway.

In attempting to run with everything they own, backpackers show an instinct for financial preservation that exceeds their instinct for life. Frankly, you're not allowed to do this because backpacks clog up the already crowded streets even more, and no one wants your hemp pants, your Grateful Dead t-shirt, or your German passport anyway. No "fanny packs" are permitted in the streets, either. Amusingly, Europeans still sport these. In 2012, a very good friend of ours *from the United States of America* was discussing the randomness of some of the morning *encierro* rules. He very seriously started telling us about how he "used" to run with a "fanny pack" to hold his stuff until the police removed him from the street one morning. Ari and I nervously glanced at each other, forced to stifle laughing. He is a terrific and brave runner, albeit a Pittsburgh Steelers fan, but he can be forgiven both of these foibles.

Finally, there are those bad runners who appear in the street for the "Running with the Steers." After the bulls and the herd of *cabestros* have run, the bulls are tucked away under the ring in preparation for meeting their eventual doom later that afternoon. Several *cabestros* then run down the street course for one final clear-out. These castrated bulls with tinkling bells wouldn't step on you if you threw yourself down in front. Nevertheless, the least noble and brave of the morning revelers seem compelled to jump in and run like it's the Miura on a Sunday morning. It's not. If you know this, and still run for fun, that's fine. If you are actually frightened by the castrated bull, you should receive "equal treatment" with a rusty saw. Most importantly, you most certainly will not have run with the bulls.

So, if you find yourself in one of these groups, give us a call and we can recommend a good balcony rental agent for you, or something milder, like maybe a nice Celebrity Cruise.

Be a Good Runner; Be a Barbarian

A good runner seeks no praise. A good runner is more interested in how you ran than in explaining how well he ran. Unfortunately, running with the bulls lends itself to delusions of grandeur. I tend to lean in that direction naturally, but have friends that don't. Our friends Owain, Bryan, and Tony Hoskins have been coming to Pamplona for years. They are son, brother, and brother. Tony is pushing seventy and is still a brilliant runner. Bryan lost a giant chunk of his calf to a horn and does not appear to have ever sought medical attention, for the goring or anything else in his life. Owain is one of the best long-stride runners every July. Tony and Owain are tall and lithe, and Bryan is built like a truck. Recently, they have been bringing Bryan's possible future son-in-law, Jordan Tipples, to run. Poor Jordan seems so blissfully unaware of his fate. They will eat him alive, but you have to respect the boy who comes to Pamplona with his future father-in-law.

This family of bull runners is so completely without pretension. Some or all or one of them is from Cardiff, Wales, so we say they are all from Wales. Anything else is too complicated. Llan-fairpwllgwyngyll is actually a village in Wales. T. E. Lawrence (a personal hero) was a Welshman. Our friends have a heavy accent, so we usually have no idea what they are saying, and they are usually approaching or departing Brahms and Liszt (or Saying Hello to Mr. Armitage, if you prefer), so we keep the questions short. Ari and I cannot recall when we first met them, but they took to Ari immediately, a sign they are good people. Every morning, they run in their black-and-white striped Barbarians rugby jersey. The older jerseys have the word "Gartmore" across the front, because the rugby team was sponsored by the Gartmore Group, a British-based investment management business. My grandfather's name is Gartley. It's an odd connection to this family. So, we have always called them "The Gartmore Boys." In 2013 I broke my ankle running in a Barbarians rugby jersey and could not be prouder. Bryan came to see me in the hospital in 2013 at my absolute lowest point and saved the day while he was getting his broken wrist casted. It is not something I will ever forget. When he and Ari took a taxi back into the old town, Bryan insisted on paying, which is something Ari will never forget. The Gartmore Boys are as honorable runners as you will find in Pamplona, and that is in the history of the fiesta. They are brave but not reckless. They are tough but not foolish. They are very friendly, very proud, and very passionate. Unlike me, they don't have to fake being unaffected. They just jump into the fray and run like the wind. They actually don't care what anyone thinks, and that embodies the true spirit of running with the bulls. Because they wear the black-and-white jerseys, when you look at photographs of the *encierro*, they seem to be everywhere at once. These Welshmen are scattered around photographs of my runs in Pamplona that are hung in my house and law office. I have more pictures of them hanging on the walls *than I have of my own wife*. They are practically actual family, and our lives are certainly intertwined. Without offense to the others, Tony is our favorite. In 2012, Tony fell over me in the Callejón and we both had to roll into the secret spider-filled chambers behind the wall (it was just a shock to look up and see someone I knew). That same year, Tony distracted the bull that gored Ari away from him. In 2009, Tony and I were together near the bull that last killed a Pamplona runner. I have a photograph in my office of me cinching up my pants while Tony leads the bull with his newspaper.

In 2013, we ran into the clan outside a newer photography store on calle Chapitela. That street is uphill to the Plaza del Castillo. It is more than a slight incline. Tony wanted to tell Ari a story. Tony was completely snobbled and carrying a very large and very full glass of horizontal lubricant. And, standing on the incline of the street, but trying to compensate and failing. Off balance, Tony was then pouring his potion on Ari's foot as he talked and gesticulated. Ari would step back downhill to avoid the spill, but Tony followed. We all watched the dance: step, step, pour, and shake your foot. Repeat. They easily went twenty yards downhill before the glass was empty. Later, I asked Ari, "What was he telling you about?" "I have no idea," Ari admitted.

Tony was also involved in what I consider the most John Wayne thing I've ever seen in Pamplona. Early in the fiesta in 2014, I was with my son Sam, Tony Hoskins, and our friend Gary Masi near where calle Estafeta turns into Telefónica. We were waiting for the herd to arrive. The first rocket exploded, and panicked runners were pouring past us. Tony started calmly talking to Sam for a good minute or two. Runners were screaming and I saw someone in blue jeans run by who had obviously failed in his efforts to hold his bladder. The runners were gathering in front of Tony and Sam and flowing around them like they were islands in a stream. Still, Tony was leaning in and telling Sam something, and he was pretty animated. It then became obvious that the herd was nearly upon us. Sam did not start running because Tony had not even flinched yet, and Sam did not want to be impolite by leaving mid-story. The crowd was starting to clear; I could now see horns. Even then, with the horns in the picture, Tony removed his pack of cigarettes from his pocket, pulled out a cigarette, put it in his mouth, returned the pack to his back pocket, *struck a match,* lit the cigarette, puffed, and *only then* started running. He ran into the ring with half the herd on his heels, and with us chasing. It was so John Wayne–like, I thought we were going to start searching for Natalie Wood in the American Southwest. Later, I asked Sam, "What was he telling you about?" "I have no idea," Sam confessed.

Don't Panic

On the other hand, if for just a moment you get between those horns—*en los cuernos*—you are forever welcome to stand among the *noble y bravo,* and tell anyone who'll listen for the rest of the day. On the most serious of notes, a good runner has his wits about him. And he is prepared for panic.

This is true in any setting, let alone in the streets of Pamplona. The human mind is a weird, funky place. During San Fermín, it is tired, ramped-up and wired, overheated and overloaded by sensory input. Plus, it's been listening to Ari explain the inner workings of middle to lower corporate management tactics for seemingly unending hours. Or, about his *National Geographic* collection. Boy, I love hearing about that, again.

It is easy to become overwhelmed by stress. Everyone deals with it differently. Some minds are conscious of it, and some are oblivious.

Years back, MTV brought some lowbrow simpletons to Pamplona, released them into the wild, and filmed their antics during San Fermín. They were nice but clueless. Ari and I watched it, of course, from a distance, and laughed ourselves silly when the episodes ran and as a weak member of the entourage lay on his hotel room floor with his head inside the little door of his nightstand and cried after only standing in the streets as the bulls ran by.

Afterward, when we feel ourselves coming unglued over the panic and stress of the *encierro,* we nervously reference that nightstand "guy." It goes like this, "Ari, I'm feeling a little 'nightstandy.'"

We've suffered our own traumas during the *encierro,* but those suffered by others have had a more lasting effect. However, everyone has to be ready for the onset of panic during San Fermín. The word panic derives from the Greek πανικός, "pertaining to the shepherd god Pan," who took amusement from frightening herds of goats and sheep into sudden bursts of uncontrollable fear. He does the same thing to us during the fiesta.

Before, during, and after running with the bulls, you will be under medical bona fide stress, which often manifests itself physically. I read in a medical text that stress causes your body to release "catecholamine hormones," such as adrenaline or noradrenaline, which causes immediate physical reactions associated with a preparation for *violent muscular action*. These include the following:

> Acceleration of heart and lung action;
> Paling or flushing, or alternating between both;
> Inhibition of stomach and upper-intestinal action to
>   the point where digestion slows down or stops;
> General effect on the sphincters of the body;
> Constriction of blood vessels in many parts of the
>   body;
> Liberation of nutrients (particularly fat and glucose)
>   for muscular action;
> Dilation of blood vessels for muscles;
> Inhibition of the lacrimal gland (responsible for tear
>   production) and salivation;
> Dilation of pupil (mydriasis);
> Relaxation of bladder;
> Auditory exclusion (loss of hearing);
> Tunnel vision (loss of peripheral vision);
> Disinhibition of spinal reflexes; and
> Shaking.

Yep, that seems about right. I believe that preparing for this physiology is essential to surviving the *encierro* and enjoying the rest of your day. Frankly, you want to be ready for anything that has a "general effect on the sphincters of the body," especially in a town where white pants are de rigueur. After we decided to never skip the fiesta ever, I decided to ask the doctor for a homeopathic remedy for the taste in my mouth I had after the *encierro*—like I was chewing on tinfoil. I learned that our body's patented fight-or-flight response is triggered during very stressful situations, and our body dumps a huge amount of adrenaline into our bloodstream to give our body the strength and intensity we need to either fight or run away. This overdose of adrenaline causes a coppery, metallic taste to flood our mouths. My doctor's advice to help avoid the taste? "Don't run with the bulls."

Panic causes the flight-or-fight response, which is otherwise known as the "acute stress response." I can provide the following example of the young runner mentioned earlier. On July 10, 2009, Daniel Jimeno Romero, a twenty-seven-year-old from Alcala de Henares, near Madrid, was gored to death and nine others were injured in what became the bloodiest run in decades. Daniel died when the horn pierced his neck and lungs. The 515 kg beast named Capuchino became disoriented and aggressive after separating from the herd all the way back at the Ayuntamiento. This raised the death toll to fifteen since record-keeping began in 1911. Daniel was treated at the local hospital but surgeons were unable to save him, and he was pronounced dead at 8:45 a.m. "He suffered mortal injuries, so there was nothing we could do to save his life," said Esther Vila, the surgeon who operated on him. "He had lost a great deal of blood." The run lasted four minutes and twenty-eight seconds. Daniel Jimeno Romero was gored to death right in front of Ari and me during the fourth day of the fiesta, and we didn't even know it. That morning, I ran into the ring with a large contingent of the herd and was unable to find Ari. Because the doors were not closing, I realized that there must be a *suelto* charging. Against the rules and common sense, I ran back out of the ring to see if Ari was all right, and to see if I could get into the mix with the *suelto*. This was foolish.

Right outside the turn for the entrance of the bullring, Capuchino, a solid dark-red Jandilla bull, was loose and charging over and over. If you spend enough time in Pamplona, you learn that the so-called *colorado* bulls are much more likely to gore and attack runners than the black bulls. When a Navarran friend first told me this, I listened, but privately doubted the veracity of the statement. He claimed that it was related to their breeding and their ancient bloodlines. I chalked it up to the type of legend that is prevalent in Basque culture, which includes stories of dragons in the forest. All the same, you can indeed trust the *colorado* bulls to come looking for you in the streets. Beware. They are crazy. They are *considered* ruddy or reddish in Spain. To our untrained eyes, they look tan. The morning newspapers instruct you otherwise, and I have lost many arguments with the locals on this issue. The area around our State of Colorado was explored by the Spanish in the 1500s and was first claimed by Spain. It eventually became part of the United States with the Louisiana Purchase and the Mexican-American War. The rocks and dirt in Colorado have a reddish tint, which is why the Spanish named it Colorado, and why the bulls carry this label.

In addition, the Jandilla breed is the most dangerous. So, Capuchino was double trouble—a red Jandilla bull. Ari escaped the crowd fleeing this lone terrorizing bull, and we both ran into the ring ahead of him. We knew someone had been gored, and Ari knew it had been right near him. It was loud and bloody. We did not know how serious the injury was to Daniel, or even that it was Daniel.

Afterward, we bought our bullfight tickets for that afternoon (David "El Fandi" Fandila vs. Jandilla breed cannot be missed). Because it was a brilliantly sunny day, we decided to hightail it to the beach. We raced to San Sebastián, relaxed on the beach too long, and had to race back to Pamplona for the feria. Since then, many, many, many speed cameras have been installed on the A-15. Many.

We hardly had time to change and charge through the crowds to the bullring. We made it to our seats as the bullfight started, and it started with a moment of silence. We did not know why. The gentleman next to us, offering us cigars, explained that Daniel had died.

I remember El Fandi quickly dispatching Capuchino in an icy, emotionless fashion, but not much else of that bullfight. Afterward we rushed to a friend's newspaper store on calle Estafeta and read about the death, and saw that the moment of the goring was captioned in a photo that featured Ari standing just a few feet away. Thirteen hours after the *encierro,* the flight-or-fight effect took hold of Ari, and hard.

Over the night, Ari became obsessed with the idea he'd be fired from his job at Lockheed Martin because he was wearing a Lockheed Martin bike jersey in the newspaper photos, which we learned were on the front page of nearly every newspaper in the world. He would not stop talking about it. It was a long night. Now, we laugh about Ari's wild imagination then. Actually, I laughed about it then, too. The lesson was that stress manifests itself, and you have to be prepared for it.

Like surfing, running with the bulls is not a sport. Why? No one is competing. There is no race, no ball, no trophy, no award, no score, and no personal or team accolades. There's no yellow jersey. The *encierro* celebrates grander topics, like brotherhood and honor and reverence. As with surfing, there are written and unwritten rules. Every one of the bulls is running together in the morning sun as brothers and a herd for the last time. They have names, and their pictures are in the newspapers. In turn, every runner should be anonymous. The running is not about calling attention to oneself. If you run bravely and with honor and valor, you'll get all the attention you need.

6

(Cobblestoned) Street of Dreams
(a daily plan)

Love laughs at a king,
Kings don't mean a thing, on the street of dreams.

—THE INK SPOTS

In 2010, moments before the rocket at 8:00 a.m., a Frenchman, dirty, shirtless, shoeless, about four and a half feet tall and more than halfway to alcohol poisoning, looked Ari and me right in the eyes and said, "I am, how you say, brown in the pants." We just carefully inched away from him for all kinds of different reasons. It's hard enough to run with the bulls, let alone laughing the entire time at someone being "brown in the pants." Moments in the streets of Pamplona are funny, frightening, disgusting, poignant, weird, otherworldly, smoky, smelly, potentially illegal, immiscible, and always memorable. Every day something occurs down in those flawless streets that merits being recounted in my fiesta journal. You wouldn't believe half of it.

We love walking the streets of Pamplona. No one, and I mean no one, can walk faster than Ari and me, slicing through the suprarational crowds of Pamplona's fiesta. We know the secret routes but also enjoy walking anadromous into a parade. I can never recall turning around and finding that Ari was unable to keep pace, even the afternoon after he was gored in 2012. We spend way too much time congratulating each other over this. And, as Ari likes to say, it's all "kicks and giggles" down on the cobblestones at 6:00 a.m. In fact, everyone is still *jolie laide* at 7:45 a.m., but the morning's levity is waning. By 7:50 a.m., even the French aren't clapping and singing anymore. At 7:57 a.m., it feels like someone crammed a ShamWow down your throat with a plunger. In the morning streets, the 8:00 a.m. rocket is as startling a sound as anything that will ever pass by your ears. You know it's coming, but you still shudder. Then, waiting for the bulls is interminable. In 2012 someone was thoughtlessly selling firecrackers to the children of Pamplona on the street corners when the police were not around. Every time one exploded any time of the day it caused the same physiological reaction in my brain as the 8:00 a.m. rocket, with the attendant chemical releases. That's how much your body will remember the rocket.

Every day I have ever run the *encierro,* someone has asked: "How will I know the bulls are getting close?"

The answer? "You'll know."

It is no exaggeration to say you will later be able to recall bits of these moments from the perspective of a third party, as in a dream and watching the events unfurl. In REM-sleep dreams you will watch your *encierro* as if you are in the middle of *A Christmas Carol.* It is indescribable. When the bulls arrive, in their mum-chanced cloud, your senses give notice before the message reaches your brain, like fingers touching a hot stove.

It is then the Street of Dreams. From the wooden and stone paddock at the top of calle Santo Domingo, uphill to that little dangerous hump at the peak; through the wide plaza, the lazy, listing left around calle Mercaderes, to the sunrise, to the sawdust or the acid-scarred stones or whatever new corner trick of the year, and the hard right onto the long and morning man-making stretch of calle Estafeta; past the door hiders and window hangers, past Carmelo's store, onto the pavers, taking my favorite left in the world onto Telefónica, past where Daniel died, past where Ari was gored, and squeezing through the Callejón and past where my ankle snapped; every morning the bulls and runners disembogue onto the bloody sand in my favorite city, and into the greatest arena in the world. *Deo volente,* I've asked that my family scatter my ashes in the Pamplona bullring sand in the end, *but don't deny me a single summer in those streets until that faraway time.* Dumping me in a pile in front of my beloved Pamplona street sweepers, or even better, with someone spraying down the streets with the giant hoses, would be an acceptable alternative.

The *encierro* course is around 825 meters long (that is over nine football fields or over one half-mile), and *every bit of a hike* even without the bulls. There are steep climbs, sharp turns, lazy listing turns, stone walls, doorways, inconceivably hard wooden barriers, wet cobblestones, manholes, slippery drains, curbs, metal gates, boarded storefronts, *hirondelles* (the swallows that fly over Pamplona), TV towers and cameras, clock towers, drainpipes, dangerously crushed plastic Coca-Cola bottles, and all manner of dross, flotsam, debris, sawdust, flags, bunting, pavers, sand, urine, blood, screams, cheers, flashing cameras, the morning and dawning sun, and a sea of humanity. And it all disappears when the beasts bear down on you. Poof: It all disappears.

I love the streets, and that their standing in history was hewn by the glorious modern Spanish fighting bull, or *toro bravo* (known also, in certain erudite groups, as *toro de lidia, toro lidiado, ganado bravo,* or *Touro de Lide*). Most are descendents of the semi-domesticated personal herds of Egyptian pharaohs and were introduced into Spain by the Phoenicians or some other unknown trading group. Enough got loose in the forest, and they reverted to wildness on the Iberian plateau. After being caught again, they were culled and bred long ago to give the fighting bull its distinct small triangle head, wide shoulders, small hooves, horns that face forward (particularly unpleasant), the extraordinary *morrillo* muscle about the neck, and the distinctive dewlap captured centuries ago in cave paintings. While I am not inclined to deem bullfighting necessary to defend, a ban on bullfighting would sentence the ancient *toro bravo* to near if not complete extinction. They have no other historical purpose on this planet.

Here, the *toro bravo* is a killing machine, who in breeding long ago lost its *retromingent,* or the human association of cowardice that comes therewith. Even an average fighting bull would show no qualms attacking a Bengal tiger or any so-called king of the jungle. If you could work out the details, most would weigh in against an orca or great white shark, too. If a matador were swinging around a Scottish battle-axe in lieu of a two-inch-wide *estoque,* the bull would still charge. A *toro bravo* never flees pain. The Spanish bull brings such kinetic energy, mass, and velocity that the pressure by which the horns explode into whatever object the bull deems justifiable equals that of an artillery gun.

I have been forced to rest my hand for balance while running on a fighting bull in Pamplona (seeking contact is never an *encierro* goal; and only when being pressed by the crowd against the bull is it all right), and its muscle and strength and mesomorphic existence is unimaginably astounding. A *toro bravo* will kill you without as much as a pang of moral misgiving. They deserve, if not require, your near-ceremonial preparation in the morning before the *encierro.*

I plan on running with the bulls every year until I can't. Many old men (and I mean in their seventies or later) run every morning still, even with the ever-increasing crowds. Some just step out their own front door at the last minute with a cigar in their mouth and stand in the doorway as the bulls pass on by. I cannot wait until it is my time to do that. When we run in front of the town hall there is a man in his sixties. Ari him calls "Paul Sorvino" because he thinks he looks like Paul Cicero in *Goodfellas* (he doesn't). He runs close to the bulls around the turn onto calle Mercaderes every morning like he is still a teenager. There are more than a few Navarran runners we've been saying hello to every morning for a long time, and we are way past the point of getting around to asking their names. I don't remember how long we've been friends with a guy who looks like a chubby Fred Armisen and sounds like Andy Kaufman. We call him Latka. We've met him in the streets with his wife and children, so we know their names but still not his.

Everyone has developed his own personal ritual for an *encierro* morning and the day that unfolds. You will create your own, as the chaos of the fiesta unexpectedly lends itself to comfortable but flexible routine. This is ours:

On the busiest days of the fiesta (weekends, July 7, dates nearest Bastille Day), Ari and I like to get out in front of the Plaza de Ayuntamiento between 6:30 a.m. and 6:45 a.m. We like to stand where we can see the clock face. You can mill farther up or down the course a little in each direction. Many English-speaking runners (and even "Canadians") often congregate in the Plaza de Santiago behind the Ayuntamiento in the early morning. Other days, and especially toward the end of the fiesta, we're down in the street at 7:15 a.m., at the latest. That means we are up anywhere between 5:30 a.m. and 6:15 a.m. By rule, we are in the hotel room by midnight, unless there is a midnight concert we can't miss, which is often. Otherwise, we are asleep by 2:00 a.m. We take more than a little ribbing from the harder and heartier revelers; however, we run each day of the fiesta, and we are not in our twenties. Those revelers miss runs all the time. We also do not sleep all day, unlike some of the more braggart party-boys. Getting a real night's sleep—or something close—is simply an issue of safety. This schedule gives us about anywhere from four and a half to five and a quarter hours of sleep each night. On average, we get less than forty hours of sleep in Pamplona, unless we happen upon a nice nap on the beach.

I believe we are the only runners who faithfully spot-clean and iron our clothing every morning, and I mean the only in fiesta history. You'll notice daily the crisp line in our pants, and that lasts the entire fiesta. I also keep our hotel room or flat immaculate as a respite from the storm that is the Pamplona fiesta. I bring supplies from home. Sharing a room for two weeks with Ari is, putting it nicely, horrifying. It's not just his patented forty-five-minute showers, or how he likes to point out that his running shoes smell like his cat, or how he meows at cats he sees on the TV or out the window. He dumps out bullring sand from his shoes and cuffs on the floor and acts surprised. Every time! He sheds body hair, and apparently has an unlimited supply. In a week, he sheds out Chewbacca onto the floor. He doesn't tuck the shower curtain properly. He uses my soap. If we have four towels, he takes three and touches the other. He also hogs any sofa (his personal storage shelf), every chair (his personal drying racks), the desk (for stacking his clothes like he's opening an Old Navy), the bathroom counter, and even that little shelf in the shower with his "special" prescription shampoo, the scariest bottle ever (his shampoo is *brown*). He reserves his most malevolent behavior for the closet. How his tiny clothes take up that much space violates natural law—it is *malum in se*.

We do shave and shower before the *encierro*. I never understand those who just roll out of bed (or out from behind a Dumpster) fog-headed, filthy, and covered in stink, and I find they usually do not comprehend the seriousness of the morning.

Since we are preparing to risk our lives, dressing for the running of the bulls for us takes on the solemnity of a matador preparing in his hotel room. The dressing of a matador is ritualistic and replete with superstition. It is an honor just to be invited to watch the dressing, or stand around in a room next to the dressing. We don't often invite anyone to watch us dress for the running, but usually don't bother to close the curtains, if you want to watch from the roof across the street.

Dressing is among the oldest rituals in bullfighting. Each piece goes on slowly, in a time-prescribed order. For us, the clothes are laid out, clean, each morning, and examined as if we were going to a wedding. We always wear the white pants and white shirt with the red sash and *pañuelo*. Take a moment in the streets and notice how good we look even late into the fiesta. Feel free to mention it to us personally.

Many eschew the white shirt tradition in the morning run and opt for a favored jersey. Every couple of years, the local Pamplonica runners try to get a movement going that would *require* runners to run in white. This dies down when someone reminds them that their own best Pamplona runners don't wear white, ever. I would say that the general rule is that when you first start running, wear white. When you've accomplished enough, you can wear whatever you want. Many try to give their "morning uniform" some personal meaning. Our friend Victor Lombardi (gored in the arm in 2003) wears a black number 88 NFL Raiders jersey. He explained to me that it started when he ran out of clean white shirts many fiestas ago and was forced to wear a black t-shirt. He liked how it showed up in photographs so much he came back the next year with his now iconic Raiders jersey. He once went to a Raiders game and met wide receiver Cliff Branch at an autograph-signing event beforehand. He told Branch that he ran with the bulls in his jersey, and Branch's mind was blown. He said, "Would you like to wear a Super Bowl ring?" and they were both photographed with ear-to-ear smiles. That is the kind of story you need to warrant leaving your white shirt back in the hotel room.

Author Alexander Fiske-Harrison runs in a red-and-white striped blazer, which makes a lot of sense after you meet him. Bostonian Robert Kiely dons a Sweeney's shirt with a giant green clover on the front every morning. I've been looking for one for years and would just love to show up one morning wearing it. Famed American runner Joe Distler takes us to the gun show every morning with his red sleeveless tee. He of course can wear whatever he doggone wants to wear.

Tying the red *pañuelo* around your neck properly is tricky. Logically, you do not want to tie something around your neck that can be caught on the bulls' horns. I have warned morning runners about this many times, and received smirks and doubting eye rolls. However, in 2012, the bulls of the Dolores Aguirre Ybarra ranch caught a runner by his improperly tied *pañuelo* and he was dragged thirty meters. How he didn't die remains a mystery. If tied correctly, the knotted *pañuelo* would have slipped off.

I've even had panicked runners grab my *pañuelo* from behind, and if the knot had not slipped, I would have been choked or yanked to the ground. You do not want to tie a normal knot. The so-called magic knot can be explained as a pseudo–slip knot (there are some "how-to" videos online), but your best bet is to ask someone who looks experienced to help.

On my feet, for many years I have worn size 12 red Chuck Taylor sneakers (just like Philadelphia's own Julius Winfield Erving II, or, as you may know him, Dr. J.), and not the traditional espadrilles (little white shoes with red crisscross ties), because the Basques do not believe in size 12 shoes, or wide shoes, and running in slippers seems too dangerous, even for a Basque tradition. Very few run in these still. Since the fourteenth century, these shoes with flat jute soles have been made from a tough, wiry Mediterranean grass, and feel like canvas or rope. They were initially designed for marching soldiers. Chuck Taylor sneakers allow me to feel the cobblestones under my feet. When I run, they provide some ankle support, and their soles are actually similar to those of espadrilles. It is my understanding that Chuck Taylor sneakers fell out of style around the world but are making a comeback, especially with the female population. I am from Philadelphia, where Chuck Taylor sneakers never fell from grace. When the next French teenager asks why I am wearing *chaussures pour jeunes filles*, we might have a situation. On July 9, 2009, as the bulls reached me in the Plaza Consistorial in a perfect herd formation, a panicked dunce tackled me high while another, unrelated, but identical dunce tackled me low, and I was flipped upside down, knocked to the side of the plaza, and just a *single red Chuck Taylor sneaker* appeared in the picture of this incident. Yes, many were amused that day. In 2013 I ran in low-top sneakers for the first time in years and broke my ankle. In 2014 I ran in a heavily padded pair of Nike Air Jordans to protect my healing ankle. I hope to return to my Chuck Taylors soon.

It should go without saying, but the shoes you run in should be comfortable and light, and should have some traction. No one should wear army boots, flip-flops, cowboy boots, or UGGs, and we have seen them all. In 2012, our good friend Bill Hillmann caused a mini-controversy by wearing Vibram FiveFingers running shoes and then falling more than a couple of times. "Money, it's gotta be the shoes." In 2014, he went back to wearing them and was gored.

I wear a brand-new red sash every year, but Ari has worn the same sash (which needs emergent care from a Medevac Air Ambulance to last an entire fiesta now) since the beginning. The locals can also teach you how to tie your sash so it slips off if it is horn-hooked. I also don't know which side the knot should go on—left or right? The general rule is that the knot goes on the side I am not wearing it on. Sometimes I think the entire city is playing a practical joke on me.

I wear a belt under my red sash (a white military woven belt), but I shouldn't. Ari does not. In the ring, I've had the baby bulls hook the belt, and that was bad, so I cannot imagine what it will be like when a big bull gets me. However, keeping my pants up is of a more urgent nature. If anyone has a better suggestion, speak up. And if you see me in the ring after the *encierro,* please remind me to loosen my belt! Many times—too many times—we have witnessed runners completely losing their elastic waistband pants (or worse, shorts) when they fall or become tangled with other runners (or worse, bulls). Running into the bullring in 2012, I was between two bulls with another runner, and no one else was around. We were in a nice straight line with a bull in front and at the back. My fellow runner tripped on a pebble, fell forward onto his face, and as his momentum took him and he skidded along the paver stones, he left his pants (elastic waist, painter's style) behind, along with a shoe. He was running commando, something I would not recommend, and I was forced to leap precisely over his bare posterior as he used proper form to cover his head with his arms. After all, there was a bull behind me. He retrieved his pants, but never his shoe, and ran off, and the footage was shown over and over and over on television back at Café Iruña. No matter how often they showed it, his pants came off *every time*.

I leave my pants at normal length until fifteen to twenty minutes before the run, and then roll up the cuffs once or twice. I know it looks ridiculous, so you don't have to point it out, but thank you to the twelve thousand interested citizens who have. I don't want to trip on my cuffs. Ari rolls his pants, too, but no one ever seems to notice.

In 2011 I wore a headband while running. I love how Jim McMahon wrote "Rozelle" on his headband a game or two prior to Super Bowl XX. I decided I would run wearing a headband to help distinguish my shaved head from all the other shaved heads in the street (for picking out photos later, of course). I got "Kharlamov" (a hated Philadelphia nemesis) printed on mine, and wore it every day. It was a regrettable, terrible fashion statement that still has not been forgotten.

We prepare in the quiet of the morning—no music; no TV. There's just the lingering odor of the travel iron, and the din of revelry in the streets below our hotel room. We do some light stretching out in the room, and I especially concentrate on holding off the annual Pamplona shin splints, and loosening my perpetually stiff neck, as it will be used to help me take some quick but deep glances over my left and right shoulders later in the morning. The sun does not rise until shortly before the run starts, so it's dark outside while we prepare, and always cool, but there's still a good buzz in the streets outside the hotel even before 5:00 a.m. No matter how many times I wake up in Pamplona, those seemingly professional roisterers from central casting amuse us to no end. How can they still be singing at 4:56 a.m.? We check the weather from the window. If it is cold or raining, it may change our preparation. Running in the rain with the bulls is not an ideal situation (the streets are even more slippery). We might briefly discuss our plans for after the *encierro* and the day, but it really is the only time during the fiesta we are quiet.

Before leaving the room, I sit on the edge of the bed and I try to convince myself I am confident, intelligent, and reasoned. I think about making decisions in the street by instinct and without pause. I will myself to be quick, still. I think about doing something incredible that morning if the opportunity arises, and why we're in Pamplona, and about the fun we will have that day, and my edacious determination to get between the horns and run as fast as I can into the bullring. In those secretive moments, I am grateful that Ari and I are fortunate enough to be able to do this every year, that we can run together, that we have for the most part remained healthy and safe, and that we don't live boring or overly cautious lives.

Ari is always ready before me, but when I catch up we stand in front of the hotel room door and take the deepest of breaths. We open the door, make sure we have a room key (Ari's job), walk down the hall to the stairwell (there is no patience now to wait for an elevator in the morning!), and walk through the hotel lobby and tumble out into the street. For many years, we have stayed in the wonderful Hotel Maissonave on calle Nueva in the old city. We love the concerned faces of our friends behind the front desk and at the door every morning, and because we are so darned charming, the hotel staff always holds a morning paper for each of us. For that, we are very grateful. It's just before sunrise when we leave for the *encierro*, but it looks more like twilight. Already, swallows are circling the city, squeaky, sharp chee-deeping and eating every mosquito available (you will rarely get bitten in Pamplona). The sky is electric blue, the streets are wet and clean (cleanish?), and there are always a few people wandering around who never went to sleep. Some are sleeping in doorways. There's always music playing in the distance. For us, it's our favorite quiet moment of the San Fermín fiesta. Ari likens it to the feeling of getting to Disneyland before it opens. It feels like they *just pulled back the plastic,* and that the whole place is brand-new, and they've just hosed down and unwrapped the park.

We carry very little with us in the morning. Other than the potential noose around my neck if I forget to tie it right, I don't want anything that might get caught on the bull horns. We put a few euros in our pockets for breakfast. For years, I did not carry identification, but now (so they can identify me at the hospital or in the newspaper) I wear army dog tags with my name, blood type, and next of kin. These would break away if the chain became tangled in horns or hooves. Ari carries a few "business cards" made for Pamplona. I take a few Halls or Binaca (in 2010, a bull from the El Pilar stepped on me and crushed my Binaca; it exploded in my pocket), to keep moisture in my mouth and my throat in working order. Halfway through the fiesta, I always start losing my voice. It is an annual event celebrated by many. I take a bottle of water that I've bought from the same stand and the same girl at the fairgrounds every night since 2004 on the way back from the fireworks (her mother has proposed an arranged marriage several times). I sip it all morning and discard it safely far outside the *encierro* course before the run.

For every run, I carry my Bobby Clarke 1972 Canada vs. USSR Summit Series coin in my front pants pocket. I most certainly do not believe in the concept of luck. However, during San Fermín, anything goes. You'll want all the luck, karma, good fortune, providence, godsends, blessings, breaks, flukes, chances, and kismet you can muster. You are welcome to ask to rub my coin any morning before the run. It never fails. No one rubbing the coin has ever suffered a serious injury. However, they have been stuck with the check at breakfast.

I am compelled to explain this coin. Robert Earle Clarke. You may have heard me sigh out loud writing this down. In Philadelphia, he is a living legend. In my home, he is untouchable. From the streets of Flin Flon, Manitoba (Canada), Bobby Clarke set the gold standard for what it is to be a man growing up in Philadelphia. As the ringleader of the Broad Street Bullies, Clarke brought

Lord Stanley's Cup home twice in the mid-1970s, but his greatest moment on these earthly confines did not occur even close to our city boundaries. In the 1972 Summit Series, the Canadian National Team found itself down 3–1–1 with three games to play in Lenin Central Stadium in downtown Moscow. Valery Kharlamov was repeatedly taking advantage of the Canadian squad, and had been for several games. Between periods, John Ferguson looked around the locker room and said *someone* needed to do *something* about Kharlamov. Robert Earle looked around the room, filled with hockey legends, and realized that the assistant coach was talking to him. In the second period, Clarke deliberately and savagely slashed and fractured Valery Kharlamov's ankle. Rendering the Russian "ineffective" for the rest of the series, and sparking Team Canada to a comeback series win, Clarke later admitted, "If I hadn't learned to lay on a two-hander once in a while, I'd never have left Flin Flon." This is like a parable in my household. Later, during the 1975–76 USSR Red Army Tour for the Super Series '76, memories of Bobby Clarke and the ghosts of 1972 made the Russians flinch again during their visit to the south side of Philadelphia at Pattison Avenue and Broad Street. This time Ed Van Impe checked Valery hard to the ice, and the Russians, *who fled the ice in whiny repose,* were exposed as cowards in our own hometown. Until the Philadelphia Spectrum was demolished, I could take you to the exact spot on the ice where Van Impe laid Valery out. After a seventeen-minute delay, the Soviets finally returned to the ice when they were warned that they would lose their salary for the entire series ($200,000 in 1976) if they did not finish out their loss to the Flyers. Someone set fire to a car in our apartment complex afterward. Eyes tear up as grown Philadelphians pass these stories onto their children. So, when I run in Pamplona, I carry my 1972 Summit Series coin to inspire me to run bravely, as Bobby would have wanted. Ironically, while I despise Kharlamov, his mother (Aribot Abbad Hermann) was a Basque who came to Russia as a refugee from the Spanish civil war.

After a decade or more in Pamplona, I know a little something about luck, which I don't even believe in. On July 12, 2014, I walked down to calle Santo Domingo at 6:00 a.m. in the pouring rain. The street was already like an ice rink. Common sense said go back to bed, but circumstances pressured us to push onward. We were running out of time to run into the bullring in spectacular fashion. My older son Sam's first runs in Pamplona had been on the seventh and eighth, and we had stayed safely along calle Mercaderes. On the ninth and tenth, we had quietly run into the ring unscathed on the heels of the herd, but without much fanfare. On the eleventh I was laid up in bed by what turns out was the beginning of pneumonia (2014 was the coldest and wettest fiesta in many decades). The thirteenth was a Sunday, and it looked like the crowds would be enormous. The fourteenth was with the Miura bulls, so who knew what would happen, and with them, the issue could not be forced (turns out, the run that morning was an agonizing five minutes, with three runners gored). So, it was decided that on the twelfth we would run into the ring, notwithstanding the rain, and, hey, it looks like it's slowing down anyway. That morning, the Fuente Ymbro breed, from Cádiz, were running. They gore runners about half of the time. The bulls arrived to where we were waiting at exactly two minutes past the rocket. I remember exactly how they were aligned, as the events following ran in my head in slow motion for hours afterward. Three steers arrived first, loping along in front of a strangely white bull. It was majestic if not ethereal, and there was almost an urge to slow down to get a better look at it as it cantered by. It remains the most wonderful bull I have ever seen, anywhere. Two more steers appeared with a black bull in between and just behind them. Then, we turned the corner on the right side of the center of the street onto Telefónica with two particularly dangerous *colorado* bulls. One kept to the center of the street, and the other (with a giant 66 branded into his right side) followed Sam and me as we moved toward the wooden barriers to avoid him. We were running forward on the course full-tilt but also moving to the right. Big 66 either slipped on the wet cobblestones or decided to gore us. As he bore down upon us, I used my left arm to slam Sam against the fence and out of the way, and at the absolutely last possible moment the bull lifted his horns. They were white, and jet-black-tipped. They missed Sam by a hairsbreadth. The bull ran me down exactly between the horns and slammed me against the barrier. A horn hooked into my left shoulder blade but did not puncture it. The impact left about a gallon of bull snot on my pants. For a moment he stayed with me, as I waited for him to violently thrash and end my fiesta, if not my life. I put my left hand on his right horn, and my right on his snout, and steered him easily away toward the bullring. Luck? More like a miracle. Maybe it was just a little Bobby Clarke magic. On video, the whole thing lasted a little more than a second. As the pawky *colorado* bull ran off, I fell over to my right, and rolled through the wet muck and under the barrier to check for holes. There were none. Even then, I had lost count of the bulls, and another black bull was to follow on my heels as I foolishly stepped through the barrier back onto the course, not following my own wise advice. Later that morning, covered in mud and worse, I was still formulating ways to exaggerate the tale when we went into Alberto Estudio Fotográfico S.L., at calle Chapitela, 18. The owner had already blown up a poster-sized photograph of the exact moment of The Great Collision Without Consequences. I bought one, of course, and another was put right in the front window of the store for the entire city to walk past in the coming days. I found many excuses to stroll by for photographs with amazed tourists. "Look, it's that guy in the window!" I hope it's still there next summer. It's on the cover of this book. That's about as close as it gets.

Sometimes early in the fiesta, Ari and I will wander down to the streets around 6:00 a.m. to hear some of the Dianas, which is morning music performed by Pamplona's formally dressed band. Later in the fiesta, we sleep instead. We used to mosey down calle Santo Domingo to buy a paper for rolling (for me, just to have something for my nervous hands), but happily take the free one now. While I carry the paper around in the morning, I discard it before the run. Some experienced runners use the paper to lead the bulls into the ring or away from fallen friends, or possibly for throwing down to distract a bull that has become too interested. I found that I was not using the hand that was holding the paper to brace or protect myself. So, I don't use it anymore. Plenty of runners still do.

If neither of us is feeling nauseated, we buy a *caldo,* off Plaza de Santiago (near the old town market). It's a warm drink, and tastes something like a salty but greasy cup of beef bouillon to me. Allegedly, it is made of chicken, but that has to be proven to me before I will believe it. Really, it's made of mystery. It's supposed to calm your stomach and wet your whistle. According a close friend, it is a "grim tradition." You really shouldn't eat or drink much in the morning before a run. You know, in case you need anesthesia for your big day in Operatory No. 3! Good news, everyone who gets gored gets their picture in all the newspapers. Try to scare up a smile or a grimace, at least, for the photographers. Pamplona bars start serving *caldo* around 3:00 a.m. It is a consommé of unknown origins made with marrow bones of an unknown animal, or dirty shoes. You can ask for a shot of sherry with it, too. Why you would do that is another question. If you get the last *caldo* from the pot, it is full of the bony dregs, and I would be surprised if you can gag it down if you are running. How the last *caldo* can be measurably worse than the first *caldo* out of the pot seems impossible, but it's true and horrifying.

We thumb through the morning newspaper (Pamplona also has the long-lost afternoon or early evening paper, too!), perusing it for fiesta photographs of ourselves and people we know, and looking at the photographs of the bulls running that day, and reading their biographies (in case we meet one later, we want to know his name). Actually, the morning paper has pictures of the bulls, with their names, their numbers, and their colors, hobbies and interests, and Zodiac signs. The color of the bull is particularly helpful information, as it helps you keep track of how many bulls have passed you by.

Bulls are said to get their fighting heart and spirit from their mother, and their physical characteristics from their father. Their reputation in the bullring does not necessarily match their reputation in the street.

Before 7:00 a.m., we stake out a spot in Plaza Consistorial, in front of the Ayuntamiento. Until 7:45 a.m., we mingle with old friends, complain about the crowds, and brag about what we did the day before and where we ate, but we try to meet someone or some group new to the fiesta every day. I hope you will try this, too: Meet someone new every day in Pamplona. Look for someone from a foreign land who does not speak a lick of English. We have made lifelong friends this way, and I can't even pronounce some of their names. In the end, this is why we return annually.

As the morning passes, when we're not talking, we stretch, and remove trash and debris from the course to prevent runners from slipping on a discarded Coca-Cola Light can or something even more thoughtless. Ari and I finalize our plan for the run. We agree on where we will meet after the run one last time. Except for some locals, who can step out of their business or office at the last moment, the very large majority of runners are crammed into the plaza. Sometimes there's singing and clapping. Recent years have witnessed the new tradition of driving a street cleaner through the crowd at its peak. The logic? Good luck, as I don't know. I guess if the truck makes it through, the bulls might. The giant truck ran over my toes once. *Still ran.*

At 7:45 a.m., we stop talking and reflect earnestly on the morning's goals. Runners gather at a small niche built on calle Santo Domingo which holds a small replica figure of San Fermín. They sing a homily and wave their newspapers while praying to the Catholic saint for protection (we are Protestants and do not do this). The song is in Spanish: *"A San Fermín pedimos* (We ask of San Fermín) / *por ser nuestro patrón* (for he is our patron) / *nos guíe en el encierro* (to guide us in the Bull Run) / *dándonos su bendición* (giving us his blessing)." It ends with shouts of "Viva San Fermín! Gora San Fermín!" (Long live San Fermín, first in Spanish, then in Basque). This is often replayed on American TV. If you want your friends at home to see you, get down close to the saint. This homage occurs three times after 7:45 a.m. before the 8:00 a.m. rocket, and it is one of the most emotive fiesta moments. Personally, I don't pray to any saints; instead, I whisper this—"Lord, guard and guide the men who fly through the great spaces in the sky. Be with them always in the air, in darkened storm or sunlight glare. O, hear us when we lift our prayer, for those in peril in the air." This is a variant of the military hymn "For Those in Peril on the Sea" or "Eternal Father, Strong to Save." It is used in *The Right Stuff*.

A few minutes before 8:00 a.m., the crowd is permitted to disperse throughout the running course. The local cops stalk the masses for drunks, backpacks, cameras, bags, and the feeble and insane—and flip-flops. This is not a good time to be horsing around—we had a friend removed from the course because someone jokingly pushed him, and he bumped into an officer. They don't have time for a protracted explanation in a foreign tongue.

When allowed to disperse, we casually walk up calle Santo Domingo or down toward the bullring at this point to claim our planned spot in the streets. There are always the panicky runners darting by, and those who enter and exit the bullring before the first bull has left the corral. I particularly enjoy, when the city officials have allowed sufficient time, a calm morning walk down calle Estafeta with the bunting and flags, and camera flashes and the thousands and thousands of throngs hanging on balconies cheering and wishing they were in the streets, too. We walk past many Pamplona-made friends who have taken up their stations and shake hands and quietly wish each other *suerte*. It is the de rigueur greeting among runners in the morning. We stop at *la curva* and shake the hands of the *pastores* and the photographers. There are more than a few runners who overwhelmingly honor us by reaching out to shake our hands on that walk. If I am not locked in on the task at hand before that, I become so as Ari and I share that eye-to-eye moment with the few men on this planet who understand our common morning cobblestoned will-o'-the-wisp: the perfect run.

Then there's the rocket, the rush and mass of people, and the bulls. We run, have our wounds treated by the Red Cross, have breakfast, do whatever it is we do the rest of the day, and do it all again the next morning. When we first went to Pamplona, I worried about how we would spend our time from 8:03 a.m. (after the run) until the next morning. As described in following chapters, this is not a problem. If we did everything we now consider "never to be missed" on our travel itinerary, we'd need a month of thirty-six-hour days.

These mornings sitting with my brother Ari for breakfast under the overhang at Café Iruña, or at street tables with a larger contingent of friends and family, after the *encierro* while nursing the freshest of fresh *zumo de naranja* (the kind you can only get in Spain), compel us to hark back to when we were kids crammed into the back bedroom of my parents' house. I enjoy it as much as anything in my entire life. We scheme about long but excessive dinners, wax thrasonical to old and new friends about the merits of the *encierro*, and quibble with the mafia over bullfight tickets. We debate who should have brought money to pay. We watch the delivery trucks, the green-suited workmen cleaning, the hot air balloons, stray dogs, bums, street performers, prissy tourists tiptoeing around trash and trash juice (the kind you find only in Pamplona), muddy but oblivious Frenchmen, and the entire cosmically and comically perfect scene. We drink coffee. Then praise the merits of Spanish breakfast meats. Most importantly, and as the sun also rises over the buildings surrounding the Plaza del Castillo, we plot our day and our return to Pamplona for the San Fermín fiesta for the rest of our lives.

And then breakfast. In the end, it's all about the breakfast.

At midnight on July 14, we never miss getting down right in front by the stage for Pobre de Mí, which happens at the Ayuntamiento. We wander out around 9:00 p.m. Eventually sometime around 1:00 a.m., everyone finally stops singing, and we all have to go our separate ways. This is as melancholy as any event can be. Yet even after the fiesta is over, it's really not over for weeks. In the words of Irishman Phil Lynott:

> *When they say it's over*
> *It's not all over, there's still the pain*
> *I'd come running*
> *I'd come running back to you again*

The physical pain we endure during and after the fiesta is a welcome reminder of our time in Pamplona, and either one or both of us is limping and straining to get around for weeks (if not months) afterward. We promise to cut back—next year or the year after that at least—and never do. We hope we never will.

We spend August and the fall season organizing our expensive bull-running photos, getting our white clothes dry-cleaned, licking our wounds, and getting our stories straight. On January 1, the countdown to return officially starts, as outlined by Pamplona's famous song *Escalera,* or "Staircase."

The lyrics recount the path from January 1 to July 7 like this:

> *Uno de enero,*
> *Dos de febrero,*
> *Tres de marzo,*
> *Cuatro de abril,*
> *Cinco de mayo,*
> *Seis de junio,*
> *Siete de julio San Fermin.*
> *A Pamplona hemos de ir,*
> *Con una media, con una media,*
> *A Pamplona hemos de ir,*
> *Con una media y un calcetin.*

In this song, after counting the months, you sing, "To Pamplona we have to go, with a stocking [or tights?], with a stocking [tights, again?]. To Pamplona we have to go, with a stocking and a sock." No one alive now knows what this business of the stocking or tights means, but it was written by Basque and Carlist lawyer Ignacio Baleztena Azcarate (1887–1972), and he never offered an explanation. It still is a good idea to bring a sock.

7

The Other 23 Hours and 57 Minutes
(what do we do all day)

"The question isn't 'what are we going to do,' the question is 'what aren't we going to do?'"

—FERRIS BUELLER

This is just about Ari's favorite line in a movie. While you are read-ing this, Ari is five minutes or less from being ready to go and do just about anything. I could call him right now, and ask, "You want to go to Best Buy?" Regardless of what he is doing, his answer will be, "Give me five minutes." Flyers game? Five minutes. Ocean City, New Jersey? Five minutes. Late-night snack in Chinatown? Five minutes. He will go to the Cherry Hill Mall or Japan or help me cut new trim for the kitchen. When? In just five minutes. Bookstore? Are you kidding—he's already there. On a whim, he will take the train with me to New York City or DC or go to Walmart to look at blue jeans. Dig a hole in the yard? No problem. He's ready to go on al-most no notice. He also always enjoys whatever we do. Dad says Ari is "game." As in, he's game for anything. I cannot ever recall hearing him complain about anything, or declining any opportu-nity to go anywhere, ever. He never wears down. In December 1994, after I was done with law school finals, I drove down to

South Carolina to pick him up from college for Christmas and we
stopped in Washington, DC, on the drive back. Together, we toured
the FBI; visited the Arlington National Cemetery, the Bureau of En-
graving & Printing, Ford's Theatre, the Lincoln Memorial, the Na-
tional Geographic Museum, the National Museum of the United
States Navy, the National Air and Space Museum, the National Zo-
ological Park, the United States Holocaust Memorial Museum, the
Vietnam Veterans Memorial; and we toured the Pentagon, where we
shook hands with a Medal of Honor recipient. In thirty-six hours.
We both have a perfectly foudroyant recollection of the tiniest fea-
tures of our traveling time together on this, our first foray into the
world alone. We have been traveling together, and often, since.
When you see us in Pamplona, rest assured, we're on our way some-
where, or five minutes from it at most.

The Running of the Bulls occurs between 8:00 a.m. and 8:03 a.m.
every day between July 7 and July 14. With (at least!) 120 minutes budgeted daily for sleep, only 1,317 minutes are left per day.
Frankly, it's not nearly enough. A couple weeks before July 6, the
Official Program becomes available online, but if you miss it there,
upon arrival in Pamplona, it's among the first things you should
buy. It lists the "official" events of each day, although there are
plenty of unofficial matters to keep you occupied. Official events
are listed from 5:00 a.m. until 3:00 a.m., and I am not kidding,
those are just the "official" events. Great news: 3:00 a.m. until
5:00 a.m. is "free time." For Ari and me, the San Fermín fiesta is a
tactical incursion; for us, precision and planning are obligatory.
We have our minutes in Pamplona planned down to the last wave
of the trainman's hand on the last train out of town. This is how
we relax. We have lunch and dinner reservations, and every minute between 5:00 a.m. and 1:00 a.m.—at least—accounted for. You
may scoff at our fastidious planning. "You have to let the fiesta
come to you" may work as a philosophy for others. We wait fifty
and a half weeks a year for this fiesta. We squeeze every drop of

life from it. The daily program includes many events for children, too. My children started going to Pamplona for the fiesta when they were ten and three years old. It is not possible for a child to suffer *taedium vitae* in Pamplona. Things that long ago became dry as dust to me still amuse my children, like European street performers. Because of the huge crowds, the fiesta is the Olympics for smarmy street performances. Personally, while some of them are creative, most just annoy me. Children go ape for them. In a pinch, I'll unload all my change lower than a 50-centime piece on the boys for them to use on street performers as they see fit. It is pretty funny to watch them budget it out over the course of the day. There is almost nothing—except the *encierro*—that is not appropriate for children. My boys keep late hours, too, but take a little nap in the afternoon. It's a good excuse for your own nap some days ("Sorry guys, but I have to take the boys back to the hotel for, ahem, 'their nap'"). There are many opportunities for small children to prove their bravery during the fiesta, and you'd be better to warn them ahead of time.

In *The Dangerous Summer*, Hemingway offers a magisterial aperçu in chapter 9: "Pamplona is no place to bring your wife."

> The odds are all in favor of her getting ill, hurt or wounded or at least jostled and wine squirted all over her, or of losing her; maybe all three. It's a man's fiesta and women at it make trouble, never intentionally of course, but they nearly always make or have trouble. I wrote a book on this once. Of course if she can talk Spanish so she knows she is being joked with and not insulted, if she can drink wine all day and all night and dance with any group of strangers who invite her, if she does not mind things being spilled on her, if she adores continual noise and music and loves fireworks, especially those that fall close to her or burn her clothes, if she thinks it is sound and logical to see how close you can come to being killed by bulls for fun and for free, if she doesn't catch cold when she is rained on and appreciates dust, likes disorder and irregular meals and never needs

to sleep and still keeps clean and neat without running water; then bring her. You'll probably lose her to a better man than you.

Of course, his counsel was a reflection of his attitude toward the wives he brought, and the company he kept in Pamplona. His practical guidance should not have been limited to one's wife—the persnickety tourist (male or female; adult or child) should be left elsewhere during San Fermín.

So, if your children are whiny, picky eaters, and can't walk distances, and can't take loud noises or crowds or jostling or getting dirty or bumped in the head, or melt down without ten hours of sleep every night, it might be best to leave 'em home and wait until they grow up. I don't bring my wife and children every year, but when they do come, it is a completely different fiesta for me, and in a good way. They love the fiesta.

Before leaving for Pamplona, it is best to sit down with a map of the city and the official program and figure out where the events are held. In the morning you will run, and the rest of the day you will walk and walk and walk. Walking is the primary Pamplona activity. Planning ahead prevents unnecessarily long walks. A rental car helps getting to neighboring towns for dinner, or getting out of the city to relax. You cannot get around Pamplona or the fiesta in a rental car—it is not practical. Equally, you should not attempt to get around by taxi. You will wait in human traffic jams longer than any walk would take. Within our first hour in Pamplona ever, we had called a taxi to take us from our hotel to the bullring. Now we look back on this and laugh. You are going to have to walk and walk. In the high heat of the day, make walking on the side of the street with the shade a habit, which is actually good advice for touring anywhere in Spain.

Remember, if you find yourself yawning out of anything but extraordinary exhaustion during San Fermín, you'll need to retrace your steps, because somewhere along the line you've lost your soul. There are thousands of official events, and unlimited unofficial events. Here are some of our favorites.

The Photo Crawl

Before our first trip to Pamplona, Ari and I read Gary Gray's book *Running with the Bulls*. Anyone thinking of visiting the fiesta should do so also. In the middle of his book Gary has various candid photographs from his times in Spain. Ari and I were struck by a picture of Gary dashing into the ring—in his patented blue trucker cap—right on the horns, or as locally said, *en los cuernos*. He's holding onto his hat, and it's still one of my favorite San Fermín photos of anyone. We became obsessed with getting what Ari dubbed "The Gary Gray Shot." So, you've heard of a tapas crawl? Well, shortly after the morning *encierro*, photography stores throughout Pamplona, especially in the old city area, start to post photo boards of pictures of the morning run. Instead of seeking tasty dishes on tiny plates, we crawl from photography store to photography store looking for great action shots of ourselves and friends with the herd. When younger, my boys loved supporting this endeavor, and actually were quite helpful, because they crawled through the crowds to the front for a closer view at the posts. Our favorite store is Foto Auma at Plaza del Castillo, 6. In 2010, another of our other favorite stores simply disappeared from calle Santo Domingo and was replaced with the Museo de Navarra. In 2005, we bought a ton of pictures from a store on a little side street near the Plaza de Toros. It is no longer there. Photography stores come and go, and move around, so keep your eyes and ears open while in the city. Buying photos of oneself in the *encierro* is addictive—and, at about 10 euros a picture, expensive. If you are on a budget, a nice drug habit might be less financially draining. The stores, of course, do not appreciate you taking a picture of their pictures, either. And, *no tocar* means *no tocar*! If you find a nice sequence of photos featuring you, the bull, and the horns, your children might be going to community college, because it is going to cost you big bucks. In our initial runs, we were happy with just about anything ("Ari, is that my shin bone down in the left corner?"). It's not unusual for runners to wear distinctive clothing (or a blue trucker cap) in an attempt to distinguish themselves from the crowd in photos.

As usual, the best things in life are free. The Holy Grail, of course, is seeing your run in photos in the newspaper. If you are pictured in the paper, you've done something really, really good, or really, really, really, really, really bad. Watch out: Newspapers also run photos of someone being cowardly with snarky headlines. In addition to the photo crawl, there's the newspaper crawl—that is, when we try to check all the papers for pictures with the bulls. There are several local city papers (some in Spanish and some in Basque), and several daily editions, and our favorite store to buy a few is located on calle Estafeta. It's called La Casa del Libro. Look for our friend Carmelo Butini Etxarte, a Pamplona fixture and an icon of the fiesta. It is very difficult to check all the shops properly without buying dozens and dozens of newspapers. If you see a friend in the papers—or me—buy it, tear it out, and put it in your pocket. There's nothing worse than someone congratulating you on a newspaper photograph but forgetting when they saw it and what paper it was in.

If you get a photo in the newspaper, you are *lawfully obligated* to carry it with you and force it upon waiters, doormen, matadors, tuba players, Frenchmen, and perfect strangers throughout the day. Increasingly, newspapers, including international newspapers, are posting photos of the run on the Internet, but there is *just something about* carrying that paper around the city. No matter how good a shot you get of yourself in danger, when you get home, prepare yourself mentally for this conversational exchange:

"You really don't look like you're that close to the bulls."

"Thanks, Mom."

Baby Bulls

Immediately after the morning *encierro*, one at a time three-year-old heifers with cork- and tar-capped horns are released into the bullring to cause mayhem and mischief. These are known as *vaquillas*. They're not really babies. They're not really bulls. They are heifers, which are young female cows that have not yet borne a calf. It's just easier to call them *baby bulls* than to say *vaquillas*. Get into the bullring, and lie down in front of the Gate of Fear, where the cow is released. Generally, it will jump right over you. Except when it doesn't. Sometimes it will lower its horns. Sometimes it will use the center of your back as a launching pad, and you shuffle around the rest of the summer like an old man. Don't ask. On weekends, the crowds are too big for us to enjoy this. But, during the week, you can usually get a couple of passes with the cows, like an amateur matador, with your newspaper or *pañuelo*.

Find some open space, and keep an eye on the cow. In 2014 I hoodwinked my older son Sam into standing in the middle of the ring, telling him that if he stood perfectly still the cow would not bother him. The joke was that no one can stand that still even with just the *vaquilla* sniffing around, and so when the cow came around he flinched more than a little, and it plowed into him at full speed and hooked his horn under Sam's shirt and out the armpit and rode him around for ten long seconds. We laughed at him for hours, but for the rest of the day he still showed the big scrape across his stomach (from just the corked horn) to anyone who would look.

It is not uncommon for matadors, even very famous matadors, to run the *encierro*. We love to talk with them afterward, but they stand in the ring so calmly, like it's just high tea, and don't even seem to notice the *vaquilla*. It's hard to talk with them and stifle the need to flinch when the cow comes nearby. Don't hit the bull or smack it from behind or grab its horns, all of which are considered jerk moves, even if you see others doing it. It seems every year some Aussie or U.S. Midwest farmer grabs the *vaquilla* by the horns and wrestles it down like a rodeo clown. This is what they'd do at home on the farm. It is their natural reaction to the event, even if they are showing off. The locals don't think it is natural, and usually they give the guy a pretty good beating. It is a fine line, but the locals expect you to show the bulls respect, and in their way. It has gotten so bad that they show a little video asking the locals to not beat the tourists who ignore the *"no molestar"* warning right after the running. Normally, the baby injures someone badly, but not seriously. Over half of my San Fermín injuries have occurred with the *vaquillas*.

In 2006, American Ray Ducharme was paralyzed after being struck by a *vaquilla*. When one lowers its horns, it is time to get out of the way. Getting smacked with the horns is like getting smacked with an axe handle: There's no axe on the end, so you won't die, but the bruise still hurts like nothing doing. In 2011, a cow knocked a couple of revelers out cold by hitting them in the head with its horns. It had a knack for it and did it over and over. As the *vaquilla* wears down from repeatedly charging the crowd, a *cabestro* is released into the ring to guide the cow back to the paddocks, so don't panic. Still, as with the *encierro*, there is a lot of unnecessary surging panic in the crowd. The *vaquillas* were as close as Ernest Hemingway ever got to actually running with the bulls, in the days when there were far fewer participants in the ring. Even today, it has a real international vibe, with a lot of hand-shaking and back-patting. Unless you're a professional athlete or opera singer, it's likely the largest crowd before which you will ever perform. Getting the cow to take a pass with your newspaper or *pañuelo*, standing in firm (or turning your back on the bull like a matador does), and hearing the crowd cheer *"olé"*—none of it gets old. It is a time to show some bravery, but unlike the dangerous *encierro*, there's time for laughing and smiling with the cow darting around. We've made some of our best Pamplona friends merrily dodging about in the ring.

Breakfast After Bulls

That's not the title of the book, is it? I could have gone either way, though. I don't eat breakfast at home. There, it's a coffee and a scowl and off to work. Even immediately after the *encierro* in Pamplona, I can't eat anything, because adrenaline (or something) is still stirring about in my stomach. But by midmorning, my appetite returns, and no matter what we've eaten over the past week, I have to have a nice big breakfast. Primarily, we enjoy prebreakfast at Café Iruña (Plaza del Castillo, 44), the café in *The Sun Also Rises*. It pays dividends to take the time to get to know the waiters at Café

Iruña. They are good men and hard workers, and deserve respect for their hard work during the fiesta. Sometimes we pack a breakfast if we are hitting the road. Otherwise, after prebreakfast, there are seemingly a million places to eat in the streets. Just ask the new friends you've made where they are having breakfast. Many restaurants spill outside onto the cobblestones and set up long tables with butcher-paper coverings and chairs for large groups. I cannot imagine that any group taking seats in the streets for breakfast will not welcome you. The city's best food market is indoors, open right after the morning run and in a circular building to the right of the Ayuntamiento, if you're looking at the town hall from the front. Look for the fruit, local cheeses, and glorious, heavenly pastry. Or you may pine for early morning churros from the Churrería La Mañueta "factory" in the narrow lane leading to the old market (as you will hear over and over in the media, its ovens rest right against the "ancient Roman wall," which makes me giggle: You can almost taste the Italians!), where the line winds on forever soon after the *encierro*. Are they selling Heavenly Hams and Springsteen tickets, too? But, yes, they're excellent, and worth the wait. I have a confession, though; I am more of a midnight churro guy. Address: calle La Mañueta, 13. Line: monstrous but fast-moving. The line makes it look like Walmart on Black Friday. Find someone who at least likes you, and make him or her stand in line.

In Pamplona, I love sitting in a morning sun surrounded by old and new friends and family after the *encierro* to nurse a couple of *café con leches,* or more, and some pastry and a loaf of bread. I like the spilt eggs and ham with friends while trading yarns with them. Ari calls it "holding court," which I am sure is somehow an insult. However, we "hold court" in two places daily. First, we are in front of the Ayuntamiento at around 6:30 a.m. Second, we are almost always at Café Iruña sometime after the morning run. Ari even signs autographs for free. It's a great opportunity to get the details of your lies about the morning run straight. But I've said too much already. Many Americans and other English-speaking visitors gather at Bar Txoko (pronounced Chock-o) in the Plaza del

Castillo after the run, too. *Txoko* means "cozy corner" in Basque. You can ask Ari about his mordant nickname for Bar Txoko, but you have to agree to keep it quiet.

Again, if you fall in with the right crowd, you can join one of the street table breakfasts you'll see miraculously emerging all over the city every morning. These are the best breakfasts. It is the best way to get to know your new friends.

Balloons

Immediately after the morning run (they must release them with the last rocket), hot air balloons appear over the city. Sitting in the Plaza del Castillo, smugly satisfied with the morning conquest, with a crystal-clear blue sky and a glass of freshly squeezed *zumo de naranja*—man—I love watching those balloons. So, if you're reading this, and you know how to get a ride in one, please let me know. In 2010, a Burger King hot air balloon managed to find its way to Pamplona. It was simultaneously exciting and frightening. In that vein, in 2011, greasy billboards advertising the Nuevo Rodeo Whopper with the slogan in English "Thanks America," without a hint of irony, appeared on the outskirts of the city. These were unintentionally funny.

Parade of the Gigantes and Cabezudos

A relatively new institution for Pamplona, the Giants and Big Heads and terrors leave the area near the Estación de Autobuses daily at 9:30 a.m. to wander the streets of Pamplona, and return to their "home" at 2:00 p.m. A map of the route for the day is printed in the daily newspaper. It changes daily. We have never-ending fun stepping out into the street and joining the parade.

Music

In the fiesta program, you will find listings of the official nonstop music. This includes traditional Basque and Navarran performances. The listings are great and excessive. You would do yourself a favor to take in some culture.

At midnight, you can usually find a truly awful euro-techno concert. That's fun. Excellent American jazz bands perform every night (morning?) at 12:30 a.m. Basques, and many other locals, are quite into American jazz. In 2012, there was talk of cutting these jazz concerts to save money, and it was met with protests. And there are at least two free concerts every night that rival U.S. state fair quality. For instance, we've seen Chuck Berry, Los Lobos, survivors of Thin Lizzy, Los Del Rio (aka the macarena guys), an Argentine Queen cover band called God Save the Queen, DJ Funky and the History Funk Club, and the Blues Brothers. They start at midnight, usually. During heady economic times, the quality increases, but during bad times it's nothing but bad bar mitzvah bands. The best ever was Marky Ramone in 2014. It was a relentless and exhausting concert. Moments before Marky came on stage, our friend Bryan Hoskins said we should back up because there would be a mosh pit. We laughed—"there's not going to be a mosh pit," we said. Then, he started the mosh pit.

Pamplona's local musical performances are quite moving, and unlike anything you'll see or hear at home. Spend a day in Pamplona, and you will learn what the local culture sounds like. There are some extraordinary voices to be heard during San Fermín. I would imagine that there are more people with significant musical talents per capita in the Navarran countryside than in most places in the world. When a child is born in Pamplona, he or she is named, and then immediately assigned a musical instrument. For instance, "His name is Javier, and he plays the trombone." It's right on their birth certificate, I think. Ari and I play a game called Count the Tubas. Count the number of people you see carrying a tuba in Pamplona. If I told you the number, you'd think I was exaggerating. The places you will see them are comical, too. Every couple of years, I see someone riding a moped, or *trying to use a urinal*, while carrying his tuba.

The official Navarran musical acts are great. If Raíces Navarres (Navarre's Roots) is singing during San Fermín, you would do well to go out of your way to see them. We're particular fans of

Natalia Narcué, who has a lovely and powerful voice, and when she sees us she always yells, *"¡Extraños!"* I think it's a compliment.

The spontaneous and unofficial music is what makes the San Fermín fiesta truly special. In the perdurable decree of our dear friend Ray Mouton, "Whenever you are in doubt during fiesta, follow the music." He is right on all accounts: If you hear music, walk toward it and only good things will happen. See a parade? Just join in. The parades of Pamplona are endless, and give passage only to the *encierro*. I guarantee you'll have to quit before the locals do.

In 2008, we arrived in Pamplona about an hour after the fiesta started on the sixth, and from behind the hermetic seal of our rental car in the *underground parking garage* of our hotel, we could already hear the not-so-distant din of the never-ending music of San Fermín. We quickly changed into our Pamplona whites, and watched band after band pass our hotel balcony below. It didn't stop until after midnight on the fourteenth. We could not remember a single moment when we could not hear music somewhere. The streets of Pamplona teem with musical notes. Just start following any group that wanders by, and eventually you'll be a full-fledged member of the band, with musicians trying to hand you their instruments or trying to buy you lunch. Invariably, I find Ari in such a mix, playing French horn #3 and perusing menus with his new best friends. Sometimes, four separate bands will meet marching through a street intersection and debate over who gets to pass through unmolested; or, they keep playing as if nothing happened. In the late afternoon, roving bands and singers move from hotel to hotel and provide entertainment for those just too weary to still be out in the streets.

There's also music in the bullring, which includes the official (and often hopelessly drowned-out) La Pamplonesa, the formal marching band of the feria, and much, much, much less formal bands of the *peñas*. These groups have become part of our favorite times. Aside from the morning run, I look forward to a *peña* deciding it's *that time* of the bullfight to play the theme from *The A-Team*.

I really don't feel comfortable going home until I've heard it at least once. The *peñas* have also added *da-da-da-dah* words to the 20th Century Fox theme song. These bands play simultaneously, loudly, and without end. At home, it would drive you to distraction. In Pamplona, it's relaxing.

There are plenty of opportunities to get an early start on learning the local music on iTunes. I try to learn the lyrics to a new song every year. I do not do well, though. My favorite album is *Ven a San Fermín!* by Raíces Navarres. Also, you can try

> *Las Peñas de Pamplona*, by Iruñeko Penak;
> *In Front of the Bull*, by Fermín Music;
> *Toros and Toreros en Pamplona*, which is an album of
> music commonly heard during the Pamplona
> bullfights;
> *Errobi Kanta Baionta*, which presents authentic Basque
> *jotas* dancing music;
> *La fête Basque*, by Kaskarot Banda;
> *Viva San Fermín*, by Hermanos Anoz; or
> *A Pamplona—7 de julio, San Fermín*, by Banda Elgarre-
> kin, which is a recording of songs you will defi-
> nitely hear in Pamplona, often by the artists on
> this album. If I am feeling sentimental about the
> fiesta during the winter, this is the album I play.

Hotel Yoldi

The "Rick's Café" of Pamplona is found on the ground floor of the Hotel Yoldi, on Avenida San Ignacio, near the bullring. If you walk right through the lobby and through the bar and café, you will find yourself out back on calle de Francisco Bergamin. Look up, and you will see the iconic yellow-and-brown backlit hotel sign. It's huge. You can see it from space. Except, Ari and I can never find it. We've set out for the Hotel Yoldi well over one hundred times and found ourselves lost every time. We take a map; we get lost. We ask a policeman; we get lost. If we leave with friends who know the way, they get lost. There is some kind of directional vortex nearby that leaves us confused, or perhaps it is the state we are in when someone says, "Hey, how 'bout the Hotel Yoldi?"

The hotel was built in 1950 and served for decades as the favored place in town for matadors to stay during the fiesta. You can hear the din of the bullring from the street out front. Ernest Hemingway met famed bullfighter Antonio Ordoñez here for the first time. Hemingway, Ordoñez, and Orson Welles hung out in the lobby during the fiesta. Hemingway wrote about Ordoñez in *The Dangerous Summer*. Ordoñez and Welles became such good friends that Welles' ashes were scattered on the Ordoñez ranch. The Hotel Yoldi is a major destination for any Hemingway fan. Yet it has successfully maintained its cosmopolitan feel, and has held off from becoming a tourist trap. It's still like it was in Hemingway's time. During bullfights, you can sit with locals and watch on the flat screens. They will explain—without provocation—why you know nothing about bullfights. After the bullfights, more locals congregate and lament how tourists are ruining their fiesta. It's great.

The real secret is the *champú* served at the bar. It is a lemon sorbet served in a wine glass that rinses the dust and heat of the day right down your throat. It is a shampoo for your spirit and your soul. You sip it; don't use a spoon. If you Google *champú*, you will find precious little, if anything, about it on an Internet that has 18,900,000 results for the search "Dr. Who Fan Fiction." Again, it is a precious secret.

We have wasted many, many hours in the hotel lobby. One evening during the bullfights we were at the bar doing our best Gary Cooper leaning, nursing our sorbet, and bickering about who just got us lost this night. Ari was explaining how he believes he has iron particles in the end of his nose like a homing pigeon's beak and can always naturally sense "geodetic north." He "cannot get lost." Right. You cannot believe how annoying I find that discussion.

From across the room, we saw the Frenchman. As a group, they love us. The French are drawn to us, and always with important political news from the front lines of civilized society,

where they have yet to discover the dangers of secondhand cigarette smoke. This one was dressed like Gene Kelly in *Anchors
Aweigh* and wasn't much taller. Without prompting he started explaining to us how he had discovered the formula for living on
the public dole and moving from party to party and meeting
beautiful women. We were fascinated.

He said "I am from France."

We said "No way."

He asked what we were drinking and we showed him our sorbet. He frowned. He had been drinking something much, much
harder. He then motioned to us that he would momentarily return,
and began leaning over the bar and whispering and occasionally
looking our way. The barman returned to him with a large silver
tray, which interested us. We then watched him mix a dozen gin
and tonics and place each of them on the tray, which frightened
us. What was this guy's plan here? While the barman was working his order, the Frenchman smugly asked us, "Can you handle?"
He held the tray at his waist and began the walk across the bar
toward us. But, in his intoxicated state, he listed heavily to the left,
and walked right past us, and out the door, and over the sidewalk.
He must not have seen that curb, because he missed it completely
and fell hard into the street. The glasses scattered, smashed, and
the tray rolled away on its edge, making a perfect half circle in the
middle of the road before stopping. Everyone looked up, and then
went back to whatever was going on before the Frenchman fell.
He got up after a few minutes and stumbled off into the night.

Thirty minutes later he returned to the café and sidled up to
us. He still looked and smelled like he fell down with a dozen gin
and tonics. But he came back as if nothing had happened. He
said he was from Paris and asked us if we had ever been there.

I said, "I've been to Paris many times," and explained how
much I love it. I told him my grandfather landed at Cherbourg right
after D-day and spent many months in Paris at the end of the war.
I told him that my family had toured the Normandy region and
that we'd been to Disneyland Paris. I told him I'd been first in line

at the Louvre—*three times*. "In fact," I explained, "we've driven all over France." And, I explained, "Ari here and I love to cross over into Biarritz during the fiesta all the time."

He stepped back and looked horrified.

"Biarritz? *Biarritz?* BIARRITZ?" he shouted. He then hauled off and kicked me in the shin and ran out into the street. I have no explanation, but the scar remains.

Ham

Is "ham" a thing to do? I can comfortably confirm that in Spain it is. Ham in Spain is a national treasure. It is a really, really big deal. The Spanish eat more ham every year than Americans eat. It's prescribed for headaches. It's a main character in romance novels. It's routinely elected to public office. There is a ham museum in Madrid. You can *easily* spend over a thousand euros buying a single ham leg. Three of the prior claims are actually true. At the bottom of the spectrum you have the *lomo,* which is a cured pork loin. It's good, but it is like comparing your grandmother's Thanksgiving turkey to a turkey hot dog. Next, there's *serrano* ham, which comes from a white pig that feeds on cereal. It is cheap and there are three grades: *serrano bodega, serrano reserva,* and *serrano gran reserva. Serrano* ham is for sandwiches. But *jamón Ibérico de bellota* is for the king's table. This is what you came to Spain for.

After what I can only assume is a formal, solemn ceremony, the mahogany-colored *jamón Ibérico* is sliced wafer-thin, served at room temperature, and spread around a slightly heated plate like tiny rose petals. This is special ham, and it is cut in a special "ham rack" called a *portajamones* or *jamonera,* with a special knife called a *cuchillo jamonero.* Most Spanish homes have this rack and knife. Whole bone-in *jamón Ibérico* have the hooves, or *patas,* still affixed. That's how you know it's bona fide. For storage, they are hung from the ceiling by rope, and small cones catch the fat that "sweats" out (their phrase, not mine). If you hold a small slice in your hand, you can watch your body heat melt the fat. Hypothetically, *jamón Ibérico* is supposed to be shared around the table, or at least it should be, Ari.

The Iberian black pig is an ancient breed (cavemen drew pictures of them in Spanish caves) that is mostly hairless, black, and tall. They are comically considered "elegant" by the Spanish. "Relax, it's just a pig" is a bad argument to start with the locals.

These pigs forage for conical acorns (the *bellota*) in the ancient holm oak pastures in southern Spain. These acorns are rich in natural vegetable oil, and the smiling pigs gain two pounds of fat daily devouring them. Generations ago villagers were forced by their governor to plant these oak trees around their pastureland to provide shade for the animals, firewood for the winter, and the aforementioned acorns for animal feed. A government policy somewhere that actually worked!

There is indeed something romantic about these black pigs chosen by their ranch owners to run free in the old forest. *Jamón Ibérico* is an expensive, special treat that alone is worth the flight to Spain.

Procession of San Fermín

On each seventh of July, starting at 10:00 a.m., the San Fermín icon is taken from the church and paraded through the city. He's always tinier than I remember. Look for the planned route in the morning newspaper. Few tourists are involved, and the native citizens turn out en masse and dress immaculately in their fiesta finest. This is a bona fide cultural event, and you cannot help but be moved by the smiling faces and joy of the Pamplona burghers. The walk from the church of San Lorenzo and back takes several hours. Pamplona's clergy, city officials, and local celebrities join in. The Plaza del Consejo is a great viewing spot. There is always an argument going on inside the crowd about the Basque flag and whether it should be a part of the procession. It's usually not. At the end, famed vocalist Mari Cruz Corral sings the traditional *jota* to the figure of the saint. She has been singing at San Fermín for over a quarter of a century, and the crowd that forms to hear her is so big she has had to move to a balcony in recent years. She is lovely.

Sorteo and *Apartado*

Together, these are the second of the three daily bull-related events during the San Fermín fiesta. First, there is the *encierro,* which is the morning running. Second, there are the *sorteo* and *apartado,* discussed in this section, which occur at 1 p.m. inside the courtyard of the bullring. Third, there is the *corrida,* which is the bullfight, which takes place at 6:30 p.m. in the bullring.

Attending the *sorteo* and *apartado* will allow you to witness the inner workings of the Plaza de Toros. The activities are repeated in every bullring in Spain before a bullfight. The whole thing is abbreviated as the *apartado.* You should clean up and see this at least once per fiesta.

You purchase tickets to the *apartado* at the bullring (beginning at around 10:00 a.m.). The line moves quickly because no one is at the front carping about seat location, because there are no seats. You can expect to pay less than 10 euros. The ticket window is at the Plaza de Toros, to the right of the Ernest Hemingway statue. Someone always scrawls a simple sign that says *"APARTADO"* above a ticket window that usually sells tickets to the bullfights.

The entrance to the *sorteo* and *apartado* is to the left of the Hemingway statue, around the side of the plaza closest to calle Estafeta. You'll want to start lining up to go inside around noon for the *apartado.* The official events start at 1:00 p.m., but the crowds get too heavy for you to be able to look around casually. Once inside the proverbial "castle gates," you will see where the horses are kept, their equipment, where the bulls are butchered, and the veterinarian's office. You will find the official legal postings about the bullfight for that afternoon. Sometimes the matador chapel is open before or after the *apartado.* Everything is painted white, and there are beautiful flowers and trees. Dignitaries and other pseudo important types mingle with representatives of the plaza, the bull ranches, real cowboys, the matadors, and aficionados. There's finger food!

Up the steps (to your right as you enter), you look down on

the maze of rectangular walls and pens, each separated by a system of locks and pulleys. You can see the bulls from the *encierro* and even the extra *cabestros* relaxing under some trees, or maybe eating at the manger. This is a very social event, and the locals dress up to "see and be seen." You can usually shake hands with the ranch cowboys, and thank the *pastores* and *dobladores* for their helpful but dangerous work. The hard work of the *pastores* and *dobladores* and the safety blanket they provide during the *encierro* cannot be exaggerated. If there are any white or brown bulls in the pens, talk among yourselves how they are more dangerous. It's a good way to get the aficionados going. It is not appropriate to call to or attempt to attract the bulls. You will definitely be escorted off the premises.

We always try to see if we can identify any of that morning's bulls from the earlier run, and pretend we actually can. Look around for the representatives of the matador teams who will be in the bullring that afternoon. They are usually talking with the ranch representatives, and weighing up which bulls will be better for their matador. Their faces are very serious. As a group, they agree on appropriate pairings of the bulls, and then draw lots from a hat to see which pairs are assigned to which matador. The names of the bulls are written on cigarette rolling paper and placed inside little metal balls. This is the *sorteo*. This is a key event, and a matador relies on a trusted member of his *cuadrilla* to make a good decision in the pairing, as a "bad" bull can make the best matador look inept and foolish. In short, the representatives are looking for bulls that show the appropriate level of aggression, and who will exhibit the instincts that make a good corrida possible.

Nearing 1:00 p.m., stake out the front row of any of the pens for the *apartado*. It's best to attend the *apartado* more than once. The first time, you can wander around and see everything. The second time, you can stake out a spot around the "main pit" immediately upon your arrival. Once inside you will understand what I mean by this. You really need to be there almost immediately after the crowd is allowed inside. This pit has a space marked "reserved."

Stand next to the reserved area, and you will meet the ranch representatives, who use the reserved area to watch their bulls. To get a spot at this pit, you will have to be a little lucky, and you will have to aggressively hold it. (Watch for pushy old ladies who show up at the last minute and pretend they "just want to peek" over the ledge! Fool me once, shame on you!) In this pit, a bull and steer enter after a series of pulleys and locks are manipulated. The steer is allowed to leave the way he entered, but the bull is caught between the doors. A *pastor* stands on the scaffolding over the pit and uses a long pole along with audible chirps to distract the bull away from the door the steer used to leave, and to get the bull to go in the door for the individual stall, or *chiquero*. Sometimes the bull (usually the Jandilla breed) just won't cooperate, and the ranch and matador representatives nearly come unglued.

The *chiqueros* are underneath the bullring seats. This event gives you the opportunity to see each bull up close and to decide yourself which will be good bulls and which will not. Your guess is probably as good as the cowboy's. Each bull disappears, the *chiquero* door closes, and each *toro* is readying for its later fate. It's a great chance for photos, and video, and it's among our favorite events of the fiesta. Again, don't try to distract the bulls. After the *apartado,* more of the plaza is opened up, and you can usually walk out in the ring sand and take photos by the Gate of Fear. This alone makes the day.

Rural Sports

At 12:00 p.m. daily at the Plaza de los Fueros (a healthy hike from the old city, but near a cool Chinese restaurant), the city holds Deportes Rural. It looks like Strongman Contests on Saturday afternoons on CBS back in the 1980s. Mountain-size men carry giant rocks, pull giant piles of rocks, saw giant logs, chop wood in every known dangerous fashion, and chainsaw *upside down* from their ankles. If there's one thing you learn in Pamplona, it's that giant men from tiny mountain towns can chop logs, and really,

really fast. Watch your fingers and toes at all times. This is worth a visit every year. When we first came to Pamplona, we looked askance at this event. As time passed, we came to learn that this competition is an important part of Basque culture. They have been lifting heavy rocks for a long time.

Ice Cream

Voltaire wrote, "Ice-cream is exquisite. What a pity it isn't illegal." An historic challenge during San Fermín is to have a fermented drink at every bar on both sides of calle Estafeta in a single night. Legend is no one's managed it, ever. We don't imbibe. But they sell ice cream everywhere during San Fermín. Try Magnum—*Europe's No. 1 Hand Held Ice Cream Bar* and the Official Ice Cream of the Philadelphia Peña and Taurino Club. We try to eat an ice cream at every place that sells them on the way back to our hotel room, from any random spot we happen to be. We never manage.

The French

Je suis désolé, mais vous êtes debout à l'endroit que je vomis normalement. Il serait peut-être utile si je fume plus près de votre visage. Achetez-moi un verre. Chante-moi une chanson. ("I'm sorry, but you are standing at the place I normally vomit. It might be helpful if I smoke closer to your face. Buy me a drink. Sing me a song.")

You will not believe your eyes when you see the massive hordes of Frenchmen that descend on the fiesta on the weekend closest to Bastille Day. More than one Spanish waiter has described them as *la pestilencia* to us. If you ever went to class in high school, you may remember that the British have old disputes with the French. The Spanish have older disputes, and the Basques have ancient ones. During the fiesta, the French are a never-ending topic of conversation. The French used to have a saying, "Africa begins at the Pyrenees." This was meant to be the ultimate insult to the Spanish. You can still really rile one up by saying, "Hey, have you ever heard the old expression . . . ."

As to Spain, they have been invaded by the French many,

many times. For instance: See Charlemagne, AD 778. In October 2013, the Spanish celebrated the two hundredth anniversary of the end of the Siege of Pamplona. In the fall of 1813, the retreating French army was finally expelled from Spain during the Napoleonic Wars, which had no agreed-upon starting cause. The end, of course, came with fooling around with the Basques, and then the Russians, which is never a successful war recipe. Future tyrants, please pay better attention in Social Studies class. The French general in Pamplona had threatened to blow up the city fortifications leaving Dodge, but was threatened by the Spanish with certain death. So he surrendered instead. What—a—surprise. During the siege, the French were reduced to eating rats and dogs, something still brought up today. That plays out like this:

> Intoxicated Frenchman: Pourquoi devriez-vous être en colère que j'ai essayé d'embrasser votre fille? (Why should you be so upset that I tried to kiss your daughter?)
>
> Red-faced Spaniard: Ir a comer otra rata. (Go eat a rat.)

As to the Basques, they live in northern Spain and southern France (known as *Pays Basque*). While they all advocate for a separate country, they share a common enemy: themselves. The French see the southern Basques as barbarians, while the Spanish side sees the northern Basques as sell-outs who pimp their ancient culture out in Disneyesque fashion. On a macro scale, Madrid and Paris use these differences to quell any rebellion. On a micro scale, loud arguments on who is "really Basque" are hilarious.

Tour Groups

This is not something to do; it's something to avoid. I find it amazing writing this down, but I dislike tour groups more than I enjoy mocking The French. You cannot take a side trip in a tour group; you have to wait until you are told it is okay to move to the next item on the official itinerary. Tour groups seem to exclusively bring people to Pamplona who speak the King's English, or some version thereof. For the most part, they are bringing groups that are too large and too drunk and too uneducated and too immature. If someone does not know how to buy white pants without guidance, perhaps he should not run with the bulls. There are responsible tour group operators who bring small groups and provide accurate advice and instruction. They use experienced runners to educate first-time runners. But if you find yourself wearing matching t-shirts, you hired the wrong company. Further, nothing endangers the fiesta more than the migration of Western business interests to Pamplona. A future with the "Running of the Bulls Sponsored by Burger King" should scare us all. Many of our British and Australian brothers and sisters are using tour groups to visit Pamplona. Alarmingly, so are Americans. If you need a walking guide on reveling, something is wrong. If you lack the savvy to walk around Pamplona during the fiesta, you probably need someone to help with pulling up your white pants. There is some dishonesty afoot also. Tour group operators love to warn of the dangers and difficulties of buying tickets to the bullfights, and then mark up their prices to criminal usury levels. It is the same with balconies and hotels. If you can't scalp tickets, or make a hotel reservation, or plan remotely ahead, you might want to reconsider coming to San Fermín. This is no place for the indecisive or unprepared. It is better to hope you don't get ripped off than to know you are getting ripped off. More importantly, people in tour groups tend to stay together in one big mass, and you will only make friends with the people you met at the airport on the trip over. Or, they are coming to Pamplona solely to get drunk. You could have just stayed in Gooloogong, Australia, and done the same exact thing in a Spanish-themed bar. In a tour group, you are more likely than not missing the fiesta. In a tour group, you are watching other people immersed in San Fermín. You are a tourist and not a traveler. This does not mean you should not ask for help. Kind strangers helped us when we started making our annual appearance, and we love to pass on the advice. So do many, many others.

"The Three Scorpions at Breakfast, 2014," or "What Happened to That Plate of Ham?"

(Courtesy of Deanna Ally)

The rocket explodes and the famed Pamplona fiesta starts (July 6, 2014).

(Photograph © Craig MacPherson)

The note said, "Ari, meet down in the front. I'll be wearing white pants." Chupinazo, 2014.

(Photograph © Craig MacPherson)

Peter hangs out at Mesón Pirineo. And, poor Xabier (in black and yellow) is crawling at Peter's feet before getting skewered on July 11, 2005 (at this precise moment, the author was hooked on fiesta forever).

(Courtesy of Peter N. Milligan)

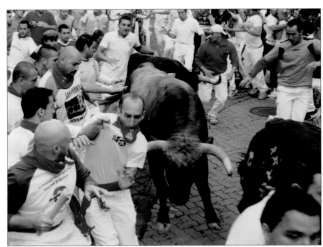

Peter is about to have a run-in with the forehead of a bull that just would not make the turn (July 9, 2011).

(Photograph © Foto Auma)

Peter falls under the El Pilar bulls (July 13, 2010). He survived; his Binaca did not. Note the concerned reaction of "Farmer Bob."

(Courtesy of Peter N. Milligan)

Peter steps away from the horns, while the bull appears to step away
from Peter (July 11, 2012). *(Photograph © Foto Auma)*

Peter runs on the left in his black-and-white Barbarian jersey and squeezes through the crowd moments before his most serious fiesta injury (July 11, 2013).

(Photograph © Foto Mena)

Peter is smacked by the bull horn (as shown from another angle in the cover photo) while running with his son Sam who is "just" a step behind (July 12, 2014). Ssshhh! Don't tell his mother. Both are wearing their infamous scorpion T-shirts.

(Photograph © Pablo Roa Ros)

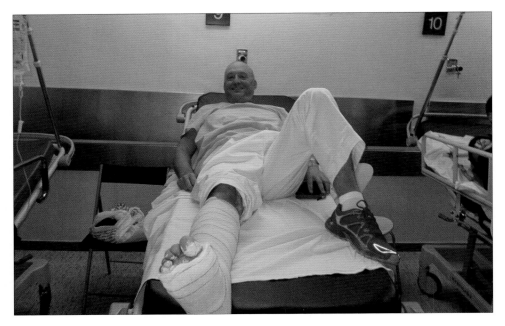

Smiling Peter, with his compound ankle fracture and third-degree burn, in the hospital (July 11, 2013). *(Courtesy of Peter N. Milligan)*

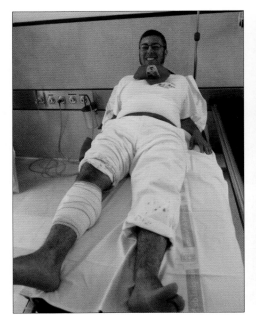

Smiling Ari, gored earlier in the morning, in the hospital (July 9, 2012).

(Courtesy of Peter N. Milligan)

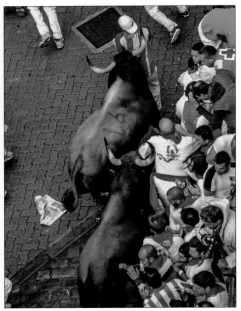

Peter and Sam run together, with father trying to keep son on the sidelines for at least a while longer (July 14, 2014). Of course, this will not last.

(Photograph © Pablo Roa Ros)

"The Morning Street Cleaning," or "I love the smell of trash juice in the morning. It smells…like fiesta." *(Photograph © Craig MacPherson)*

Peter's son Jackson takes off for parts unknown. Fiesta will do this to you, too. He returned three hours later speaking French.

(Courtesy of Peter N. Milligan)

A member of the Royal Entourage for the Parade of Giants. Fleeing children, and grinning parents, not pictured.

(Photograph © Craig MacPherson)

Famed Caravinagre (or, "Señor Vinegar") prepares to bop a local child on the head. This is completely normal in Pamplona.

(Photograph © Craig MacPherson)

Peter, Ari, and Sam celebrate the end of fiesta at Pobre de Mí.

(Photograph © Craig MacPherson)

Local Pamplona citizens gleefully flee the firework bull.

(Photograph © Craig MacPherson)

Peter blows out the candle, ending his fiesta. "Time for 'someone' to carry my bags down to the car," he reminds Ari. *(Photograph © Craig MacPherson)*

A few candles refuse to concede the end. Sadly, it is indeed over.

(Photograph © Craig MacPherson)

But for free. We still have to ask for help. Having outside, overseas interests charge extraordinary fees to help people attend the fiesta is contrary to the spirit of the fiesta, and may San Fermín strike them stupid. Or stupider.

The Miura

The Miura bull breed is from Seville, Spain, and it is measured as the bravest and the noblest. Even their arrival in Pamplona for the feria is an occasion. They have been causing fear in the bullring since the late 1800s, and in Pamplona, they almost always run on Sunday. They are giants. In *Death in the Afternoon*, Ernest Hemingway writes:

> . . . *there are certain strains even of bulls in which the ability to learn rapidly in the ring is highly developed. These bulls must be fought and killed as rapidly as possible with the minimum of exposure by the man, for they learn more rapidly than the fight ordinarily progresses and become exaggeratedly difficult to work with and kill.*
>
> *Bulls of this sort are the old caste of fighting bulls raised by the sons of Don Eduardo Miura of Sevilla . . .*

Then in *The Sun Also Rises*, Hemingway writes:

> *Montoya smiled. "To-night," he said. "To-night at seven o'clock they bring in the Villar bulls, and to-morrow come the Miuras. Do you all go down?"*

The Miura line traces its roots to five historic bull breeds: the Gallardo, Cabrera, Navarra, Veragua, and Vistahermosa-Parladé. They are not only large but have a reputation as cunning and problem-solving. They're thinking. Like velociraptors "testing the fence for weaknesses, systematically. They remember."

They had gone over twenty years without goring anyone, but started goring runners recently and resolutely. In 2009, a bull named Ermitaño gored runners a shocking five times. In 2014, this breed gored three runners.

Matadors are noticeably unnerved by the Miura bulls, and turn their backs on them much less often and from points farther away than they do with other breeds. These bulls are appreciably larger than other bulls, which are already big to begin with. A bull named Islero gored and killed beloved bullfighter Manolete on August 28, 1947. Islero had poor eyesight and chopped with his right horn. He was considered a dangerous bull in the paddock. In the town of Linares, Manolete reached over the bull's horns and thrust his sword deep up to its hilt. Islero gored Manolete in the groin with the right horn. His femoral artery was severed. Unlike many, if not most, modern-day matadors, Manolete excelled at the *suerte de matar* (the kill). The lesson should be luculent—if the Miura killed the greatest killer of all time, it will not hesitate to cut you down on the cobblestones.

A group of American *mozos* started wearing suit coats many years ago during the morning *encierro* to honor the Miura. Most are associated with Amigos de Miami, and, to a man, they are all superb runners. More so than many Spanish from outside of Navarre, they show respect to the bulls by both their running and their conduct in the streets. Truly gentlemen, they will help you in Pamplona without hesitation. Without knowing this tradition, we started wearing neckties to the Miura bullfight, and to dinner afterward—for the same reason. We could take to the streets skipping and buck naked and get fewer curious glances than the looks generated by the neckties. Miura Sunday is always a great crowded day of the fiesta and worth celebrating. You cannot run the *encierro* in a necktie unless it is a clip-on. If a bull got a horn underneath, it would be the last necktie you'd ever wear.

Garlic

Plaza del Ajo, or "Garlic Square," is in the Plaza de las Recoletas. Strings of (giant) garlic are sold from stands during the fiesta. The rest of the year the square is named after the convent nearby (the

Agustinas Recoletas). The garlic sales used to be a huge part of the fiesta, but now it appears they are selling sentiment more than condiment. Often you will see old fiesta photographs with men wearing the large strings of garlic around their necks for the trip back to their village. Now you can buy garlic at the supermarket, so demand has decreased. However, it's still a nice taste of the 1950s, and I hope Pamplona manages to keep the tradition going forever.

Riau-Riau

In the middle of the party, it's hard to remember that real, regular people live here. For the Navarrans and Basques, there is nearly always some political issue brewing. Some are silly, and some are deadly serious. Most are beyond our comprehension. I am hardly an expert in Spanish and Basque politics. I am not unsympathetic to those seeking to govern themselves, or those who desire to be left alone. Hey, live free or die, right? While bouncing merrily along a backstreet in Pamplona, Ari and I once stumbled into a silent protest by Basque locals regarding the Spanish government's refusal to relocate ETA prisoners to prisons closer to their families. Seems perfectly reasonable, right? They stood silently with photographs of their incarcerated family members, and with ashen faces. I was permanently struck by the realization that they'd lost so much in the last century, their fight was reduced to demanding their families be kept close together, even if behind prison walls. It's not something I'll soon forget. I also am not an expert on the deep-rooted and enduring wounds of the Spanish civil war, a war with no winner. George Orwell's *Homage to Catalonia* is an extraordinary and frustrating account of the siege of Barcelona during the Spanish civil war. In the United States, we can hardly comprehend a war of Communists vs. Fascists vs. Anarchists.

Unless it's canceled during high levels of political stress (and it usually is), on the sixth of July at 4:30 p.m., the local residents gather for the *riau-riau*, or at least hypothetically they attempt the *riau-riau*. Simply put, tradition requires the City Council parade from the town hall to the Church of San Lorenzo along calle San

Saturnino and calle Mayor, and the route is only about 500 meters long, but along tiny streets. To show their displeasure with elected officials, a crowd gathers to slow, to frustrate, or prevent the procession. It is patently satisfying to stand out in the street and block the politicians from getting to church. Can you imagine this happening in the United States?

Everyone stands in the street, pretty peacefully, in my experience, while La Pamplonesa plays *Vals de Astráin* over and over and over and over (and over and over) as the City Council members creep along the blocked route. Oh yes, and over and over and over and over and over and over. You will be humming this tune in your head until October. This event has been going on and off since 1914. In 1980, the walk required 181 repetitions of the song. The five-minute walk took over five hours. In 1972 the politicians quit after moving only a few feet in just under an hour. In 2012, it was canceled (again) after a huge brawl broke out in front of the city hall, and Ari and I left when we saw the first thrown bottle. Flying bottles scare us infinitely more than bulls. The abstract reason for the church walk is so that the politicians can take in the celebration of the Visperas Cantadas, which lasts about forty-five minutes. There are around two thousand seats.

La Pamplonesa is not only the fiesta's but the town's official marching band. In 1919, it was formed with thirty-seven musicians and given the impossibly creative official name of The Pamplona Music Band. It was first paid by the city to help out in the San Fermín fiesta in 1920. The band takes part in all the events organized in the street; the *chupinazo;* the *riau-riau;* the procession on the seventh; the daily early-morning Dianas before the *encierro;* and Pobre de Mí. They even have some spontaneous concerts in the La Taconera Park. Just ask one of the musicians in the street when they will be playing a free concert.

Basque Puppets, and Other Ways to Scare Children

Check the fiesta program for times, but Menudas Fiestas are held for children at the Plaza Conde de Rodenzo daily. It's a bit of a brutal walk from the old city, but it's free. There are dozens of "stations" with activities for kids, many of which are moderately unsafe, or completely unsafe (such as 2013's "Sky Dancers," the human football, *target shooting*, tightrope walking, "acrobats," stilts, trampolines, and rock climbing), and none of it would ever be permitted in the United States. The 2013 English guide advertised "large polyester animals" and the menacingly named Dracoland. Our culture simply cannot abide such a glorious opportunity to pick off a few weak kids from the herd. This is where you can prepare small children for getting injured as adults during the fiesta. These stations are so much fun it is simply unbearable adults are not permitted to partake. But, you should never say: "Hey, it's Spain, it must be safe. They wouldn't let us do it unless it was safe." Bring tiny Band-Aids and finger splints.

There are also staged shows, including Basque Puppet Shows, which are so truly creepy they'll haunt your dreams forever. Remember the Sid and Marty Krofft puppets on the *Barbara Mandrell and the Mandrell Sisters* show? Yeah, these are worse. Your children might not be scared, but you will be.

See the Bulls, Down by the River

As each bull breed arrives in Pamplona, they are held in pens near the start of the running course. Although the exact times seem to change yearly, in the midafternoon you can see the various breeds waiting for the *encierro* and the corrida. In general, it is open from 11:00 a.m. to 1:30 p.m. and 4:30 to 8:30 p.m. Walk downhill on calle Santo Domingo, turn left, and cross the River Arga over the bridge at Puente de la Rochapea. To view the bulls costs only a couple of euros, and is well worth it. The bulls are behind thick glass in a large paddock, and you can causally inspect each breed (from a few feet away) and photograph them before they run you down in the street some morning. You will hardly ever see a tourist. There are fairgrounds nearby with rides that look like they belong in a Catholic Church parking lot. In 2014, the fair options included an amusement called Mr. Bean: The Ride. That sounds inviting.

El Día del Niño

Each fiesta, a day is set aside for the local children. This includes heaps of unofficial events. Also, small children and babies are presented for a "church blessing." Families line up in their Sunday best at the end of calle Nueva to walk past the saint's icon and present flowers, balloons, etc. It is a happy part of the fiesta, and fun and relaxing to watch the families from a comfortable bench out of the sun. In the afternoon there is a "children's" running of the bulls, where a plastic bull head on a wheelbarrow contraption is used to chase little kids around. In the past, cows were released to chase middle school–aged children. It was dropped after a couple of children were injured. There is talk of bringing back this glorious event.

Sunday Night

Pamplona takes on a different vibe on Sunday nights. It is an astonishing night for people-watching. Tour companies steer their customers away from Pamplona on Sundays because of the large crowds, and the Frenchmen. We usually head to the beach during the day. However, Sunday night is always the best night of the fiesta, when the locals are out in force in their nicest clothes. Joining them are the French, the tourists, the drunks, the street performers, the beggars, the celebrities, the musicians, local farmers and cowboys, children and gangs of local teenagers who have finally slipped the reins, as well as the filthy hordes that have been sleeping in the park since Friday night. Everyone is out in the streets, from king to urchin; from great-grandmothers (or older) to newborn babies. It's like visiting a cantina on Tatooine. The city pulsates and the earthquake-needle rests somewhere between hullabaloo and bedlam. Sunday nights are tediously and throbbingly crowded; if that bothers you, you have come to the wrong fiesta. Walks from your hotel room to wherever you are going are exhausting. But you will laugh harder, eat better, immerse yourself in more sights and sounds, and make more friends than on any other night. It is a

great night to have bullfight tickets in hand and dinner reservations with friends for afterward. The best fiestas have two Sunday nights.

Guiri Day

Sponsored by the good people at Kukuxumusu, an outstanding
and recurring foreign visitor to the fiesta is honored and recognized every fiesta. Kukuxumusu also runs sanfermin.com, which
is by far the best site on the web for San Fermín guidance, and has
stores selling their excellent wares on calle Estafeta and elsewhere.
The presence of Kukuxumusu in Pamplona is superfluous and
synonymous, as are their designs for t-shirts and posters, and their
mascot (tastefully named "Mr. Testis"). It would be a lesser fiesta
without them.

If you've been carefully reading this book, you already know
what Kukuxumusu means. I have some of their stickers on my car.
In the USA, I have been asked several times by strangers if it is associated with the Ku Klux Klan. These people are morons.

Fountain of the Navarrería

The St. Cecilia fountain is located in Navarrería Square. For many
vistitors from Australia and New Zealand and other places with
a funny English accent, this is the primary event of the fiesta. No
kidding. Their tour group packages really emphasize this "tradition." They all drink without moderation at the Mejilloneria, then
climb the St. Cecilia fountain and dive into the locked arms of their
mates below. 'Cept they are all drunken dopes and can't always
catch well. Some of them can't climb well, or even remember what
they were doing the moment before. Every year, "oops" echoes
through the streets, and someone suffers a monstrous injury, as a
"jumper" becomes a "faller." A fairly large percentage of local citizenry look on at this tradition with disgust, but it still makes
for good pictures in the newspapers. I cannot emphasize this
enough—I hope this "event" is banned forever someday.

The 1788 fountain had been removed for roadwork and refurbishment in 2009, and rumors circulated that it would not be returned, essentially to end the carnage. That year, we watched with some amusement as the wankers, tossers, and yobs wandered around in confusion. "I say, Old Bean, where's our fountain?" It was returned, but in 2012, the city announced that jumping from the fountain was illegal. As far as I could tell, the funny fence they put up stopped no one. In 2010, a woman was still in a coma when we left town after she fell while climbing the St. Cecilia fountain.

Parade of the Mules

At 5:30 p.m., the mules used to drag the newly deceased bulls out of the bullring, along with the horse-mounted *alguacilillos* (constables), parade from in front of the Ayuntamiento through the Plaza del Castillo and into the bullring. The *alguacilillos* are the sheriffs for the bullfight president, and they communicate his orders to the matadors and unlock the Gate of Fear. They serve a mostly ceremonial role today and are dressed in uniforms from the sixteenth century. Later they lead the matadors into the ring. Before the parade starts, children are allowed to sit on the mules for pictures. My little boys loved getting hoisted up onto the mules for photos, but they are outgrowing this tradition. And Ari *absolutely refuses* to pose for photos anymore. Post a few shots of him unwittingly standing near the backside of a mule online and he never lets it go. Bands play and everyone marches with the mules, but you can watch, or anyone is permitted to step out in the street and join the parade. I recommend the latter, especially with children. Or, you can catch the whole thing at the end, about half an hour later, at the Plaza de Toros—the parade goes to the left of the Ernest Hemingway statue and enters the ring at the same place as the matadors. In a city of millions, only a few dozen people are at the matadors' entrance in the afternoon. This is where the matadors and their *cuadrilla* enter the ring before the corrida. In the hour before a bullfight, this is a good place to hang if you want to see the matadors up close, even the most famous. They pull up in their fancy Mercedes minivans, get out in their *traje de luces* (the "suit of lights"), and glad-hand a bit before going inside. Sometimes their handlers have tickets to give out, and sometimes they have merchandise (photos, key chains, locks of hair, etc.)—or, as Ari calls these items, "freebies." It is harmless fun, and you can get good close photographs of the matadors.

The Corrida

Discussed in chapter 9 in detail, there is a bullfight every afternoon at 6:30 p.m. during the fiesta. It lasts until almost 9:00 p.m. Pamplona is a memorable place to attend a bullfight. Bring a snack.

Other Than the Corrida

During the fiesta, there are many other events in the Plaza de Toros in addition to the afternoon bullfights. On the sixth of July, there has not yet been an *encierro,* but there is a bullfight in the afternoon. It is the *rejoneador,* bullfighting on horseback. Attend this and you will audibly and involuntarily gasp more than once. It seems like the horses are constantly inches from dying, yet they miraculously escape time and time again. Even Hemingway did not want to see horses die. There is also the Concurso Nacional de Recortadores, which is usually scheduled once or twice during the fiesta (check the yearly calendar). Here, young Navarrans and Basques jump over or dodge charging bulls or put a ring on their horns. The similar Festejos Taurinos is free but held also only once or twice per fiesta and is also worth attending for the *novillero* (novice) bullfights, and to watch the guys who jump the charging bull on motorcycles. Obviously the decision to jump a charging *toro bravo* on a motorcycle started with some kind of luminous Reese's Peanut Butter Cup moment. "Hey, I love Spanish bulls!" "Why, I love motorcycles!" "Wait, why don't we . . ."

Plaza de la Cruz Concerts

Every night during the fiesta, concerts and dances are held at the Plaza de la Cruz at 8:00 p.m. You don't have to be over eighty years old to dance, but the atmosphere is strictly old-time-y Pamplona. Many of the men there danced during the Spanish civil war, too. Local kids play on the swings, and you can wrestle someone's grandpa for a spot on the benches. In Philadelphia, if you go to the trouble to dig out a street parking spot in the snow, you can save it with a lawn chair left in the spot. This is tradition, and people have been *murdered* for violating the code in Philadelphia. In comparison, if you get up to dance in the Plaza de la Cruz, you cannot save your bench seat with a hat or handkerchief, even if you are eighty years old. I may look younger, but I am 110 years old in fiesta years. If you have to pick just one night, choose the night the band Carisma is performing. Four words: *Spanish Achy Breaky Heart.* Trust me, and you'll thank me later.

Dining

As noted earlier (and as discussed in chapter 10), Navarre is a culinary capital of the world. Lunch and dinner can be truly special during the fiesta. Make early reservations.

Firework Bull

Nightly, at 10:00 p.m., from the Plaza de Santiago, the town's children are brought out to be chased after by their own special bull. It's on fire. And, it's exploding! Basically, a guy carries a life-sized plastic bull that's covered in fireworks and set on fire. Then, in keeping with timeless fiesta ideals, it chases kids through the streets. It sounds safe, right? You'd be surprised, but it isn't. These fireworks have burnt holes in my shirt, and burnt my hair and head, and I've choked on the smoke, but only *every time we've ever seen the firework bull.* My boys absolutely love this, and it is fun to watch their faces, and the glowing but potentially engulfed faces of the local children. In Pamplona, as in the four corners of Spain, this is completely normal. You cannot miss seeing this spectacle.

Until recent years, the firework bull *always* started at the Plaza de Santiago. Recently, the city began experimenting with starting it in less crowded areas, or even having multiple firework bulls going at once. Often, when it starts at Plaza de Santiago, the firework bull crowd and the remaining *peña* revelers marching from the bullring meet on calle Estafeta for the Mother of All Log Jams (MALJs). Check the newspaper and the daily schedule for where the bull is lit on fire and where it is going.

Fireworks

Every night, at 11:00 p.m., a different city of the world sponsors a presentation of Fuegos Artificiales. Most are from Spain, but some are from North America, Africa, and other European countries. In the spirit of competition, they fortunately try to outdo each other. The contest results are published in the morning newspapers. Usually they print the competition "scores" in a funny bar graph inside a cartoon firework explosion. Some nights, the fireworks are spectacular. Some nights you'll say, "Those were the greatest fireworks I've ever seen." Some nights, they'll shake the ribs out of your chest. Unequivocally, I say, "Thank you, Pamplona." There is no better way to start off the wrap-up of a day than setting off an absurd amount of fireworks. I cannot understand the soulless cretins who skip the nightly show. We have friends who have been going to Pamplona for years—*decades*—and have never gone out to see the fireworks. They have brain damage, apparently. Other than the *encierro*, Ari and I come to Pamplona for the fireworks more than anything.

Until I was injured in 2013, we had missed the nightly fireworks only five times. First, we could not find a parking space returning from a dinner outside the city on a Saturday night right before the Chuck Berry concert in 2008. Second, we went to see the Pretenders in San Sebastián in 2009. Third, in 2010, we got caught in bad weather in San Sebastián after sneaking off for a quick dip into the Bay of Biscay and some *pintxos*. Fourth, we stayed in the old city for Spain's World Cup victory in 2010. Fifth, dinner ran long at Túbal, in Tafalla, in 2011. There is also a dispute about whether we missed the fireworks one night in 2007 because Ari was "sick." However, he refused to have a mature discussion on the subject. Then, in 2013 we missed them on the eleventh and twelfth after I broke my ankle. On the thirteenth, I dragged myself well over two miles from our hotel to dinner and then to the bus station in a cast from my toes to over midthigh with crutches designed for Ari or some other famous short person, and only two days removed from serious surgery on my ankle. The pain was ghastly, but *there was no way* I was missing the fireworks (or dinner!) three nights in a row.

It is my understanding that Spain has other fiestas where fireworks are the central attraction. I cannot comprehend a fireworks display better than what Pamplona puts on every night. Every night they match any July 4th or New Year's Eve display in the United States. Usually they beat the July 4, 1976, Bicentennial fireworks in Philadelphia, which is generally considered the greatest in American history.

As of this writing, the best place to view the fireworks is in the field by the "new" bus station on calle Yanguas y Miranda. If you are not there, you cannot see the fireworks displayed on the ground—just the ground show is impressive. I don't want to sound like an old lady, but bring a plastic bag so you can sit on the ground and not get your white pants dirty. You can quietly thank me later. The "new" bus station opened in 2008. It is an impressive and sprawling structure underground. It had a Kentucky Fried Chicken inside, but it has since closed. The 2008 fiesta was cold and rainy, and the bus station was opened to stragglers and campers overnight. By the end of the fiesta, it was a shantytown and its "new" luster was lost forever.

The *Encierrillo*

This is the "little *encierro*," which starts "around" 11:00 p.m., or when it's dark. It's the middle of the bulls' tour through the center of Pamplona to the bullring. Few people even know about this.

First, the bulls are brought to Pamplona and placed in pens located across the River Arga to the left of the Puente de la Rochapea on calle Santo Domingo. This activity is the *desencajonada*. Second, bulls for the next afternoon's corrida are brought across the river in the dark to another pen at the northern end of calle Santo Domingo. This is *el encierrillo*. It is nice and calm and quiet. Third, the bulls are released from that pen to run all the way to the Plaza de Toros. That is the morning *encierro*. It is not nice and calm and quiet.

Hypothetically, you can get a free pass to the little *encierro*, but they are only available a few days before the fiesta, from the office of Pamplona City Council's Culture Department on calle Descalzos. Historically distributed "first come, first served," and now by lottery, you can only get two. There are only two hundred passes available per day. They actually publish a list of who got passes in the newspaper, presumably so you know which neighbor to bug about it. The tickets are all distributed long before most people arrive in Pamplona. There are two ways to get these passes in town. First, strike up a friendship with a local, and he or she may give you one. Second, buy a free pass from a tourist company that bought them from someone else. They charge excessively for these free passes, and on principle we never do this.

To see the little *encierro* without a pass, wait along the side of the street, beyond the fence on lower calle Santo Domingo, or on the slope above the street. This area is usually crowded. Or find a place on the steep, grassy bank by the road. There is a direct view from Paseo de Ronda and from the Rotxapea, next to the Puente de Curtidores. Do not make loud sounds or talk or try to distract the bulls. Once the bulls start moving, the event is completely silent. If you cannot cooperate, you will enjoy the free accommodations at Hotel del Policía. We never see this because it conflicts with our court-ordered obligation to attend the fireworks. However, this is an historic event of the fiesta.

In chapter 13 of *The Sun Also Rises,* Jake and Montoya discuss the *desencajonada*, which is the event where the bulls are released from their crates into the paddock. Hemingway gives a great description of the event. To my knowledge, this is not open to the public anymore. It happens before we ever get to town, anyway.

Night of the Drums

This is called the *Struendo,* and it celebrated its fiftieth anniversary in 2011. While in Pamplona, keep a careful watch for the round stickers that announce the Night of the Drums—they just start showing up. This is not an official event, but organized by a local *peña.* It is massive and spontaneous. On the appointed date, everyone meets at the Plaza de Santiago at midnight. Sometimes it seems like the entire population of Pamplona shows up with their drums, musical instruments, kazoos, whistles, and every other thing imaginable that makes noise, including pots and pans. The *peña* wheels its giant ten-foot-tall drum around on a cart. Hundreds, if not thousands, of people are involved. The din created is astonishing. You can usually buy a toy drum and join in. Or, just be ready to snap your fingers loudly.

Beginning at the Plaza de Santiago, everyone bangs or toots in unison and marches around town. You might as well join in—it sounds like it's somewhere in your hotel room anyway. Again, this is one of those situations where you'll collapse before they do. Some years we say, "Great, it's Night of the Drums!" Other years we say, "Oh no, it's Night of the Drums!" Little kids are superfluous in the drum march, and my boys love this night.

However, if your children cannot make it until midnight and beyond, the children have their own Day of the Drums at noon on the same day.

Tomatoes

I have terrible news. The tomato fight you see on TV is not in Pamplona. That fiesta is called La Tomatina, and it is held in the Valencian town of Buñol, over 500 km from Pamplona. And it is held on the last Wednesday of every August. I cannot even imagine the story we would have to come up with at home to stay in Spain from July 15 through the last week of August. I suspect the better tack would be to add a half day to the trip every year for the next fifty years so that it is not noticeable how long we're gone. I have to break the bad news that this does not occur in Pamplona to about a half million people a year. A lot of people think the running and the tomatoes occur in the same city at the same time. Rinky-dink versions are held around the world in happy places like Reno, Nevada, and Dongguan, China. In 2013 a U.S. company was advertising a traveling fiesta with "bull runs" (but with silly cows) and "tomato fights," which required a registration fee. Very, very sad.

Anyway, if you want to throw things, there is a much better Spanish fiesta than La Tomatina. I prefer San Pedro Nolasco's Battle of the Rats. Every year on the last Sunday in January in El Puig, the townsfolk eat a lot of turnips and then throw dead rats at each other. We know people who collect dead rats in an old freezer so they have lots of ammo come January. They also hoist clay pots over the street while revelers attempt to break the pots with sticks. Some pots are filled with candy; others have dead or even live rats inside. Either way, candy or rats fall into the crowd below.

Chupinazo and Pobre de Mí

The fiesta de San Fermín starts at noon on July 6 with the *chupinazo* in front of the Ayuntamiento. During this event, protect your feet, hands, and head from broken and flying glass. While banned from in front of the Ayuntamiento, glass is still a serious issue in other sections of the city during the *chupinazo*. A friend of ours wore flip-flops during the *chupinazo* in 2008 and shredded her feet in broken glass. It ruined her fiesta.

Since 2011, police have established checkpoints to stop glass bottles from being taken into the party (also, "paint-filled balloons" are barred). It has worked somewhat. The number of injuries has dropped dramatically. In a crowd of thousands and thousands, the internecine meanness of only a few fools can wreck the day. Reducing glass was a start, and I suppose the city will eventually take actions to curb the *nastiness* of the ceremony, and until then,

I suggest not attending. There is not another moment of the fiesta that is so unpleasant or randomly dangerous. Getting hit in the face with a glass bottle (a girl was seriously injured in this fashion in 2010) is unlike the risk of injury in the *encierro*.

On the other hand, the fiesta de San Fermín ends on July 14 at midnight with the Pobre de Mí ceremony. Everyone left standing at the end of the fiesta packs out in front of the Ayuntamiento—get out there by 10:00 p.m. for a close view. Get down in front and to the right for the best view of the fireworks. The time until midnight always passes in a whoosh, as you have undoubtedly made countless new friends during the fiesta, and the time is perfect to talk with old and new friends, discuss post-fiesta plans, and exchange email addresses.

You will need a white candle to properly enjoy Pobre de Mí. All night, local gypsies wander the area selling white candles in plastic cups. Really, this is your last good chance to be burned during the fiesta. Don't let it pass! Melted plastic cups burn skin much more efficiently than candle wax alone. I have scars on both hands. If you plan ahead, a soda can carved open with a pen knife works much, much better than a fiery plastic cup.

Nearing midnight, the Pamplonesa plays songs, and everyone sings the song "Pobre de Mí." The uncomplicated lyrics are:

> Pobre de mí, pobre de mí,
> que se han acabado las fiestas,
> de San Fermín.

This translates as "Poor me, poor me, for the fiesta of San Fermín has come to a close." You have plenty of time to pick up the rhythm and tune to the song, because they sing it about a thousand times. Our official *peña* version: "Pobre de mí, pobre de mí, something something about Santa, and San Fermín." No one remembers how this started, but we can usually get a couple hundred people to join in singing it incorrectly. Join us in this annual scrofulous tradition.

At the end, you take off your *pañuelo* and hold it overhead with your burning candle. This allows the maximum amount of hot wax to burn your face. The mayor announces the official closing of the fiesta, and tons of fireworks are exploded right overhead. Tons. If you've conditioned yourself to resist fearing for your life during the prior days of the fiesta, the raining ash won't concern you much. Don't get it in your eyes. The crowd sings as long as it can, and until shoulders and arm muscles painfully burn while holding *pañuelos* and candles overhead. It is rather moving. It's hard to hold back the tears; some relate to the end of the fiesta, and some to the permanent shoulder damage. As the crowd dissipates, many walk to the Church of San Lorenzo (at calle Mayor, 74, which has housed the Chapel of San Fermín since July 6, 1717) to tie their *pañuelo* on the gates. I understand that the parish priest takes a dim view of leaving the candles, as someone has to clean that mess up. So, don't leave your candle! The older generations of the city's citizens march around and sing through the night. Their song appears to me to be celebrating the fact that the tourists are finally leaving. By morning, it is hard to see signs in the city that there had been a fiesta at all.

Some inspired recusants refuse to give up the fiesta, and start running with the first public bus (in lieu of the bulls) that comes up calle Santo Domingo at 8:00 a.m. on July 15. Amusingly, the city hall did not fancy this unofficial addition to the fiesta, and stopped the 8:00 a.m. bus to suppress the running of the buses. This only served to foment the quasi-anarchists associated with this group. In 2011, they celebrated their twenty-fifth anniversary as an anonymous movement, still shouting, "Fiesta does not end when [mayor] Barcina says!" To that, who can disagree?

8

A Side Trip to Our Most Excellent Adventure
(leaving the fiesta behind sometimes)

Strange things are afoot at the Circle-K.

—**TED,** 1989

*Famously, Ernest Hemingway nearly always found time to get side-
tracked on a side trip from the San Fermín fiesta. He pays homage
to these anti-Icarian expeditions seeking cooler temperatures and
quiet in* The Sun Also Rises. *(Chapter 11: "'It's awful cold,' Bill
said." Boy, Bill was right. We've slipped on the ice on the mountain
near Roncesvalles in July when it's 120 degrees in Pamplona.)*

In *Hemingway's Paris and Pamplona*, Robert F. Burgess describes the
famed author's actual time spent in Burguete, and "daily hikes out
to visit the old town with the tin-roofed monastery at Roncevalles
[*sic*], or to pack lunches and make the long hike to enjoy trout-
fishing along the Rio de Fabrica and Irati Rivers."

In *Running with the Bulls* (which my mother gave me for Christmas in 2004, and inscribed as follows: "This is in no way to be
construed as encouragement"), Valerie Hemingway recounts picnic lunches on the River Irati with girls in bikinis and wine chilling

in the river. In 1959, Mary Welsh, Hemingway's fourth wife, broke her toe slipping in the stream. Valerie is very critical of Hemingway's reaction, which she describes as equally annoyed and jealous. "He quickly calculated what an inconvenience it was to have a crippled mate demanding his attention and devotion. I observed a darker, meaner side of the writer." He acted like this broken toe was going to slow him down in the fiesta, which is exactly how I felt about Ari when he got "a cold" during the fiesta in 2008. With a cold, how faithful was he to his promise to be attentive and devoted to me?

If you stay in Pamplona from the sixth through the fourteenth and never leave town for the beach or the countryside, you are cheating yourself of the entire experience. I love driving out of town, and watching as the number of people wearing white pants and red sashes steadily diminishes. Even better is the trip in reverse, as you come back into town for the afternoon feria. The person who sees the first pair of white pants does not have to pay tolls.

Within miles and minutes outside of the city you reach the mountains, where the temperature can plummet fifty degrees. There's extraordinary hiking, and there are historical sites and monasteries all over Navarre. One of the world's greatest urban beaches is about an hour's drive north at San Sebastián. Local towns near Pamplona have amazing restaurants.

This may come as a shock, but Pamplona becomes, on occasion, very crowded, especially on the weekends. Many Navarrans, Spanish, and Basques who live reasonable distances from Pamplona have off from work and come to the fiesta. Then there are the invading hordes (aka "The French") gathering in the city on the weekend nearest the celebration of Bastille Day. The French have one thing— one single thing—going for them. They don't come in tour groups. They stumble across the border and sleep, all of them, I think, under our hotel window. It is amazing how many fit down there.

From the beginning of our time in Pamplona, when it started to feel like 1979 at The Who concert in Cincinnati, Ohio (and it will), we started checking bus schedules for getting out of town for a while, especially for a couple of hours in the afternoon, or at least for lunch. We did stop taking the bus years ago. Can anyone explain why buses run daily except on the biweekly weekend bank holiday? Spanish banks have more days off than there are days in the calendar! Even the "nice" person behind the bulletproof glass at the bus station doesn't understand the Leap Year Bus Schedule Rules implemented during the Roman Empire. Now we have jobs, and we use a rental car. We split the cost, and I can drive a manual, so it is not that bad. Don't get me wrong, I like riding the bus. You can kick back and relax, and it's easy to make new friends. However, I have grown to detest the consumer hatred that motivates the design of Spanish schedules, and that a degree in astrobiology is necessary to interpret them, and that you're locked into someone else's schedule. I don't want to worry about making a deadline lying on the beach. This is why we rent a car.

Also, Pamplona gets hot. Trees whistle for dogs. The mountains on the edge of town whisper "By Mennen." Some days, it's so hot that—even with millions of visitors—you don't hear a sound in the street at 2:00 p.m. Everyone simply collapses. On these days, "lying in the grass in the park" does not satisfy my need for cooler temperatures. If you are staying the entire fiesta, you must seek higher ground or coastal beaches.

When leaving the city, please beware of the intoxication checkpoints. You cannot drive out of town without passing one. Since we don't drink, it's never a problem. However, we have friends whose time in Pamplona was ruined by getting caught. A tip: If you are not wearing sunglasses, you have a better chance of getting waved through without getting tested. They are looking for people covering bloodshot eyes. Personally, I enjoy predicting to the nice officer with the Uzi guarding the checkpoint that my blow in his tube will be *"perfecto."* He doesn't think I'm funny, either.

When returning to Pamplona, it is not uncommon in the late afternoon for there to be security checkpoints when driving back into town. I understand from our friends that these are nothing more than a show of force designed to keep so-called Basque ter-

rorists away from the fiesta. These checkpoints have mounted artillery with a military ambiance, complete with uniformed men
ready to throw menacing spike strips should you attempt to flee.
Usually, we are waved through because we are obviously not
Basque. However, there have been increasing demands for me to
present my IDP, or "International Driver's Permit," which is a com-
panion document (hatched by the United Nations in 1949) to your
own country's driver's license. I had been pulled over in Europe
dozens of times before anyone made a request for this worthless
permit. Technically, Spain does not recognize a U.S. driver's license, but it does the IDP. The State Department permits a couple
of organizations to process your IDP, including AAA. You fill out
the form, send them a passport photo with a *photocopy* of your driver's license and $15, and they send back a cheap little booklet say-
ing in Spanish (and many other languages) that you have a valid
driver's license. That is what is accepted as an IDP. It is a ludicrous
process, but worth getting to expedite any checkpoint stops.

There are many, many options to rest your weary fiesta bones.

The Beach—San Sebastián

San Sebastián. In Basque, it's Donostia, or even Donostiaka. In any
language, this place is amazing, if not downright heavenly. In our
first year visiting Pamplona for San Fermín, we didn't even know
it existed. After our first visit we seriously debated whether or not
to go back to Pamplona. On a nice day, this beach town is the love-
liest place on earth. The beaches and restaurants of San Sebastián
are commonly known to us as the Mother of All Side Trips (MOAST).
We love San Sebastián. Some years, if the weather is right, it's
hard to differentiate from which town we are side-tripping.

The drive to San Sebastián is easy, with cool mountain tunnels and through beautiful countryside. Starting in 2010, there
have been frequent speed-trap cameras along the route, and especially at the tunnels. There are plenty of places to pull off and
look at the valleys and mist. San Sebastián is less than an hour's

drive north from Pamplona. Just keep driving until you hit the beach.

In San Sebastián, look for the parking garages along Paseo de La Concha, as street parking is reserved for the earliest of arrivers and the king, apparently. Seriously, by 11:00 a.m. in the summer, especially on the weekends, parking in that town is a drag. And make sure Ari remembers where we parked the car, or you end up walking around town all afternoon and nearly miss the fireworks. Hey, Ari, you had one job!

There are two beaches facing the Concha Bay—Playa de Ondarreta and Playa de La Concha. The former is more for families with little kids, which—clearly—you want no part of. Farther down and next to the Kursaal Congress Centre is Playa de la Zurriola (sometimes called Playa de Gros), which is open to the sea and popular for surfing. It is a man-made beach, mostly, from the 1990s, with the installation of the jetty.

La Concha is considered to be the number one municipal beach in the world. Behind this beach is the famous boulevard for a *paseo*, with a very helpful time/temperature tower—remember, the corrida starts at 6:30 p.m., and you have to drive back in time.

A time-honored tradition in every Spanish town—big or little—is the *paseo*. As afternoon passes into evening, around the time when Americans would be watching the nightly news, the locals emerge to walk. After running with the bulls in the morning and lolling about on the beach all day, the *paseo* in San Sebastián is among life's greatest pleasures. The path starts at the town hall and continues to Miramar Park all along La Concha beach. The white wrought-iron railing running along this promenade, covered in wreaths and flowers, is known the world over.

Ari and I take this walk after showering off the suntan lotion, and use it to prepare our appetite for a *pintxos* crawl. It is not uncommon for us, and the many walkers, to stop and lean on the iconic railing and gaze at the sights on the beach below, or at the sun reflecting off the sea, or at Santa Clara Island in the distance. One particular evening, as we were enjoying this angular repose, we noticed a very large and hairless Frenchman (don't ask how we knew he was French; we just knew) stripping off his clothes to reveal his pink Speedo. As he stretched and touched his toes and flexed, we giggled and elbowed each other, and exchanged some choice comments with some older locals who were also pointing and laughing, the international language for "Hah, a pink Speedo."

To our horror, facing the sea, he then stripped off that pink Speedo in a single fluid motion. He laid out his beach towel and lay down—buttocks north—to enjoy the last hours of sunlight right under us on the beach. While San Sebastián is close to France, it is still in Spain, and nudity (especially male nudity) is not allowed. A crowd was forming and recoiling at the sight. Instinctively, I reached into my pocket and retrieved several EU "cent" coins (centimes). Ari has a great bit where he demonstrates how cheap the metal used in the coins is by floating them in toilet water. Pretty much I save them just for that. I balanced several on the railing and flicked them off into the air. The first several missed, but soon the trajectory was found, and they were routinely landing on the Frenchman's bare back and, even better, bare cheeks. Still, the Frenchman did not stir. So, the grizzled old men (likely veterans of the Spanish civil war, or worse) started digging in their pockets and passing centimes to me to continue the air assault. We were merrily at it when the police arrived. Municipal police have a sense of humor, so they marched him up the ramp still naked, and into their waiting car. At least he had enough change to tip the cabby after paying his fine at the station.

Down the steps to La Concha beach, there is an inexpensive pay area to rent lockers, towels, soap, and showers. Actually, I don't think you rent the soap. They do not want you to take the towel on the beach, so don't. When you turn your towel in after your shower, you get some of your money back. It is unclear how this place turns a profit.

The facility is very economical and clean, and tourist-friendly. There are also some sandwich shops, which serve *paprika-flavored Doritos,* which I warn you now are gross. You're better off packing a lunch, or grabbing something from the various fruit stands near the beach to hold you over for a nicer meal in the Parte Vieja (the old city), wherein you will find some of the finest restaurants and *pintxos* in the world. You can buy ice cream on the beach.

For 1 euro, you can rent a chair, which—to blend in like a local—you should face away from the water and toward the sun in the morning hours. With the chair, there is some complex ticket exchange. You get a ticket, and need the ticket to turn in the chair. Or, you can just leave the chair on the beach, because you get nothing back for turning in the chair with the ticket. At least we don't. If someone can explain it to us, we'd be very grateful.

While crowded by midday, it's as civil as any beach I've ever been to (no radios or horseshoes, and no jerks and almost no children). There's a gentle wave on the beach, and a very significant tide. At low tide, you can scurry to the left over the slippery rocks to Playa de Ondarreta. I don't know why, but we always do this. After risking our lives, we usually turn back immediately after confirming, "Yep. It's still here."

Before Isla de Santa Clara, there are two swimming platforms. One has a sliding board, and the other a "high" diving board. Bull runners who can swim to these platforms are held in the highest regard; others continue to maintain their junior status, Ari. Personally, I have to recover out there for about a half hour, while eighty-year-old Basques dogpaddle by. At low tide, the platforms are closer, but scary giant kelp disconcertingly tickles your feet when you swim out. These platforms are an excellent place to meet fellow travelers, and I've kept in contact with more than a few for years—people I only met waiting in line for the sliding board.

While the fiesta persists, there is usually in San Sebastián a strange meeting of the eyes and sharing of exaggerated stories on the beach among those ducking in from Pamplona. Learn the secret handshake. We especially enjoy these chance encounters with kindred spirits, and the exchange of information. Where you from? Where you staying? How'd you get here? How long are you in Spain? Where'd you eat? Did you run? Did you see that bull? Did you swim to the diving platform, too? Do you think Ari even knows how to swim?

In San Sebastián we get a thalassotherapy treatment, which is an ancient treatment for aches and pains, of which there are many associated with "running on cobblestones." I think that in Basque thalassotherapy means "spraying you in the face with cold sea water while old ladies watch and laugh." Thalassotherapy spas are found only in northern Spain and southwestern France. Whether a spa is a thalassotherapy spa or just a spa is governed by law. It must be near the ocean. La Perla Spa in San Sebastián is the best (around 25 euros for two hours—it is right behind La Concha). Jumping between freezing and boiling seawater, and the fine steam baths, ice showers, and saunas—all of this gets us through to Pobre de Mí. Plus, you get to wear a cool shower cap. Ari brings the shower cap he bought the prior year to Pamplona and, for mystifying reasons, leaves it in the hotel in Pamplona and is forced to buy a new cap every July. He must have saved enough by now for a museum wing on the History of the Shower Cap.

More than occasionally, a brutal winter storm will destroy La Perla Spa (no joke—every couple of years a rogue wave destroys it), and we are forced to find a replacement. In San Sebastián, the other establishment we like is Hydra Wellness & Spa, Hotel Maria Cristina, Paseo Republica Argentina, 4. In the town of Hendaye, on the French side, you'll find the famous Serge Blanco Thalasso Center right past the ferry at 125 Boulevard de la Mer, Hendaye. In Saint-Jean-de-Luz, France, we love Thalassotherapie Hélianthal at Place Maurice Ravel. Embarrassingly, each place knows us by sight, and greets us by saying, "Aren't you the guys who made all that noise last summer?" Or, "At least it looks like Ari shaved his back this year."

After cleaning up at the showers, it's time to eat. We head into the Parte Vieja. Facing the beach, just walk to the right along La Concha. Once you've crossed Alameda del Boulevard ("Avenue of the Blvd." in Basque?) and behind San Sebastián's own Ayuntamiento, you've reached the highest concentration of Great Food in the Hemisphere. Here, you have two options: sit down or *pintxos* crawl. You almost can't miss. This is explained more in chapter 10.

After you've experienced San Sebastián, there are seemingly unlimited and generally remote and nontouristy natural and historic sites to soak in to escape the din of San Fermín. You could spend your entire life exploring northern Spain. These are our favorites.

Roncesvalles—Sorogain Hiking Trail

The Roncesvalles area is our favorite hiking spot outside of Pamplona. Roncesvalles is a province of Navarre and northeast of Pamplona, and it's found in the Aezkoa Valley. Less than an hour's drive from Pamplona, it's in the Pyrenees and only a couple of miles from the French border. In 2009, we were a good hour into the hike, on the side of a mountain, in the cold mist, and we met a family driving a station wagon from France into Spain *over the mountain* on a dirt road. They asked only if there was somewhere to buy beer from the direction we were walking. Seemed legit.

Also, Roncesvalles is the annual winner of Best Place to Destroy Your Rental Car. In fact, all around Roncesvalles, there are many other options to lose or destroy your rental car during a hiking excursion.

With forest trails, rivers, meadows, beech and fir trees, mountains, a reservoir, old shepherd huts, hikes from Roncesvalles are amply outlined online. Our favorite hike is the Sorogain trail (off the N-135), which leads into the hills, where we have found ice from hailstorms the night before, and very low temperatures, even when Pamplona is sweltering. There are many little ancient stone huts, or dolmens, that the Basques took over to use while they were herding sheep, or fighting Franco. To keep matters confusing, on maps they might call dolmens *Trikuharri* or *Jentiletxe.* They are a great place to picnic.

Often you'll find cattle, sheep, and other livestock, all with the classic Basque cowbells, wandering the hills with you. Basque shepherds we startle are always friendly, but appropriately amused by our huffing and puffing through the hills. In 2006 we surprised one who was dozing and smoking a pipe in one of those ancient huts that had long ago lost its roof. He was wearing a black beret that he used as a hat and not for show. He carried a staff and had a black woolen sweater wrapped around his neck like he was invited for wine and cheese in the Hamptons but was watching over a couple hundred sheep and some cows and hairy ponies. He and his dog suspiciously examined us like we must have been lost, and we were the only Americans he had ever met. He was not impressed. He told us a long story in Basque and pointed in the direction we were walking and ominously tugged at his left eye repeatedly mentioning a *tartalo* that lived around the bend. We enjoyed his incomprehensible story and continued on in search of the *tartalo.* He watched us walk on like we had escaped from an asylum, and we later found out why. A *tartalo* is an enormous one-eyed giant that eats people and sheep. The classical story is that two Basque brothers took refuge while hunting in a cave during a storm. It was a *tartalo*'s cave, and he captured the brothers and said, "One for today and the other for tomorrow." He ate the older brother and fell asleep. The younger brother escaped, stole the *tartalo*'s ring, and stuck a stick in the giant's eye. He hid in a flock of sheep wearing a sheepskin, but the ring started yelling, "Here I am, here I am!" The *tartalo* blindly groped for the ring, which the younger brother now could not remove from his finger. He cut off his finger and threw it over a cliff, and the *tartalo* followed over the edge to his death. How a giant's ring fit on the Basque's finger to begin with is not explained.

Roncesvalles—Ibañeta Pass

In the actual town of Roncesvalles, we often visit the Colegiata, built by King Sancho VII el Fuerte (the Strong), which houses his giant tomb. Behind an iron grill, you can see a bit of the chain (broken by Sancho) that had been used to guard him in the Muslim chieftain's tent. Who locks a tent door with a chain anyway?

Above the town is the famous Ibañeta Pass. A stone marks the spot of the legendary battle (aptly named the Battle of Ronces-valles). Also known as *Orreaga* (or Valley of the Thorns) in Basque, Roncesvalles is famous for the legend and history of the defeat of Charlemagne and the death of Roland on August 15, 778, during the battle of Roncevaux Pass, when Charlemagne's rearguard was destroyed by the Basques. It is romanticized in the epic poem *La Chanson de Roland*. Charlemagne was the first European emperor after the collapse of the Roman Empire. He was French and spread Roman Catholicism in Europe. Roland was a nephew of Charlemagne and led the rearguard. When he knew the battle was lost, he blew his "olifant-horn" so hard, ensuring that Charlemagne knew his rear was exposed, that he burst his temples; then he threw his sword, named Durandal. In the poem, the Basques are portrayed as Muslim sympathizers, which could not be further from the truth—it was Middle Ages propaganda from the French Catholic Church. In reality, after besieging and demolishing Pamplona, Charlemagne began carting ill-gotten booty (Muslim bribes) north and home. The Basques declined to play ball, and Charlemagne destroyed parts of town. The rearguard of Charlemagne's army was then decimated by the Basques in and around the Ibañeta Pass. Exploiting the story told in *La Chanson de Roland*, the Catholic Church changed the Basques to Muslims, and started selling souvenirs all along the way.

Legends of Roland's bravery were even used to pump up the Norman troops at the Battle of Hastings. So, Western history in a nutshell: Edward, Harold, William, Normandy, Halley's Comet, channel crossing, Hastings, arrow in the eye, and tapestry. Done, and done. All thanks to the Basque running of Roland out on a rail. Oh, and mountains of Charlemagne's gold were lost in the fog of battle and have never been found. When hiking near the Ibañeta Pass, we always turn over a few stones and logs in the forest. Just in case.

From the back of the Roncesvalles Abbey, the hike to the pass is about an hour's walk (steep) through beech forests. At the top you'll find a bell used to guide pilgrims from the Middle Ages through the fog. On the way back you'll find—not unexpectedly—the abbey you left from. You can also drive up to the pass, which is imminently more satisfying. This is a great place to drive to, unless you leave the emergency brake off and your rental car careens down a hill into a tree and some Italian guys help you for about an hour to dislodge it. Then, your day is blown and Ari brings it up every time you park the car, forever. The Ibañeta Pass is not just the scene of Charlemagne's greatest loss, but Number 3 on my personal list of greatest rental car abominations. Among friends, this is known as "The Avis Rental Car vs. Gravity."

See, there are many things that Ari will never understand. Like the rules of baseball. Or the pleasure of reaching things set on top of the refrigerator. At the top of the list is driving a stick shift. My father only drove a stick, so I learned to drive a stick. Somewhere, this skill evaded Ari, like learning to speak German. He simply cannot be taught. In 2007, the fiesta was brutally hot, and we set out for the Ibañeta Pass. In the prior year, Spain had spent considerable euros converting this ancient sight into a tourist attraction. A lavish tourism office was constructed, along with paved parking, unhelpful information signs, and a bar. It is still Spain, after all. In the initial years of this century, Spain was flush with euros, and poorly planned prestige construction projects flourished, sort of. In Pamplona, they built an airport next to the airport (sadly, not a joke). In 2008, the global economy sank, Spain's grotesquely so. The media dubbed the too abundant housing for-sale signs as "Spain's new national tree."

That particular day, while Pamplona was 100 degrees Fahrenheit, we drove northeast for less than an hour into the mountains, and it was less than 45 degrees. Now, there are many distractions during the fiesta, and it is generally known that I often forget to engage the emergency brake when parking. And, for those who have never driven a stick shift, if you park and leave the car out of gear, and fail to engage the emergency brake, the entire car can roll off wherever. And if the parking lot is on the side of a mountain, like at the Ibañeta Pass, it can roll for quite a distance.

We parked, disembarked, and then the car rolled twenty-five yards downhill and struck a seedling beech tree. We didn't even try to stop it, because we'd learned about the futility of such efforts during smaller versions of this accident. Coming to rest against the tree, the undercarriage of our small rental car wedged on a giant granite rock, which is how we learned it was a one-wheel drive car. I revved the engine a bunch, as we were mesmerized by the spinning tire. Again, it was the fiesta. We needed a tow truck, and we hiked up the hill to the brand-new visitors' center. We introduced ourselves to the young girl working behind the counter, whose real name was Zeberiogana, which in Basque means "barely interested and unhelpful." She explained that the nearest gas station was over 45 kilometers away, and that they did not have a telephone, even though they had a full bar. She did not want to come out to see the car. I mean, we are pretty charming, and it had no effect on her. While she did not explicitly state it, she implied that she really did not care if we froze to death in the forest. We were on the side of a mountain, so there was no cell phone coverage. There were no other tourists on the mountainside yet that afternoon.

Ari and I walked down the road a while and found a farmhouse. No one was home to beg for help, but we did steal a nice mound of firewood from behind their barn, and we tried to wedge it under the spinning wheel. I know now that the plan was destined to fail, but again, it was the fiesta. The spinning wheel did chuck a few logs at Ari, who narrowly escaped dying in the most bizarre fashion imaginable.

After an hour or so of rocking the car, some Italian tourists arrived. They seemingly materialized out of nowhere, and a dozen or more poured out of their van. We explained our predicament, and a large axe was produced from their truck. A few wandered into the bushes and started cutting down small fir trees. Without explanation, they piled them under the front of the car, as if they'd dislodged an Avis Seat Ibiza wedged on a granite rock near the